The Complete Idiot's Ref

Ten Reasons to Cook wit

1. You will enjoy having help in the kitchen, a   proud to have contributed to the meals.
2. Kids will become more healthful and adventurous eaters when they're involved in the cooking.
3. Mixing, measuring, and pouring will help develop hand-eye coordination and motor skills.
4. Reading recipes will help improve their reading skills.
5. Mixing and measuring will put math skills into action.
6. Experiencing the physical and chemical changes in foods will make science come alive.
7. Exploring food from other countries or from other regions in their own country opens kids' minds to history and geography.
8. Following recipes will help develop the skills to organize and to think logically.
9. Cooking and talking together side by side will bring you and your kids closer.
10. Kids' natural curiosity and creativity can teach *you* a few things.

Ten Tips for Success with Kids in the Kitchen

1. Have fun and keep your sense of humor.
2. Cook with your kids only if you both are not rushed, irritable, or hungry.
3. Keep it simple. Start with easy recipes or even bake from a mix.
4. Always read the entire recipe with your kids to make sure you all know what to do.
5. Get out the equipment before you start.
6. Prepare all your ingredients before you begin and put them away as you use them.
7. Start kids off with doable, age-appropriate tasks. Begin with washing vegetables, measuring and mixing ingredients, or setting the table.
8. Don't worry about the mess, but do clean as you go. Use cooking and baking time as clean-up time.
9. Spread out newspapers or waxed paper on counter tops to make clean-up a snap.
10. Praise and encourage kids as you cook, even if they make mistakes.

alpha
books

Top Ten Cooking Safety Tips

1. Always supervise kids, especially when they're using knives and appliances. Teach them to ask for adult help.

2. Cook with clean hands and wash them frequently as you handle foods. Dry your hands thoroughly before plugging in appliances and so items won't slip out of your grasp.

3. Tie back your hair, wear an apron, and roll up your sleeves before cooking.

4. Use a stool, not a chair, to reach for items in cupboards. Close cupboard doors when you're finished.

5. Always use thick, dry pot holders to grab pot handles, hot utensils, oven racks, and oven doors.

6. Turn pot handles toward the inside of the stovetop to prevent accidents. Lift lids away from you to prevent steam burns or splatters.

7. Clean up spills immediately.

8. Teach kids never to play with knives or to leave them on counter edges or piled in the sink. When cutting, tuck under the fingertips and thumb holding the food and cut away from yourself.

9. Don't reuse kitchen tools used with raw meat, poultry, fish, and eggs without cleaning them first.

10. Anticipate and be prepared for emergencies, such as fires and cuts.

Kids' Kitchen Math

3 teaspoons = 1 tablespoon or ½ fluid ounce

4 tablespoons = ¼ cup or 2 fluid ounces

5 tablespoons plus 1 teaspoon = ⅓ cup

8 tablespoons = ½ cup or 4 fluid ounces

16 tablespoons = 1 cup or 8 fluid ounces

1 pint = 2 cups or 16 fluid ounces

1 quart = 4 cups, 32 fluid ounces, or 2 pints

1 gallon = 4 quarts, 128 fluid ounces, or 8 pints

1 pound = 16 ounces

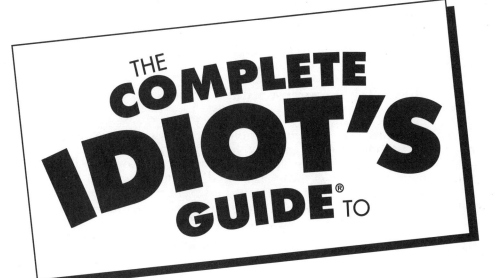

THE COMPLETE IDIOT'S GUIDE® TO

Cooking with Kids

by Joan Cirillo

alpha books

Macmillan USA, Inc.
201 West 103rd Street
Indianapolis, IN 46290

A Pearson Education Company

Dedicated to my parents, Nancy and Peter Cirillo, for teaching me to seek and appreciate good food.

And to my family, Roger, Julia, and Lizzie, for sharing that lifelong adventure.

Copyright © 2000 by Joan Cirillo

THE COMPLETE IDIOT'S GUIDE TO and Design are registered trademarks of Macmillan USA, Inc.

International Standard Book Number: 0-02-863525-6
Library of Congress Catalog Card Number: Available from the Library of Congress

02   01   00   8   7   6   5   4   3   2   1

Interpretation of the printing code: The rightmost number of the first series of numbers is the year of the book's printing; the rightmost number of the second series of numbers is the number of the book's printing. For example, a printing code of 00-1 shows that the first printing occurred in 2000.

Printed in the United States of America

Publisher
Marie Butler-Knight

Product Manager
Phil Kitchel

Managing Editor
Cari Luna

Acquisitions Editor
Randy Ladenheim-Gil

Development Editors
Linda Ingroia
Michael Thomas

Production Editor
JoAnna Kremer

Copy Editor
Amy Lepore

Illustrator
Jody P. Schaeffer

Cover Designers
Mike Freeland
Kevin Spear

Book Designers
Scott Cook and Amy Adams of DesignLab

Indexer
Angie Bess

Layout/Proofreading
Terri Edwards
Donna Martin
Gloria Schurick

Contents at a Glance

Contents

Foreword

I like *The Complete Idiot's Guide to Cooking with Kids* because it gets kids and parents involved in cooking together. With both parents working these days, they often don't have a lot of time to spend with their kids. This gives parents a good way to spend quality time and to teach us kids about the kitchen and cooking while learning and having fun. Let kids push the buttons on the blender and help with appliances, too, but of course, with *adult supervision*. I *always* have an adult with me when I cook.

People often ask me what my favorite thing is to make. Well, being a kid, I love desserts. When I was little, I made up a recipe called mini-cheesecakes. I love to make them because I get to use the blender and my mom usually lets me do everything by myself. They're my favorite things to eat, too, especially with cherry or blueberry topping. You'll find lots of dessert recipes in this book.

I like being a chef. Being the World's Youngest Chef, I have been lucky enough to be on TV shows like *Late Night With David Letterman, Mister Rogers, Figure It Out,* and many others. I even got to go to England to do a show there called *Barrymoore.* It was lots of fun. I took mini-cheesecakes to the Queen, but fruit wasn't on her diet that day. Drat!!!

If you are worried about having a messy kitchen, relax—it all comes with cooking. I know that I always have to do the cleaning up with my mom and dad, and this is always kind of fun, too! Mom always says "If you make a mess, you have to help clean it up." Besides, washing the dishes is sort of like playing in the water, and I like to do that, too. Here's a little hint: If you clean as you go, it's a lot easier. This book has lots more tips on organizing and clean-up in the kitchen.

These recipes are easy to follow. I know that a lot of kids are getting interested in cooking at a young age—I did—so with just a little bit of help from mom or dad, they can pick up this book and make hot oatmeal or cinnamon toast without too much trouble.

Always remember to watch your grandmas when they cook, too. I learned a lot from mine. (You'll find lots of tips about cooking with relatives in this book.) I try to watch and learn from everyone I can. I even attend one-on-one classes at Johnson and Wales University in Rhode Island during the summer when I'm not in school. I have a friend there named Chef Rick Tarantino. Rick and I sometimes make up recipes together. We even got to host and cook at an Academy Awards Party in Los Angeles. Boy, was *that* fun! It was for the benefit of underprivileged kids through The Audrey Hepburn Children's Fund. I'm on the Kids Board of Directors.

So in closing, let the kids try these recipes and help you in the kitchen. I'm sure you'll have as much fun as they do. Kids, remember to always listen to mom and dad in the kitchen. After all, if the house burns down, you don't want to be the one blamed (just joking).

Keep cooking,
Chef Justin Miller

Justin Miller, the Heinz Ketchup Kid Connoisseur, has over 150 television appearances to his credit. He designs his own chef's clothes through Angelica Uniforms in Chicago, and he attends Johnson and Wales University during the summer. And, of course, he cooks.

Introduction

I wrote *The Complete Idiot's Guide to Cooking with Kids* because I want you to experience the same pleasures and benefits from cooking with your kids as I have with mine. I know that bringing kids into the kitchen can be intimidating. You worry that your kids are going to cut themselves or set the house on fire. And what about the mess? Believe me, that's no reason *not* to get in there and cook. And *The Complete Idiot's Guide to Cooking with Kids* shows you exactly how to do it.

Before You Dive in

Cooking with kids is great fun, but you also need to be prepared. *The Complete Idiot's Guide to Cooking with Kids* is written to start you off with the basics, to keep you going, and to carry you through to more challenging aspects of cooking together. Ideally, you should try to read through the whole book before you start pulling out the pots and pans with the kids. If you can't do this, definitely read Part 3, "Kid-Proofing Your Kitchen," and Part 4, "The Building Blocks of Cooking," from beginning to end. The information in these chapters is designed to help you and your children feel comfortable and confident in the kitchen. Understanding this information is critical to your success. Go over these chapters with your kids and encourage them to make comments and ask questions. And check Appendix A, "Kitchen Lingo Glossary" for information on terms and techniques.

What You'll Find in This Book

As a parent, a food and lifestyle journalist, and an educator, I've become convinced of the positive power of cooking with kids. My children—Julia, 15, and Lizzie, 12—have been in the kitchen with me all their lives, and I've watched how learning to cook has bolstered their skills and self-confidence. Julia, who was a vegetarian for several years, gravitates toward making salads, dressings, and pasta dishes. We can always count on her to bake up a great batch of brownies or popovers, too. Lizzie started out as our risotto and stir-fry chef and generally takes on any kitchen task. These days, she thinks of herself as an expert at making delicious snacks and concoctions. Each of my daughters can cook a complete dinner on her own and they often do. They're not superkids. I've just taught them cooking techniques and how to prepare healthful and nutritious food, and we've enjoyed every minute of it.

I've designed this book to introduce you to the joy of cooking with kids and to give you the confidence to be proficient in the basics and beyond. You'll see and experience why letting kids cook sharpens and enhances their academic and social skills and gives them skills they'll need and use for the rest of their lives.

This book is divided into six parts, beginning with understanding why cooking is so good for kids and ending with getting in the kitchen with them and actually doing it. Here's what you'll find in each part:

Part 1, "Welcome to the World of Cooking with Kids," lets you in on secrets educators have known for decades. You'll learn who's cooking with kids and why it's so good for them. If you have any doubts about whether the mess is worth it, you'll be convinced that it is when you read about how cooking benefits your kids socially, intellectually, and emotionally.

Part 2, "Getting Kids Curious About Food," gives you ideas about getting your kids interested in food, cooking, and new tastes. The section opens with finding food in everyday things around us and moves on to discovering your own family roots and traditions. Chapters on savvy food shopping, making lunch, and sitting down to dinner offer you tips on how to involve your kids in these everyday activities.

Part 3, "Kid-Proofing Your Kitchen," provides all the basics you'll need to equip your kitchen and to have a safe cooking experience. You'll start by going over kitchen safety rules specifically geared toward kids, and then you'll learn how to teach kids to operate appliances cautiously. You'll find out about all the utensils and equipment you'll need for cooking and baking. Because I've experienced holding my breath when my children first started using knives, I've included plenty of information about the ins and outs of cutting, from teaching kids the basics to getting them to practice good knife-safety habits. Finally, a few bouts with food poisoning in the family have made me very sensitive to the subject of food safety. And as a food and nutrition educator with the Oregon State University Extension Service, I'm kept informed about this changing field. You'll learn the latest about food safety and how to protect your family from food-borne illness.

Part 4, "The Building Blocks of Cooking," is like a condensed beginner's cookbook. It opens with chapters covering the fundamentals: learning the mechanics of reading recipes and proper mixing and measuring techniques. You'll take a personal tutorial on cooking techniques in the next chapter and end up with a blueprint for dealing with kitchen mishaps, complete with a primer on making emergency substitutions for ingredients.

Part 5, "Fun with Food," introduces you to some of the more adventurous aspects of food. So many parents have asked my advice about using spices and herbs that I decided to include a mini-lesson about them. Subsequent chapters will introduce you to fun kitchen experiments; ways to play with and garnish your food; making your own dairy products; and discovering food adventures through cooking clubs, food-related parties, and other cultures.

Part 6, "Now You're Cooking: The Recipe File," offers a wide range of recipes including some of my favorites as a kid and my kids' favorites. Because I know that children really do like more than just "kids' food," you'll find recipes that the whole family will want to eat for dinner, including many from countries around the world. Friends and acquaintances have generously shared delicious family recipes that have stood the test of generations.

Each recipe is written clearly enough for kids to follow it with adult supervision, although don't be surprised if your kids can do some of them on their own. They begin with a rating and an alert about where adult help is needed. The list of equipment will help you get organized. A clear set of numbered instructions along with notes and variations will have you cooking in no time. (Don't be put off by the length of the instructions. They just include lots of information about what you might encounter while cooking.)

Look for these icons in the recipes. 🌓 signals adult help is needed. 🔄 means the recipe does not require any cooking. 🔪 indicates no sharp knives are used in the recipe. The Easy recipes don't require much skill and are a good starting point. Easy/Intermediate recipes introduce a bit more technique or may require some help from an adult. Intermediate and Advanced recipes are more challenging, but don't be intimidated. Some of them, like the yeast bread, only require more effort and time.

With the help of the Kitchen Lingo Glossary, you'll never get stumped by a kitchen term or cooking method. In The Resource Guide, you'll find listings that will help you and your kids learn about food and cooking. These resources include a handy list of toll-free numbers and mail-order sources for everything from food safety tips to recipe giveaways. You'll find reference lists for magazines, cookbooks, and food-related books along with Web sites geared toward kids and food. The Food Guide Pyramids and The Nutrition Facts Label appendixes will be quick and easy references for meal planning and shopping.

Extras

Throughout the book, you'll notice sidebars with helpful information that you won't want to miss. Let your kids guess at some of the lingo and be sure they read through the "Kid Quiz" sidebars throughout the book.

Kid Quiz

Kid Quiz boxes are designed to engage kids in fun and interactive learning. They'll learn about various aspects of the kitchen, cooking, nutrition, and food. The quizzes highlight information covered in the chapter and are designed to pique your young cook's curiosity.

Bigger Bites

Sometimes you just want to know more or to find a little extra help in the kitchen. Check out Bigger Bites sidebars for the latest information and resources.

Heads Up!

Even the best chefs have to anticipate problems and be aware of potential dangers. Heads Up! sidebars warn you about cooking hazards with an eye toward young and new cooks.

Learn the Lingo

Read Learn the Lingo boxes for definitions and descriptions of different terms that explain or expand on information in the chapter.

Kitchen Clue

If you're looking for helpful hints and advice to make cooking go smoothly, Kitchen Clue boxes are the place to find them.

Kid Comment

The Kid Comment boxes appear in the recipe chapters and contain personal reactions from our young recipe testers.

Acknowledgments

Thanks go to my family—my daughters, Julia and Lizzie Cooke, and my husband, Roger Cooke—for all their support and ideas, and of course, for the many hours they spent testing, tasting, and critiquing. Big hugs to my mother, Nancy Cirillo, for her transcontinental sharing of recipes and years of experience in the kitchen.

The recipes were tested not only by my family, but also by some 20 families throughout Oregon. Many thanks to the following families and kids who either generously shared family recipes or brought the recipes in this book to life with their cooking experiences and insights.

Kathy Albert and Hannah, 12
Chef Claire Archibald of Café Azul, Portland
Demetra Ariston
Suzanne and John Bishop and Robert, 9; Mary, 6; and William, 4
Ellen Bogart
Elizabeth Carlisle-Sullivan and Samuel, 5
Molly Clarey and Megan, 9; and Campbell, 6
Helen Cunningham
Carol and Edward Dayoob
Gil Cavanagh
Julie and Martin Goebel and Caitlin, 13
Helen Hazen and Inga, 11
Cynthia and Dorothy Hillis
Mary Chomenko Hinckley and Blake, 11; and Allie, 9
Pat Kaplan and Madison, 13; and Taylor, 11
Diane Kirk and Kayla, 10
Connie Kuenzi
Nicole Kurosaki
Mary Loughran

Siobhan Loughran and her sons James and Joseph Taylor, 8 and 5, respectively
Cyndy Maletis and John, 12; and Andy, 11
Helen Mandel
Judy Matarazzo and Harrison, 6
Yolanda McVicker and Lucy, 14; Sammi, 8; and Kevin, 5
Lorinda Moholt and her grandson, Austin Moholt-Siebert, 3
Peggy Noto and Torben, 8; and Emma, 5
Nancy Pike
Halle Sadle and Sam, 13; and Jake, 10
Carrie Silva
Shirley Thompson
Patricia Waldoch
Maureen and Fred Wearn and Colleen, 14; Christopher, 13; Jeremy, 10; and Anna, 8
Chef Catherine Whims of Genoa Restaurant, Portland

My appreciation also goes to, in particular, my editors, Linda Ingroia and Michael Thomas, for their astute insights and enthusiasm, and to editors Emily Nolan, Jim Willhite, and Jane Sigal for their help launching this project; to Marjorie Braker, Carolyn Raab, Pat Aun, Renee Hylton, and the staff at the Oregon State University Extension Service for continually expanding my horizons and sharing their time and extensive resources; to Linda Braun and the American Egg Board for their resources and support of kids' cooking; to Karen Davis, Anne Sterling, and the Kids in the Kitchen Committee of the International Association of Culinary Professionals (IACP); to Peggy Paul (director) and the Oregon Dairy Council for continually sharing their wonderful nutrition and kids' cooking resources; to Toni Allegra, Peggy Deen, Janie Hibler, Cynthia Hillis, Patsy Jamieson, Kathryn Kurtz, Lorinda Moholt, and Naomi Kaufman Price for their friendship and support; and to Betty Shenberger for her unfailing good humor.

The author wishes to thank the parents and the following for permission to use photos of the children in this book: Herff Jones Photography Division; International Association of Culinary Professionals (IACP); Lake Oswego Photographers; Lifetouch National School Studios; R&R School Photography.

Trademarks

All terms mentioned in this book that are known to be or are suspected of being trademarks or service marks have been appropriately capitalized. Alpha Books and Macmillan USA, Inc., cannot attest to the accuracy of this information. Use of a term in this book should not be regarded as affecting the validity of any trademark or service mark.

The following trademarks and service marks have been mentioned in this book:

Adopt-A-School, Better Homes and Gardens, Bisquick, Carnation, Chef's Catalog, Crayola Kids, Dole, Fight Bac!, Fleischmann's, Gold Medal, Healthy Kids, Jessica's Biscuit, Kellogg's, King Arthur, Libby's, McCormick/Schilling Company, Meredith, Nestlé, Nickelodeon/Yankelovich Youth MONITOR, Nutella, Oldways Preservation & Exchange Trust, OXO GOOD GRIPS, Pyrex, Quaker, Red Star Yeast, Seeds of Change, Sesame Street, The Baker's Catalogue, The Incredible Edible Egg, Tone, Williams Sonoma, Wondra.

Part 1

Welcome to the World of Cooking with Kids

You're probably asking yourself, "What's so great about cooking with kids, and why is it suddenly such a big deal? Is it really worth the mess and the extra time it takes?" Explore the world of kids' cooking and find out.

In the next two chapters, you'll see how boys and girls are discovering cooking as a creative and empowering activity. And they're finding inspiration from plenty of outside sources. Read about the exciting cooking opportunities kids are enjoying and how chefs, educators, and food professionals are turning our kids on to taste, cooking, gardening, and new cultures. You'll find out why cooking with your kids—even if you do it only now and then—is such good quality time. See how you can improve their social and academic skills and give them a head start on mastering skills they'll need for the rest of their lives.

Chapter 1

So You Want to Cook with Your Kids?

In This Chapter

➤ Why more kids are cooking these days

➤ Kid-oriented cooking programs and classes

➤ Messes and mishaps: Overcoming your kitchen fears

➤ The rewards of cooking with your kids

So you've decided to take the plunge and cook with the kids. But you're feeling just a little leery about how it's going to turn out. Will they make a mess, start a fire, lose control? Relax, have faith, and pat yourself on the back. You're about to embark on one of the most exciting, rewarding, and nurturing activities you can do with your kids. Just reading this book will calm your fears and give you a head start in the kitchen. And, in case you need a little more convincing, this chapter tells you who's cooking with kids, why it's such a growing trend, and why you'll want to be a part of it.

Kids in the Kitchen

No doubt about it. Cooking with kids is hot these days. All across the country, kids are becoming more at home in the kitchen. And they're not just making brownies. They're fixing breakfast, packing lunches, making snacks, and helping get dinner on the table.

"There's been a steady climb in the number of kid 'chefs' over the last four years," reported the 1999 *Nickelodeon/ Yankelovich Youth MONITOR*™. The youth trends survey, taken every two years, studied a nationally representative sample of 1,633 children ages 6 to 17 in the fall and winter of 1998.

Consider the survey's findings:

➤ 88 percent of kids age 6 to 17 fix meals

➤ 26 percent of kids 9 to 17 years old usually make meals for their family, up from 15 percent in 1995.

➤ Among kids fixing their own meals:

> 75 percent fix snacks
>
> 66 percent fix breakfast
>
> 51 percent fix lunch
>
> 31 percent fix dinner

➤ Choice, freedom, and fun are motivating the 9- to 17-year-olds who said they like to cook. Asked why they like preparing meals:

> 67 percent said they can choose foods they like
>
> 61 percent said it was fun to cook
>
> 57 percent said they can eat when they want
>
> 51 percent said they can eat as much or as little as they want
>
> 47 percent said they can invent new and different combinations

Kid Quiz

What's your favorite food to prepare and, if you cook it, do you use the microwave, stove, oven, or something else?

Who's Cooking with Kids and Why

What's happening and why is it happening now? After a decade of writing and reporting about family lifestyles, kids, and kids cooking, I've learned a few things. For starters, our kids are more food savvy and curious than we ever were. They're learning about the Food Guide Pyramid in school and talking about what they should eat to stay healthy.

A growing gardening movement in the schools is providing them with opportunities to learn about and grow foods. And food professionals and educators, long aware of the benefits of cooking, have boosted their efforts to teach kids how to cook.

Couple this with the fact that our culture has become increasingly conscious about health and exercise and concerned about teaching kids good eating habits. (Over a third of the kids surveyed, 35 percent, check nutrition facts labels for calories and fat, according to the *Nickelodeon/Yankelovich Youth MONITOR*.) And never before have we had so many different foods at our fingertips. These days all kids have to do is go into the local grocery store to learn about foods from around the world.

Lifestyle changes are also pushing kids into the kitchen. Moms are no longer the main meal makers. In 31 percent of households with kids, the kids are the primary meal decision makers, according to a 1998 national sample conducted by NFO Research for the National Pork Producers Council. (The sample surveyed 1,054 primary household cooks and 386 children.) With two-career and single-parent families, kids are becoming increasingly more independent with more input and responsibility in the home, including what goes on the table and into the cupboards.

The *Youth MONITOR* reported that chores are on the upswing for kids 9 to 17 years old. In addition to the jump in kids fixing meals, 57 percent of kids surveyed reported that they cleaned house (compared to 46 percent in 1995) and 38 percent said that they do laundry (as compared to 29 percent in 1995).

Bigger Bites

Cooking classes are becoming increasingly available to kids through culinary academies, cooking schools, and summer camps. Check with your local cooking schools and culinary organizations, recreation departments, and camp guides to see what's happening in your area. Check Appendix B, "The Resource Guide," for organizations, particularly the International Association of Culinary Professionals to find out about cooking professionals in your area.

New Opportunities for Kids to Cook

Just look at some of the exciting developments and opportunities kids have to learn more about food and cooking.

➤ In 1997, chef members of the American Culinary Federation (ACF) started going into schools around the country to teach a 10-week after school cooking program. Called the "That's Fresh Cooking Team," the program teaches kids about nutrition, food shopping, and basic culinary skills and techniques. The goal is to have chefs in all 300 ACF chapters cooking with kids in their communities.

➤ Chefs, parents, farmers, and community leaders are going into schools to teach kids how to prepare foods other kids eat around the world. Called "Adopt-A-School," the eight-part program is geared toward kids ages 8 to 12 and is sponsored by Chefs Collaborative 2000, in partnership with Oldways Preservation & Exchange Trust.

➤ Cooking is increasingly becoming part of the homeroom teacher's day. The "Cooking with Kids" program, developed by the Oregon Dairy Council with the Oregon Department of Education, has spread throughout Oregon and other states around the nation. Antonia Demas, founder of the Food Studies Institute, is working with school districts across the country to teach kids about healthful, low-fat ethnic foods such as legumes. (These high-protein sources include beans, lentils, peanuts, soybeans, and peas.) And chefs have become the new visiting celebrity. Kids are just as likely to learn from a local chef as to learn from a policeman or fireman.

➤ Culinary schools, such as the Culinary Institute of America (CIA), are bringing kids to their campuses. At the CIA in Hyde Park, New York, kids aged 8 to 15 can attend culinary college. Responding to public interest, the CIA recently created two new baking classes for kids.

➤ Kids are learning about and growing food in school gardens. Two leaders in this movement are Chef Alice Waters, owner of Chez Panisse restaurant in Berkeley, CA, and the California Department of Education. Ms. Waters, the apostle of organic food and seasonal cooking, conceived and launched the Edible Schoolyard at the Martin Luther King School in Berkeley with its garden-based curriculum. Meanwhile, the Department of Education has set a goal to create a garden in every school.

➤ Food professionals who belong to the International Association of Culinary Professionals (IACP) have banded together to create a Kids in the Kitchen network to promote and support the idea of teaching kids to cook and to connect people who are doing it. IACP holds Apple Pie Workshops in schools and community centers around the country to give kids a positive cooking experience, side by side with food professionals.

➤ The American Institute of Wine and Food has been educating thousands of kids about taste and flavor with their "Days of Taste" program across the country. This is a far cry from the home economics classes of past decades!

➤ Kids' cooking has become increasingly popular and visible with the growing numbers of classes in cooking schools and kids' camps (79 camps with cooking classes were listed in the 1999 *Peterson's Summer Opportunities for Kids and Teenagers*); the proliferation of cooking products and cookbooks geared toward kids; an increase in stories in the media about kids cooking; and frequent advertisements that show kids preparing meals.

Contact organizations in your area to see what opportunities are available for you and your kids.

Bigger Bites

Team Nutrition was created by the USDA in 1995 to create innovative public and private partnerships to focus on kids and their food choices. The goal is to promote healthful diets through the media, the schools, the community, and the family. Find out about activities in your area through your local cooperative extension service office, listed under the county/city government services in your local phone directory. Or access the USDA through your local U.S. Government office phone listings or on the Web at www.usda.gov.

Why Kids Love to Cook

The fact is, kids love to cook. The kitchen attracts them like a magnet. Remember when your kids were toddlers, how they were always underfoot, wanting to be a part of the activity at the stove? Cooking is like playing to kids. As they get older, the mixing and measuring has the same appeal as the dumping and pouring at the water and sand table in preschool.

As they move into grade school, being able to grasp through cooking the skills they're learning in the classroom—such as reading and math—is stimulating for kids. Many of the young recipe testers for this book expressed their excitement at being able to "click" with measuring, reading, and following directions in their recipes.

Kids are mesmerized by the everyday kitchen chemistry we take for granted, such as when an egg turns into an omelet or a popover puffs. Making food is magical, creative, and gives kids something wonderful to eat at the end. And when they're

around parents or caregivers in the kitchen, they respond to the bonding and nurturing that goes on during a cooking project.

But What About the Mess and Kitchen Mishaps?

Take away the rosy glow and you're still left with some hard-core realities. Kids may love to cook, but they do make a mess. And the kitchen can be a danger zone with its appliances, stoves, and knives. If you're going to cook with your kids, you have to take the messes in stride. That doesn't mean you can't teach your kids good habits. (In subsequent chapters, I'll share my best tips for minimizing the mess and cleaning as you go.) But when you cook with kids, you have to turn on your sense of humor. Kids are incredibly capable, creative, and inventive in the kitchen, but if you're worrying about the mess, you won't be free to discover this side of them.

Mishaps are bound to happen, but they don't have to turn into disasters. You'll learn all about handling them in Part 3, "Kid-Proofing Your Kitchen," which includes chapters on kitchen mishaps and the basics such as kitchen safety and appliance use.

Keep in mind that some of the most creative dishes are born of mistakes. In fact, when I tested my "Mom's 1-2-3-4 Cake" for this book, I added more liquid than was originally required, and the result was fabulous!

Staying in Control

Another nagging fear about cooking with kids is that things will just spin out of control or turn sour. I once convinced my friend Susan Hauser to try some cooking as a way of bonding with her middle-schooler. She decided to bake with her daughter, and the next thing I knew, I had this frantic message from her on my answering machine: "Joan, help! I took your advice but my bonding backfired. Our cooking session turned into a tug of war and my daughter eventually stormed out of the kitchen."

Learning to avoid these problems comes with knowing how to anticipate, set up a game plan, and use a little old-fashioned psychology with your kids. I've translated years of experience cooking with my own kids and others in schools to give you detailed information that will limit these problems. Take the time to read through this book and you'll soon be heading for success with your kids in the kitchen. And remember, even if you're feeling frazzled, the kids are learning and having a great time.

Kitchen Time Is Quality Time

Despite some of these very real fears about being with kids in the kitchen, I'm convinced it's among the best quality time you can spend with your kids. As a parent, I've delighted in seeing my kids grow in competence and master skills they'll use for the rest of their lives. It's eye-opening to see how kids approach cooking and to watch their inventiveness. And your kids feel nurtured when you take the time to teach them how to cook and produce something good to eat. When you read the next chapter and find out the far-reaching and positive impact cooking will have on your kids, I think you'll agree that it's worth all the effort.

Kitchen Clue

Use kitchen time as a way of bonding and enjoying quality time with your kids.

The Least You Need to Know

➤ More kids are cooking. A national youth trends survey found that 88 percent of kids aged 6 to 17 fix meals and 26 percent aged 9 to 17 usually make meals for their family. The latter is up from 15 percent in 1995.

➤ New resources, ranging from school gardens to classes in nutrition and cooking, are becoming more available to our kids.

➤ Chefs, food professionals, and educators across the country are increasingly going into schools and supporting cooking with kids programs.

➤ Kids and messes go hand in hand—especially in the kitchen. Be sure to keep your sense of humor about you.

➤ Cooking with your kids is a way of creating and enjoying quality time with them.

Chapter 2

Why Kids Belong in the Kitchen

In This Chapter

➤ What kids learn when they cook

➤ Why kitchen time is quality time

➤ How cooking builds upon and improves classroom skills

➤ How kids discover new cultures and traditions

➤ How cooking promotes social, physical, and emotional development

➤ How kids learn life lessons through cooking

I've yet to meet a kid who doesn't like to cook. And that's a good thing. Because while kids think they're just having fun in the kitchen, they're really developing and sharpening skills they'll use for the rest of their lives. In this chapter, you'll discover the amazing benefits of bringing kids into the kitchen.

Learning While They Play

Ask a child to make something in the kitchen and they're likely to dive right in with gusto. No wonder. All that mixing, measuring, and pouring (and munching along the way) is just like playing. It's as appealing and absorbing as making mud pies or building sand castles.

For kids and adults alike, cooking is a creative experience. You start with an idea—a recipe—mix up and cook ingredients and, in the end, you have a delicious, edible treat, one that you created with your own hands. What better way to feel good about yourself and satisfy your appetite?

Kid Quiz

What do cooking and playing have in common?

They're both fun and creative. When you cook, you put together lots of different ingredients to create something new and good to eat. You also need to be careful to follow the safety rules of the kitchen just as you would the rules of a game.

This sense of creativity and accomplishment results in some very real benefits for kids. When your child is able to engage in a project with a beginning, middle, and end, and see it through to the finish, he or she winds up with a very real feeling of accomplishment—not to mention the good food shared with family and friends and the praise awarded for all that hard work.

Kids may think they're playing, but in reality their cooking projects

➤ Stimulate their curiosity about foods and ingredients.

➤ Cultivate their imagination and creativity.

➤ Develop skills and abilities that carry beyond cooking, such as organizing and quick thinking.

➤ Boost their self-respect.

I credit my daughter's kindergarten teacher, Susan Conway, with opening my eyes to the emotional rewards of cooking with kids. One day I was telling Susan that Lizzie liked to help me in the kitchen. Susan saw cooking as a great opportunity to boost Lizzie's self-confidence and even cut down on the sibling rivalry she was experiencing with her older sister, Julia.

"Give her a niche in the family and make her feel like an expert at cooking," she suggested. I began encouraging her to help out with cooking and praising her efforts. And I saw firsthand how she blossomed. Lizzie felt really important in our family and was proud of her growing kitchen wisdom. And, because she was developing her own skills, she didn't feel the need to compete as much with Julia.

Down the road, Julia noticed her sister's growing proficiency and decided that she wanted to be in on the action, too. Fortunately they gravitated toward different areas. Julia liked to bake cookies and brownies and make salads and salad dressings. (The latter, in part, stemmed from her decision to become a vegetarian.) Lizzie was more of a generalist and thought of herself as my little assistant, no matter what we were making.

Kitchen Time Is Bonding Time

When kids have a good cooking experience, they feel good about themselves. They're proud of their accomplishments and their ability to create wonderful food from raw ingredients. And something magical also happens with the adult with whom they're cooking. A special type of bond develops as you work together in the warm and nurturing environment of a kitchen.

Being alone with a youngster in the kitchen also fosters communication in a nonthreatening way. I like to compare it to what I call car time—the time when you're alone in the car with a child on the way to a soccer game or a ballet lesson. Ever notice how kids open up about what's happening in their lives when they've got you all to themselves in the privacy of a car—and they don't have to look you straight in the eye?

The kitchen works the same way. When you're both focused on a common goal and you're alone in the kitchen, you can find out all sorts of things about what's happening in your child's life. I regularly have my kids cooking by my side just to catch up on what they're up to.

Kitchen Clue

To boost kids' self-esteem, be sure to praise their efforts along the way and especially their final culinary creations. Make them feel good by showing off their food on a fancy plate or in a prominent spot on the table. Let kids proudly bring their own creation to the table at mealtime.

Could It Make Them Smarter in Math and Science?

You may have heard that cooking improves kids' academic skills. Well, you've heard right. In fact, all that measuring does help them put into practice the math they've learned in the classroom. And when they see liquids turn to solids, watch water boil, or discover how yeast causes dough to rise, they get firsthand science lessons.

And that's not all. Working in the kitchen can improve your child's reading skills and expand his or her vocabulary. Following a recipe lets kids practice their reading and reinforces the usefulness of good reading habits. (You may motivate your reluctant reader to keep at it after all!)

Kid Quiz

When you mix and measure in the kitchen, what school subject are you practicing?

Math. You're practicing fractions when you measure parts of a cup, and you're doing math when you add ingredients together.

The world of food exposes children to all sorts of new words and concepts. Kids may wonder how you pronounce unfamiliar words, like cumin, and want to learn what they mean. You can tell them and let them smell and taste the spice and talk about how to use it. And they'll probably get curious about the information on the side of the flour bag or the cornstarch box and ask you questions about the nutrition labels and ingredients you use for a recipe. Keep 'em asking! My friend Siobhan Loughran says baking her mom's Irish soda bread with her 5-year-old, Joseph, has been "the biggest teaching aid I ever had." Her son used to say he was going to be a cowboy.

"Now he wants to measure, read, and understand all the instructions for the recipe and read the printed information about the ingredients," says Siobhan. "When you ask him what he wants to be, he says he wants to be a cowboy chef." (You'll find her family bread recipe in Chapter 29, "The Baker's Rack.")

Mastering Motor Skills and Organizing

It's no accident that therapists encourage children with learning disabilities to cook. In fact, special education students here in Portland, Oregon are assigned recipes to cook with their families as homework. Learning to organize ingredients, follow recipes, and understand directions helps kids learn how to work in sequence. Similarly, all the stirring, chopping, mixing, and pouring required in cooking sharpens hand-eye coordination and improves motor skills.

Kitchen Clue

Make the most out of measuring by turning it into a mini math lesson. Use the recipe as a jumping-off point. For instance, if a recipe calls for a quarter cup of liquid, ask kids how many quarter cups equal a cup and measure it out with water. They'll enjoy seeing firsthand the practical application of math learned in the classroom.

Working on a recipe also promotes logical thinking. Children begin to understand why it's important to follow directions and work step by step.
They see the cause and effect of procedures and
working in a systematic way. And the focus, pre-
dictability, and order of working in sequence, in
turn, produces a calming effect.

Another positive result is that kids learn how to
cooperate. When youngsters have to read through
a recipe, get out ingredients, and work with you
to make a dish, they're learning the give-and-take
of working with someone on a project. Time and
again, we cooking teachers see the best side of
kids come out in classes when they have to work
as a group toward a common goal.

Kitchen Clue

Help promote logical thinking by
explaining why you need to follow a recipe step by step. Kids
learn about the cause and effect
of the sequence as you work
through the recipe. For example,
when you're baking, explain that
you crack the eggs first so that
you can get them out of the
shell. Then you beat them and
add them to liquid ingredients.
Then you add the liquids to the
solids and after this, you can stir
to make a dough.

A Window on the World and Traditions

Cooking helps kids learn about geography, history, and other cultures. When kids learn about
and prepare ethnic dishes, they build a direct link
to the foods and lifestyles of people from other
countries. Making a dish from a foreign country makes that culture more real for you
and your children. When 9-year-old Allie Hinckley tested my recipe for Mexican Hot
Chocolate, she was intrigued by Mexican customs and told her mom she wanted to
study Spanish and learn more about Mexico.

Familiarity with foods from other cultures also exposes us to the customs and ways of
a society different from our own. When children can accept something as basic as a
culture's food, they're more likely to be open to the people of that culture. By introducing children early on to other ethnic groups through food, we may help to over-
come prejudices that may develop later in life.

And what about your own family's food traditions? Chances are a grandparent, parent, or relative cooked with you and taught you to make dishes you enjoyed as a
child. Even if you didn't do the actual cooking, you may recall favorite dishes or traditions shared by your family. The kitchen offers a wonderful way to share these traditions with your own children and their friends.

Bigger Bites

Keeping a world atlas near the kitchen helps you turn cooking into a geography lesson. When you cook the foods of another culture, find the country from which it originated on a map. Ask yourself and your child if you know anyone of that ethnic origin.

Kids Eat What They Cook

If food is the way to someone's heart, then cooking is the way to a kid's stomach. Ever notice how kids eat what they've had a hand in buying, preparing, or cooking? Getting kids involved in the kitchen is probably the best way to get them to eat well and improve their nutrition IQ.

When kids are responsible for making food, they're invested in that food. They feel a pride of ownership and control over what they're eating. If nothing else, they're curious and determined to see how their culinary concoction turns out. And that translates into their willingness to eat.

Heads Up!

Don't shortcut your children's creativity in the kitchen by always stepping in to complete tasks. It may take some patience, but give kids time to discover their particular kitchen style and work on their own—with your guidance, of course. They'll get the hang of things sooner than you think.

That's why so many nutritionists suggest that when you want to improve your child's eating habits, you should get them involved in buying and making their own food. Some even believe that cooking may help prevent eating disorders, such as anorexia and bulimia. The theory is that the more kids learn about nutrition and what's good for their bodies, the more aware they are about the damage they can cause with poor eating habits.

Learning Life Skills and Valuable Lessons

The fact is, we all have to eat. And when kids learn how to fend for themselves safely in the kitchen, they get a jump-start on a skill they'll need and use the rest of their lives.

These days everyone worries about food safety, and for good reason. Media reports about health problems resulting from tainted foods are becoming all too common. But you can empower your kids and help them feel more in control when you teach them how to recognize food that's gone bad or show them how to store and handle food properly so it won't spoil. When they learn how to wash their hands well, sanitize cutting boards, utensils, and counters, and handle raw meats or eggs, they're learning valuable lessons that will keep them healthy and safe.

And just think. Once kids get hooked on cooking, they can even begin to pitch in at dinnertime or, as happens in some families, take responsibility for making one meal a week. Now isn't that a pleasant thought?

The Benefits of Cooking at a Glance

Here's a snapshot of the many benefits kids derive from cooking:

Sharpens These Academic Skills and Puts Them into Practice

➤ Math

➤ Science

➤ Reading

➤ Writing

➤ Vocabulary building

➤ Geography

➤ History

Fosters Intellectual Skills

➤ Cultivates imagination and creativity

➤ Stimulates curiosity about foods, ingredients, and chemical reactions

➤ Teaches and promotes logical and sequential thinking

➤ Helps children learn to organize

Promotes Social and Emotional Development

➤ Boosts self-esteem and self-confidence

➤ Empowers children by teaching them skills and responsibility

➤ Fosters cooperation and working with others

➤ Promotes sharing and communication

➤ Inspires bonding with others

➤ Develops feelings of well-being and pride about completing a project successfully

➤ Promotes security by offering children a finite project with an achievable, immediate goal

Improves Physical Skills

➤ Develops hand-eye coordination

➤ Improves motor skills

Provides Quality Time with Adults

➤ Promotes well-being and bonding

➤ Offers fun short-term projects

➤ Provides the opportunity to discover family food history

Exposes Children to Nutrition and to Other Cultures

➤ Familiarizes children with different food groups

➤ Helps improve eating habits

➤ Exposes children to other cultures and ethnic cuisine

➤ Teaches how to handle food safely

The Least You Need to Know

➤ Kitchen experiences can increase your child's self-esteem, self-confidence, imagination, creativity, and curiosity.

➤ Consider cooking time quality time—an opportunity to foster communication, cooperation, and bonding with your child.

➤ When kids cook, they sharpen their academic skills, learn to think logically, improve their motor skills, and even learn about other traditions and cultures.

➤ When kids make their own food, they eat better and learn valuable life skills, such as healthful eating and safely preparing nutritious food.

Part 2

Getting Kids Curious About Food

Now that you're convinced it's worth taking the plunge, how do you get your kids interested in food and new flavors? Start by involving them in everyday tasks. They'll like the new responsibility, and you'll like the help.

The next time you go to the market, bring them along and let them help you select the food. Let them fill their own lunch box or set the dinner table.

Have fun exploring the food around you. Check out new recipes in newspapers and magazines or watch a cooking show. You can even find food in your own backyard: Take a look at your family's culinary traditions and talk to relatives about them.

The next few chapters give detailed pointers on how to set out with your kids and your family on this culinary adventure. You'll learn how to bring these ideas to life. Have fun hunting and discovering the food around you!

Chapter 3

Food Finds Around Us

In This Chapter

➤ Getting kids interested in food

➤ Letting kids help in the kitchen and at the market

➤ Exploring food at restaurants and in the community

➤ Discovering food in fairy tales and stories

➤ Finding food in the media, on the Internet, and on the computer

---

So now that you know all the good things your kids can get from cooking, how do you get them started? Chances are your kids are already somewhat interested in and involved with food. Every time they open the refrigerator door, whether it's for a drink or a snack or to help get food ready for dinner, they're directly involved with food. The trick is to get them thinking about food differently—getting them to notice the food they eat, to wonder where it comes from and how it is made. This chapter takes a look at finding food in the most common places but looking at it in uncommon ways.

How Can I Get My Kids Interested in Food?

The best way to get kids interested in food is to make it mean something to them. Help them make connections between food and their everyday activities. Take the Food Guide Pyramid as an example. Your kids can probably recite for you the different food groups, but do they think about which ones they're eating during the day? If you show them how powering up with healthful foods will help them ace that test in school or play a better soccer game, eating right becomes more important to them.

Give Kids Easy Kitchen Tasks

One of the simplest ways to get kids started in the kitchen is to give them some easy tasks. Next time you go to make dinner or a meal, stop and think of what your kids can do to contribute. Be sure to let them know how important their efforts are to getting the meal on the table. The encouragement will help build enthusiasm for the task.

A safe and easily achieved task is getting the salad ready or washing vegetables. Kids love being at the sink. It's like water play to them. You can teach them how to wash greens and how important washing is to get rid of any dirt, germs, or chemicals that might be on the food. With recent reports about pesticides and their impact on children, thorough washing has become even more important. Make the connection for them between the task and the reason for doing the task.

Heads Up!

Choose kitchen tasks for kids carefully. Tasks that are too difficult or too involved could discourage them and cause them to lose interest. Think about what they like to do, such as measuring and stirring, and then give them an appropriate task.

Other simple and safe tasks include mixing and measuring foods, getting food out of the refrigerator or cupboard, or being the timekeeper and letting you know when something is cooked.

Kid Quiz

Can you think of five easy and safe things you can do to help get food ready for dinner?

Wash the vegetables, make the salad, measure ingredients, mix and stir, and keep track of the time things take to cook.

Let Them Help You Market

I admit that taking little kids into a supermarket is not a parent's dream. My neighbor recently confided that she hires a baby sitter so she can shop in peace, and I admitted I used to do the same. But when the kids get into grade school, a trip to the supermarket or the farmers' market can be a great way to not only teach them about foods they eat every day, but also can open their eyes to new foods.

When you take the kids shopping, you involve them in the nitty-gritty of family life. They feel like they're contributing by helping to select foods and loading and unloading grocery bags in and out of the car. And, depending on your community, and your children's ages, they can help you shop. When I lived in New York City, there was no way I would let my kids out of my sight. But now that we live in a smaller and safer community, and they are older and able to walk around the market by themselves, they're a big help in getting through the shopping list.

Even when your kids are tagging along beside the shopping cart, they can help you choose foods by looking at the nutrition facts label, reading ingredients, and comparing the unit pricing labels. Taking them into the produce section, with its beautiful colors and displays, can also be eye-opening. So many new foods from other countries are becoming available locally that seeing what's new in produce is an education. (For other tips on involving your kids in shopping, check out Chapter 5, "The Savvy Food Shopper.")

Go "Behind the Scenes"

My husband and I have always been the kind of people who like to go "behind the scenes." In other words, we like to find out more about what we're looking at and ask questions about what goes into the making of something.

Start thinking about farms and other food-related places where you too could go behind the scenes. For instance, are there any food producers or manufacturers in your community? Could you visit a local bakery—when they're not busy—and find out about breadmaking? I once arranged to take a class of youngsters to visit the Portland Pretzel Company, where the kids learned how pretzels were made and got to make their own. They loved it! Look through the yellow pages or newspaper ads for ideas. Don't be bashful—people love to share their stories and will be flattered that you have an interest in their work.

Bigger Bites

Go behind the scenes at local food manufacturers or farms to find out more about the food around you. Food producers often offer tours, if not to individuals, then usually to school groups. Talk to your children's teachers about arranging a visit.

Let's Eat Out

Taking the family to an ethnic restaurant can be a novel way to spend quality family time. For a few hours you can expose yourselves to another culture and learn a little about the foods that are a part of life in other places around the world.

The novelty of ethnic foods, especially finger foods or dishes that come flaming to the table, naturally attracts kids. Wrapping fresh Vietnamese spring rolls or Mexican fajitas, dipping bread into Swiss fondue, or scooping African food up with bread, is fun for them and exposes them to other ways of eating.

My kids to this day remember the Chinese restaurant we used to frequent, where the waiters were intent on teaching them how to use chopsticks. The waiters would fold the wrapper into one small piece and wedge it between the tops of the chopsticks. They then wrapped a rubber band around the top of the sticks to keep them together and create a spring-like utensil. (Try it sometime. It makes the chopsticks easy to use and gives kids the thrill of eating with them.) We like to look for small, family-run places where owners are willing to talk about their food and culture. Check local restaurant reviews, guides, or your yellow pages to find out about restaurants.

Eating out has other advantages. Our friends the Weavers have made it a point to take their kids to ethnic restaurants several times a month. They say it gives them a stress-free chance to catch up and have a delicious meal. In the process, the kids have developed healthful eating habits.

It's often interesting to follow up a meal with a visit to a local ethnic market or the supermarket. Ask the owner where he or she buys food. We also like to link our travels with visits to local restaurants. If you're planning a trip to a foreign country, look for a restaurant specializing in that country's food. Eat there before you travel to become familiar with some of the foods and again when you return home to compare the local version with what you ate abroad.

Bigger Bites

Visiting a local ethnic market can be an eye-opening experience about the foodways of different cultures. Don't be shy about asking proprietors or other shoppers to explain how they use different foods and products. It's one of the best ways to begin to understand the foods. You could also find a cookbook specializing in the cuisine for an easy reference.

Tune In to TV Cooking Shows

Believe it or not, some kids get hooked on television cooking shows. Think about it. Many of these shows are lively, entertaining, and educational—not to mention inspiring. Several years ago, I interviewed Michelle Dinkes from Trumbull, Connecticut, for a national story on kid's cooking. The then 13-year-old had a whole list of favorite shows she watched on the TV Food Network. She started watching them when she was 12 and was so inspired she'd cook her family meals and even improvise and add her own herbs and spices. Today, Michelle tells me she's still cooking and watching her shows. Her school workload is heavier so she's doing the family cooking mostly during vacations. But she's still finding time to bake twice a week for volunteers at the Yale–New Haven Hospital.

If your kids, like Michelle, begin to watch TV cooking shows, be sure they don't try what they see on TV without supervision. Explain that TV shows use a lot of tricks to make food look good and that some of the techniques might not be appropriate for their skill level.

Find Food in Magazines

If you're interested in cooking, just go to a newsstand and you'll have your pick of magazines devoted to some aspect of cooking. They all fill a particular need, whether it's learning to make coffee and tea or learning cooking techniques or entertaining. For everyday cooking, women's magazines are a good bet. Let the kids browse through them and see what sparks their interest. These magazines have monthly cooking features, usually geared toward the season, a theme, or a holiday. And don't overlook the product ads. They usually offer quick and easy recipes—involving their products, of course. You may also find special promotions and pull-out recipe booklets for the particular products.

Magazines geared toward kids or families also publish monthly cooking columns or feature a kids' cooking lesson. Features in *FamilyFun* magazine, in particular, offer interesting and easy projects for kids, with the view that their parents are their cooking coaches. In Appendix B, "The Resource Guide," at the back of this book, you'll find the names of several magazines that contain regular cooking features.

Read the Weekly Newspaper Food Section

Another way to get kids interested in food is to have them check out the weekly food section in your local newspaper. Ask them if any of the recipes appeal to them and see if they'd like to try any for lunch or dinner. Then suggest they help you make the recipe. They can start their own recipe file and clip out the ones they've made or would like to try someday.

Kitchen Clue

Come the Christmas and Thanksgiving holidays, I always make a point of stocking up on women's magazines. They have special baking and cooking sections from which you and your kids can pick up new recipes and tips for holiday entertaining.

Look for kids' features and see if your local paper has a kids' cooking column. Sometimes the free community weeklies run features on kids' cooking. My kids are fortunate because our daily newspaper, *The Oregonian*, has been a pioneer in devoting space to kids' cooking. The editors started a weekly kids' page, titled YUM!, in April 1994. The page offers cooking features, a nutrition column, and other kid-related food stories. Kids or their families can write in to submit recipes for the child-of-the-week feature. The newspaper runs a picture of the child, his or her comments about their recipe, and the recipe.

Enter a Recipe Contest

Ever think about entering a recipe contest? That's a sure-fire way to get kids thinking about food and coming up with ideas for food combinations. Many of the big food companies regularly sponsor contests, and some of them have started gearing them toward kids. Keep your eyes open for contest announcements in your local newspaper food section, women's magazines, and at Web sites on the Internet. Appendix B has a list of food-related Web sites.

Go Cookbook Shopping

Take a Saturday afternoon to visit a local bookstore and browse through their children's cookbook section. You'll be amazed at how giving a child a cookbook of his very own promotes interest in food and cooking. Don't be afraid to get the cookbooks dirty or mark your comments or changes on the recipes. (It will be fun for them when they get older to see what they liked to make.) The same goes for using the recipes in this book. Star ones you've tried and make notes about what you like or don't like and ingredients you'd like to substitute.

There's Food in That Fairy Tale

Fairy tales and children's books are filled with hundreds of references to food. Many, like *Strega Nona* by Tomie de Paola or *The Real Princess* by Hans Christian Andersen, are magical stories based on food. The first involves a magic pasta pot and the second a princess and three little peas. Food plays a minor or significant role in others. Think of the tales of Winnie the Pooh with his honey pot or Goldilocks eating the porridge at the Three Bears' house.

Kid Quiz

Can you name some stories based on food or some of the foods your favorite story characters like? Do you eat any of these foods? What do you like about them? Would you like to try to make a recipe based on the food?

Children's literature becomes a wonderful jumping-off point for kids to explore food. Take advantage of these food references when you read with your kids. You can talk about the food, what it tastes like, what kids do or don't like about it, and whether it's healthful.

Kids might also be more willing to taste and make certain foods if they're linked to characters they like in books. Trying to cook the foods from fairy tales or cookbooks spawned by book series can also be exciting for kids. A favorite for our neighbor, 8-year-old Anna Wearn, is the *Box Car Children Cookbook*. The cookbook, like other series cookbooks, includes recipes from the adventures of characters in the series. And then there are cookbooks based on the American Girl dolls. The dolls represent different historical periods, and the cookbooks contain recipes from the different periods in history. Both my daughters and their friends have enjoyed exploring these earlier days through the recipes.

In addition to series cookbooks, I've also discovered cookbooks devoted solely to characters like Winnie the Pooh and Peter Rabbit, and recipe collections that include foods from many fairy tales. Check the shelves of your local library or bookstore for these books.

Kitchen Clue

Get kids cooking and eating new foods by making foods from their favorite fairy tales or stories.

Finding Food on the Internet

The Internet has become an excellent source for food games and information. Most of the major food companies have Web sites with recipes and detailed information about their products. Several have a special kids' corner on the Web site with activities and information especially geared toward kids.

If your kids like playing on the computer, they'll enjoy exploring some of the kids' sites and finding food links. Challenge them to find what they think is the best kid's Web site.

Computer Fun and Games

Also look for computer software that features the Food Guide Pyramid and food-related games. Kids have fun guessing about the foods they should be eating. One CD my kids have really enjoyed is the *5 a Day Adventures* put out by the Dole Food Company. (Information about this CD and Web site is listed in Appendix B.)

Learn the Lingo

5 a Day refers to the dietary recommendation to eat at least five fruits and vegetables every day. The fiber and nutrients contained in fruits and vegetables contribute to a healthful diet.

Kid Quiz

How many sites with interactive food games can you find on the Internet? Write down the sites and rate them according to how much fun they are and how much you're learning.

The Least You Need to Know

➤ Prompt kids to get interested in food by giving them simple tasks like washing vegetables or mixing and measuring ingredients.

➤ Encourage kids to find recipes they'd like to try in magazines, the local food section of the newspaper, and cookbooks.

➤ Get kids interested in ethnic foods and customs around the world by eating in ethnic restaurants.

➤ Children's literature and fairy tales are rich with references to food. Pique kids' curiosity about food by eating or making the foods that their favorite fictional characters like.

➤ Cooking shows, computer games, and the Internet all offer learning opportunities and food adventures for kids.

Chapter 4

Discovering Your Family Food Roots

In This Chapter

➤ Discovering your family's culinary history

➤ Searching out and organizing family recipes

➤ Creating a family cookbook, memory box, and album

Looking within your own family for food traditions is another way to get kids interested in the foods around them. This chapter explores different ideas and ways to spotlight food in your family. You'll find tips for creating a family culinary tree, collecting and writing your family recipes, making a family cookbook, and extending your culinary search into cultural and art projects.

Make a Family Food Tree

A fun project for the whole family is to make a family culinary tree. Get started by setting it up the way you would a regular family tree, with the names of the members of your immediate family and branches showing your various relatives.

Now write in the country each relative is from and the kind of food he or she makes. Have your kids help you contact relatives to collect information and ask them if they have any favorite recipes. If anyone specializes in a particular dish, add that next to the name. Include the history of the dish or any special alterations your family has made to the dish. This tree will serve as an outline for starting your research.

Kid Quiz

Can you think of any food traditions in your family or any special dishes relatives make that you particularly like?

Find out where each tradition came from and how it got started. Ask your relative if he or she will teach you how to make that favorite dish.

Finding Your Food Roots

Once you have identified your family members and set up your tree, expand it by searching for information about your *culinary* heritage. Think about your food traditions and how they started. Find out if any relatives were chefs, restaurant owners, or involved in a food-related business. Put all your research in a spiral-bound notebook, on large index cards, or in a loose-leaf binder. Place the actual tree at the beginning of the research. Separate information into categories, such as family history, and by recipes, such as entrées or baked goods. You can add to your notebook as you get more information.

Here are some questions you can ask yourself and relatives to gather culinary history:

Learn the Lingo

The word **culinary** is an adjective that means "of the kitchen or cooking." It also describes something that is used in or is suitable for cooking.

➤ What country are your ancestors from? Do you still have any relatives in that country?

➤ What are some of the food specialties particular to your family and that country?

➤ Do you have any living relatives who still make these foods? Can you contact them to get recipes or to find out about the food?

➤ What are your family's holiday traditions?

➤ Does your family cook any seasonal foods?

➤ If your family has created any new traditions, what are they and how did you get started doing them?

➤ What are some of your favorite recipes?

Discovering and Writing the Recipes

Your tree and culinary history book will take shape as you discover and gather recipes from relatives. When you get recipes, write them up the way you would see them in a regular cookbook. Use the following sample as a guide or create your own format for recording the recipes. See Chapter 11, "Getting to Know Your Recipe," to learn more about how recipes are put together.

Sample Family Recipe

Name of the recipe and who gave it to you

Number of servings the recipe makes

How hard the recipe is or how long it will take to make

Any special comments about the recipe (for example, "Our family always makes these cookies during the holidays")

Equipment you need to make the recipe

Ingredients used in the recipe (include any favorite brands of foods used)

Recipe instructions

Any special comments or tips about the recipe

Notes about the history of the recipe

> The person who gave me the recipe is my _____ (relationship to me). He/She was born in _____ on _____.
>
> He/She got the recipe from _____.
>
> His/Her family liked to make this food on _____ (holidays, birthdays, and so on).
>
> Other customs or special ways of serving the dish are
>
> _____.

Taking Care with Family Recipes

One of the big problems with wonderful family recipes is nailing down the specifics of how something is made. How often have you tried to repeat a recipe your mother makes but it never seems to come out the same? Warn your kids that you have to work with relatives to find out exact amounts of ingredients and details about timing, equipment, and methods of cooking. My mom's a fabulous cook. Like many

Heads Up!

When you write down recipes from relatives, pay attention to details. Ask for exact quantities of ingredients, sizes of equipment, and the method of cooking or baking. Read over the recipe and ask about anything you don't understand.

cooks, however, she often eyeballs the amount of an ingredient, or she'll add a spice or a seasoning by testing and tasting. I'm constantly having to quiz her about the details of her recipes, such as exactly how much a handful of an ingredient is, what type or size pan she uses, or how long and at what temperature she cooks something to achieve its lovely texture, flavor, or color.

Impress upon your kids that one of the best—and most fun—ways to really get the recipe right is to cook it alongside the person who makes it. Have your notebook and liquid and dry measuring cups and spoons right on hand. Warn your relative that you're going to be looking for exact quantities. Before he or she puts in a handful of an ingredient, measure it first. It might seem like a lot of work, but I'm convinced it's the only way to get the recipe right. It's also fun to share the experience of making the dish with the relative.

A Kid's Cooking Scrapbook

After you and your kids gather some recipes, see if there are any you want to try cooking together. Make your own recipe collection of what you've cooked by putting the recipes on index cards, punching a hole in one end, and collecting the recipes on a large ring. Put it on a hook or in a drawer near the stove. When your kids want to

Kitchen Clue

Make your own family cookbook from favorite recipes you've gathered from relatives. Everyone will enjoy seeing your collection, and it will be easy to cook from an organized book. Add your own special comments or notes to the recipes as you make the dishes.

cook, they'll have the recipes right at hand. It also will be exciting to see how the collection grows.

You can make a scrapbook, too, by taking some photos while you're cooking and recording your children's impressions of their kitchen experience and how they liked the finished product. Having visual proof boosts kids' confidence in their cooking abilities and makes them feel great about their accomplishment.

When my daughter Lizzie was in third grade, we made a braided yeast bread for a school project. She insisted that we take pictures as a way to illustrate the steps of the recipe. She pasted the photos along with the recipe steps, which she hand wrote, onto large sheets of oaktag, punched holes on the side, and bound the sheets into a "book" with ribbon. The book made a lovely keepsake, and the photos are a nice reminder of our shared kitchen project. We still have a picture on our kitchen wall of her braiding the bread. When Lizzie tackles a tough or new kitchen project, the photo is there to encourage her and to remind her that she can do it.

Creating a Family Cookbook or Memory Box

You can collect all your recipes and photos and put them together in a cookbook or a memory box. Your kids might find some old photos or artifacts when they talk to relatives. My dad was an Army mess sergeant during World War II, and we have some wonderful photos of him cooking in camp.

Keep your eyes open for equipment, too. You might even find a relative who is willing to part with an old kitchen tool that's out of production today.

Scrapbooks are all the rage these days, so you might get some good ideas for organizing your material from a scrapbook company. Check copying centers, too, to find out whether they can bind your book with a plastic spiral binder, copy pictures, and laminate a cover.

The following are some different approaches to organizing your project:

➤ Type up and print out recipes on the computer and organize them like a cookbook into categories such as appetizers, salads, entrées, and desserts. Add sheets with your photos, artwork, or any bits of history. Use a family photo or your children's drawings to make a nice cover that can be laminated.

➤ Write or print recipes on large index cards and organize them into categories. Punch holes through the corners and collect them on a ring or put them in a box.

➤ Make and decorate a memory box to hold photos, recipes, and any special cooking tools or mementos. Your kids can make a collage from magazine or family photos to cover the box.

Bigger Bites

Get ideas for assembling your family scrapbook at one of the new scrapbook stores. Look for them in shopping malls or check the listings in the yellow pages for locations. Copy centers also offer ways to bind your family cookbook and copy recipes with color photos of the relatives who gave the recipe.

Activities Beyond Your Family Cookbook

Making a family cookbook goes beyond just gathering recipes. Here are some other activities you can weave into your family's cookbook gathering experiences:

➤ Turn it into a history and geography lesson. Pull out the atlas and see where your ancestors were born.

➤ Check the encyclopedia for customs, dress, and traditional foods from your family's country of origin. Find out if particular dishes or ingredients have any special meanings behind them.

➤ Look in published cookbooks for recipes similar to yours and see how they vary from your own family's version. Look for some history or background about the recipes.

➤ Let your children take and write the notes about the recipes to sharpen these skills.

➤ Turn the book into an art project, and let your kids draw their own pictures of the dishes.

The Least You Need to Know

➤ Spark your children's interest in food and cooking by having the whole family explore your culinary heritage.

➤ Search out family recipes for a fun and educational experience for your kids.

➤ Collect special recipes and bind them into a cookbook or make a memory box with photos.

➤ Expand learning about your family cooking traditions into activities involving history, culture, and art.

Chapter 5

The Savvy Food Shopper

In This Chapter

➤ Bringing your kids to the supermarket

➤ Shopping seductions and how to avoid them

➤ Being a smart shopper

➤ Reading unit labels

➤ Exploring farmers' markets, U-pick farms, and farm stands

When it comes to exposing kids to food, a supermarket can be a giant classroom. Taking kids to the market is educational, but it also can turn into a tug of war. The kids might want to hit the junk food aisles or head straight for the latest product advertised on TV.

You can have more control over your shopping excursions when you know how to avoid merchandising traps. You then can use the market as a place to spark your kids' interest in foods that are not only new but also nutritious, and you can teach them how to be smart shoppers.

This chapter tells you all the things your grocer doesn't want you to know. It's full of useful tips and ways to explore other shopping outlets, such as farmers' markets and U-pick farms and stands. Read on to learn strategies for becoming a savvy shopper.

Why Bring the Kids to the Market?

Kids are eager learners, and a food market, whether it's an outdoor farmers' market or a supermarket, offers lots of opportunities to learn about food. You can empower kids by letting them have input on food decisions that affect the whole family. Chances are, if they get to help choose what goes on their plate, they'll eat it. They might even become more interested in how it's prepared and gets to the table. And that's not all. You instill both self-esteem and a sense of responsibility when you get your kids to actively participate in the daily goings-on of the family.

Heads Up!

If the kids get antsy while you're shopping, give them a job. Have them read and compare unit cost, nutrition, and ingredient labels. The activity promotes logical and critical thinking, and it gets them to put their math skills to practical use.

The Market Supports School Skills

Food shopping also can be a way to reinforce things kids are learning in and out of school. When kids figure out the cost of an item, they're putting math skills to use. They're also learning life skills about budgeting and money management.

Seeing ethnic foods in the aisles of your supermarket shows them that they live in a world of many cultures, some of which they're probably studying.

Reading nutrition, unit price, and ingredient labels promotes critical thinking. Your kids will learn to control how they spend money and what foods they put into their bodies. In fact, each section of the supermarket, from the dairy case to the produce aisle, offers kids a window to learning about different foods.

Heads Up!

Supermarkets are designed to encourage impulse buying. Staples such as milk and meats are hidden in the back of the store so you're forced to go down aisles of tempting goods. Some marketers refer to the aisles as the "prison." You're trapped until you get to the end, and you're forced to wheel past all those enticing products.

What Your Grocer Doesn't Want You to Know

Do you ever go into a grocery store for just a few items and walk out with a cart filled with food? It's no accident. Grocery stores, now more than ever, are designed to seduce us and to part us from our dollars. Their layout and merchandising are cleverly planned based on behavioral research and marketing techniques. Couple that with the ads our kids see on TV, and we're conned into buying foods we don't necessarily want or need.

Shopping Seductions

You can gain more control over your buying habits when you're aware of standard merchandising lures. Here are some tricks of the trade:

➤ Colorful and shiny fruits and vegetables typically are piled near the entrance to attract you and visually draw you into the store. Ditto for good-looking signs telling you the hottest store bargains.

➤ Soothing music, a pleasant atmosphere, and lighting are all designed to make you comfortable and to keep you happily shopping.

➤ Supermarkets are becoming increasingly open and airy with the current trends in marketplace design. Merchandise is displayed in areas resembling quaint shops.

➤ Delis entice shoppers with their café-style environment and appetizing smells. You can buy a full take-home meal or eat it right at the store.

➤ Home meal replacements—ready-to-eat foods that replace ones you normally would cook at home—are increasingly taking over supermarket space. They're attractively displayed to help you solve your dinner problems. The same goes for convenience foods. Watch out, though. You're paying for the convenience.

Learn the Lingo

Home meal replacement (HMR) *is a supermarket industry term for ready-to-eat meals targeted at consumers who want food that is quick and easy and that tastes homemade. The HMR trend began in the '90s and is in flux as food producers try to figure out what consumers want. HMRs can be frozen food, fast food, ready-to-eat cold salads, or heat-and-eat dinners, such as a roasted chicken with mashed potatoes.*

Impulse Buying

Next time you're at the market, be aware of some of the following marketing techniques that further entice you to buy impulsively:

➤ Loss leaders, items that supermarkets put on sale and take a loss on, are advertised to get you into the store.

➤ Staples, like milk and bread, are hidden in the back of the store. You have to walk through aisles of tempting items to get to what you really want.

➤ Seafood, meat, and poultry displays, the top-sellers, are positioned in the back of the store. Notice how you can see them from just about every aisle.

➤ Eye-level items on the shelves, the ones you naturally look at first, are the most expensive.

➤ Snappy displays catch your attention at the ends of the aisles. You might think the items are on sale, but that's not always so.

➤ Products that pair well are displayed together to get you to put not just one but both in your cart. Ever notice how lemons are in a bin next to the fish and croutons are beside the lettuce?

➤ The same pairing often occurs with departments such as the soda and wine next to the deli.

Kid Quiz

Can you guess where the most expensive item would be on the supermarket shelf?

At adult eye level, where an adult's eye would glance first. When you're shopping, check out the items above and below eye level for better prices. Look for store brands because they are cheaper than national brands.

How to Be a Smart Shopper

Now that you know all the tricks, what can you and your kids do to be sure you're getting the best food at the best price?

➤ Never shop when you're hungry. You're likely to make bad choices and pop open a bag of chips or cookies while shopping.

➤ Shop with a list and stick to it. It's a time-honored tip and it works. (Of course, if a higher-quality product, such as a prime cut of meat, is on sale, see if you can substitute it on your list.)

➤ Read ingredient and nutrition labels so you know what you're getting. You might be impressed by a product, but when you start reading the ingredients, you may be surprised. Remember: Ingredients are listed in order of the amounts used in the product. The first ingredient will be the most plentiful and so on. The juice you think is full of fruit might actually have more sugar and water than fruit. (See Appendix D, "The Nutrition Facts Label," for a sample Nutrition Facts label.)

➤ Read and compare unit price labels. These show the cost of an item by the unit—by the ounce, pound, quart, or other unit. Look for these labels on the display shelves directly above or below the item.

➤ Don't automatically reach for the eye-level item. They're the most expensive on the shelf. Look above or below for comparable foods.

➤ Buy in bulk. Food in bulk is sold out of bins. You scoop the amount you want from the bin. It's usually cheaper because you've cut out the packaging costs. An added feature is you get to buy exactly the amount you need. Check the unit price, though, to be sure the cost is cheaper than your favorite packaged item.

➤ Look for no-brand, generic, or store-label foods. They're usually cheaper than nationally known brands. Check the quality and cost against your favorite brand.

➤ Beware of coupons. You can wind up paying more because coupons usually apply to brand-name items that are more expensive. You also can wind up buying foods you don't usually eat just because you think you're getting a bargain.

➤ Stock up during sales on items you use frequently.

Heads Up!

When comparing unit price labels, check the amount being compared and make sure it's the same for both products. You might have to do some quick math if one label is priced by the pound and another is priced by ounces.

Reading the Unit Price Label

Reading unit price labels is easy and useful, and it can save you money. You can compare the price of similar brands and find out which is the better value. Also, most people assume that buying bigger is always cheaper. Sometimes, though, when you compare the unit prices (the price per pound, for example) of larger items to smaller packages, you'll find there's not that much of a difference. (There might be a sale on the smaller item, for example.) If you buy larger quantities of fruit or sliced bread but eventually throw out a lot of it, you wind up losing money. So keep in mind how much of the food or product you'll actually use before grabbing the super-grand size of anything.

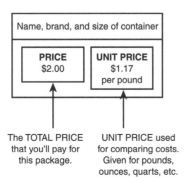

The TOTAL PRICE that you'll pay for this package.

UNIT PRICE used for comparing costs. Given for pounds, ounces, quarts, etc.

A unit price label helps you compare the cost of items.

Making the Farm Connection

One of the best ways to teach kids about food is to take them to the source, whether it's a farm or the farmers' market. You'll find locally grown produce at its best and, at the same time, be supporting the efforts of local farmers.

Kid Quiz

Do you know what a farmers' market is?

It's a gathering place where farmers can sell their produce to the local community. A farmers' market is a fun place to visit, and you can talk to farmers, learn about new produce, and buy your food for the week.

Farmers' Markets

Come summertime, our family spends virtually every Saturday morning at the Portland Farmers' Market. We stroll leisurely, meet friends, and stock up on fresh produce for the week. We also learn how to use foods at the free cooking demonstrations given by local chefs and visiting cookbook authors.

Our farmers' market, as in other communities across the country, is a wonderful gathering place that provides an opportunity to learn about food. The kids have the chance to touch and smell produce at their leisure. We all enjoy talking to the local farmers and seeing new varieties of fruits and vegetables. We can buy anything from dozens of varieties of garlic to cheese and honey. Much of it is organic.

The prices are cheaper than the local supermarket because we've cut out the cost of the middleman. We buy directly from the source, support local agriculture, know what we're getting, and learn more about the food.

Pick Your Own Produce

When I was a kid, we used to go into the woods in Pennsylvania and pick blueberries. We'd carry them home in buckets and make blueberry pancakes and blueberry sauce. My kids remember how, when they were little, they'd join other kids in the neighborhood to pick wild blackberries from bushes around our yard in Connecticut. Everyone would wind up in our kitchen to invent some berry concoctions.

Bigger Bites

Want to find out more about farmers' markets and find one in your area? Log on to www.ams.usda.gov/farmersmarkets/. You can click on the names of states throughout the country to learn contact information about the local farmers' market representative and markets throughout the state. The site also offers facts about farmers' markets and how you can establish them.

Berry picking is a summertime ritual for children and adults alike, and these days—thanks to a burgeoning U-pick farm industry—it's easier to do than ever. Picking your own berries and fruits and bringing them home to cook or just to put on top of ice cream is a fun and educational family outing, and it connects everyone to their source of food. Come the fall, you can pick apples and visit the pumpkin patch. Check with your cooperative extension service or the yellow pages to find out about U-pick farms near you.

Farm Stands

Visiting farm stands and buying produce directly at farms is another way to teach kids where food comes from. We especially like to go out to the country in the fall when we can choose from many varieties of colorful squash and apples. Visiting farms also teaches kids about what grows in what season and how to eat seasonally.

Buying Seasonal and Organic Produce

Not long ago, organic produce was found only in natural foods stores and at great cost. You also could get it if you had a farm connection or joined a co-op. But our awareness of the damaging impact of pesticides, our desire to sustain agriculture, and our demands for quality, seasonal produce have nurtured the organic foods business.

Kitchen Clue

Farmers' markets, farm stands, and U-pick farms offer families a chance to make a connection with farmers and the food we eat. For a fun family outing, visit these farms and then bring the food home and cook something together.

Many supermarkets now carry organic produce in their regular produce sections. Although the costs are still higher than nonorganic foods, the prices are becoming more affordable. The concept of organic produce has moved into the mainstream.

As with any health claims, you should be aware of foods labeled organic. Be sure the produce is certified organic. This means that the growing methods have met the strict standards and review of a local organic certification board.

Some Words About Warehouse Clubs

Warehouse clubs have become increasingly attractive to shoppers because of their low prices and bargains. Shoppers pay an annual membership fee to gain entrance to these enormous warehouses selling items in large quantities. The variety of merchandise, ranging from fresh produce to designer jeans, is staggering.

The food offerings in these warehouses are diverse and tempting, especially as they've kept up with the demand for home meal replacements and convenience foods. In my many years as a warehouse member, however, I've learned three basic things:

1. Prices on some items are not always the cheapest. It still pays to shop around.

2. Buying in bulk is not always best. It's a pain to unload the car, I need extra space to store bigger items, and some foods go bad before I can use up the large quantities the club provides.

3. I always seem to spend a lot more money and buy a lot more than I planned.

Here's my solution: I go to the warehouse store only when I need certain items that I use regularly. I go with a list and give myself a time limit. I try to stay very focused when I'm shopping, and I rarely take my kids. You might consider following these guidelines if you choose to shop at a warehouse club.

The Least You Need to Know

➤ Getting your kids to help you shop is an excellent way to encourage them not only to learn more about the food they eat, but also to shop for it wisely.

➤ The layout and design of supermarkets, as well as the merchandising techniques used by grocers, can encourage impulse buying. Be aware of the tricks that can cause you to purchase more than you intended.

➤ Check and compare nutrition, ingredient, and unit cost labels to make smart food choices.

➤ Take kids to farmers' markets, farm stands, and U-pick farms for fun and educational outings, to help them learn to eat seasonally, and to connect them to their food source.

Chapter 6

Let's Make Lunch and Sit Down to Dinner

In This Chapter

➤ Involving your kids in making lunch

➤ Learning how to make personalized and creative lunches

➤ Packing healthy lunches and using leftovers

➤ The benefits of sharing family meals

Now that you and your kids know all about being smart shoppers, why not use your trips to the market to plan school lunches? Making lunch is one of the easiest ways to get kids involved in food. They learn how to handle foods safely and how to take responsibility for what they eat.

In this chapter, you'll find plenty of tips for packing, personalizing, and presenting lunch so the lunch box always comes back empty!

And when it comes time for dinner, why not try to get the whole family together to sit down for a family meal? Even if you can only manage it once a week, the benefits of eating together are numerous. You'll read about why it's worth doing and learn tips on how to get everyone around the table.

If They Make It, They'll Eat It

Without question, my kids are happiest when they've chosen and made their own lunch. They have no parent to blame for the same old peanut butter and jelly sandwich, and they can make exactly what they want to eat. Involving kids in lunch decisions does take some planning, but you'll find it's definitely worth the time you invest. For starters, kids like having control over their lunch choices. They feel good about taking charge of what they're eating, and in the process, they're learning how to take care of themselves. It's also an easy way to introduce them to how food is safely prepared, stored, and handled, and it gets them ready for bigger cooking projects. And if you look at lunch as a time to try new foods, your kids can begin to zero in and expand on their food preferences.

After years of making my kids' school lunches, with and without them, here are some of our best lunch-making tips:

➤ Talk to your kids about their lunchroom environment and lunchtime politics. Find out if they have a microwave in their classroom and if they have to rush through lunch. This affects what goes into the lunch box.

➤ Take your kids to a farmers' market or the grocery store on the weekend to look for foods and to plan the week of lunches. You might be surprised to learn about their willingness to experiment with new tastes.

➤ Suggest new foods for lunch and try them out at dinner or snacktime before sending them to school. My kids, for instance, like sushi and jicama and grew fond of these foods at home before we put them in the lunch box. When classmates look at them funny, they can say with conviction: "Try some. It's delicious."

➤ Make lunch the night before to avoid the morning rush and to give kids time to get involved. You're also likely to make better food choices without the last-minute rush.

Heads Up!

Rushing to get lunch ready in the morning can lead to unappetizing and unhealthy lunches. Plan lunches during the weekend for the coming week and make them the night before to avoid the last-minute rush. Bring kids to the supermarket and have them choose their food.

Kitchen Clue

Want to find out what eating lunch at school is really like? Make a lunch date with your kids (if, of course, they are comfortable with the idea). It's a great way to catch up during those busy weeks when everyone is going in different directions. You'll experience lunchroom dynamics, and you'll see what other kids are eating. Be sure to check first with the school office about visitor policies.

➤ Clip out lunch ideas or recipes from your daily newspaper's food section or women's or food magazines and tack them on the refrigerator door. Suggest that the kids try making them with you for the next lunch.

Getting Creative

Kids love it when they open their lunch bag and find a sandwich that's colorful or eye-catching. An old trick is to cut sandwiches with a favorite cookie cutter or one with a holiday theme.

Here are some ways to get creative:

➤ Cut fruits and vegetables into different shapes such as roses, mini-trees, and people.

➤ Make a sandwich "boat" by attaching a piece of cheese for a sail and using a toothpick for the mast.

➤ Make designs and faces on sandwiches with cheese strips (for smiles), raisins (for eyes), or vegetables (for noses).

➤ Make vegetables into animals. A pepper can become a bunny by adding snow peas for ears and slivered almonds for teeth.

➤ Cut sandwiches into mini-puzzles or even animal shapes, like a fish, that come apart.

Lunch Box Surprises

Finding a surprise in the lunch box is a great pick-me-up for kids at school. I always used to slip in notes, and my kids really liked it. Think of what's happening during the week for ideas. Is there a big test? Send a good luck note. Here are some other ideas for lunchtime surprises:

➤ Write your own fortune or saying for the day and tuck it into a special place.

➤ Buy a package of fortune cookies and include one occasionally.

➤ Clip a funny picture or cartoon from a newspaper or magazine and put it at the bottom of the lunch box.

➤ Write a joke or a funny riddle and tuck it in between the wrapped foods.

Kitchen Clue

Personalize your child's lunch by cutting sandwiches into shapes with cookie cutters, sending special notes, using decorative napkins or straws, and packing special treats. Kids always feel great when they get these surprises, and this little bit of effort goes a long way in getting them to eat their lunch.

➤ Write down some of the Kid Quiz questions from this book or make up your own. You can discuss the answers after school.

➤ Instead of using that plain old white napkin, pack one that is colorful or that has a decorative theme. During the holidays, include napkins with holiday figures. Add a surprise decorative paper plate.

➤ Buy a funny-looking straw and pack it along with the thermos bottle.

➤ Send chopsticks instead of a fork. (Be sure your child knows how to use them so he or she won't be embarrassed.)

➤ For a special treat, pack a few chocolate kisses with a note that says "I love you."

Packing Lunch Right

Packing a lunch box properly can be a real challenge. More than once I've found myself swearing at the lunch box, trying to squeeze everything in without smashing the fruit.

When packing lunches, be sure to start by washing your hands and making sure the lunch box is clean. Keep hot foods hot and cold foods cold to prevent the growth of harmful bacteria. Be sure lunch foods are fresh and seal them in plastic wrap, aluminum foil, sealable plastic bags, or airtight containers. Don't forget to check the expiration date before you stuff in that piece of string cheese or cup of yogurt.

How to Keep Foods Cold

These simple steps will help foods stay cold and keep them from spoiling:

➤ Invest in an insulated lunch bag or box with enough room for cold packs and thermos bottles.

➤ Place frozen blue ice or cold packs, zipped into a self-locking plastic bag, next to foods that need to stay chilled.

➤ Use frozen juice packs or frozen grapes, enclosed in a resealable plastic bag, to prevent sweating. The juice and fruit will thaw by lunch and will keep food cold in the meantime. (My kids like it when the juice doesn't thaw. They just cut off the top of the pack and eat the crystallized juice with a spoon like a slushy. Frozen grapes are tasty, too.)

➤ Use frozen bread for the sandwich.

➤ Chill the lunch box and thermos bottles before packing. Freeze the lid of wide-mouth thermos bottles the night before. If you don't have time, fill the container with ice water, cover, and let it rest for five minutes. Empty and dry the container and immediately fill it with the chilled food.

➤ Tell your kids to store their lunch in the refrigerator at their destination. If that's not possible, have them set it in the coolest spot possible and away from heat vents.

Kid Quiz

What can you do to your lunch box to cut down on germs?

Keep it clean and empty it out as soon as you get home. Wash it well with hot water and an antibacterial soap. Be sure to rinse off and dry ice packs and put them back into the freezer.

How to Keep Foods Hot

Follow these tips when packing hot foods:

➤ Pack stews and soups in a wide-mouth, preheated thermos. Preheat the thermos by filling it to the top with boiling water and then closing the lid. When you're ready to fill it, dump out the water and be sure your foods are piping hot. Close the cap tightly.

➤ Keep cold packs or foods you don't want to heat away from the warm thermos. Insulate them from the heat with several layers of napkins.

No More Smushy, Soggy Sandwiches!

Nothing turns off a hungry kid quicker than opening up a lunch box to find a soggy, mushy mess inside. Here are some ways to keep foods crisp and dry:

➤ Layer the heaviest ingredients at the bottom and the most delicate ones on top.

➤ Seal sandwiches or wraps tightly in aluminum foil or pack them in a plastic sandwich box.

➤ Use toasted or frozen bread.

➤ Cover the inside of both pieces of bread with a sandwich spread, such as mayonnaise, margarine, or peanut butter, to protect the bread from wet filling.

Kitchen Clue

Miniature foods are always a lunchtime hit. Some fun foods include sandwiches cut into four pieces or lunch meats on mini-rolls; small cheeses, such as baby gouda and foil-wrapped cow cheese; tiny boxes of raisins; and mini rice cakes stacked and filled with cheese or peanut butter.

47

➤ Dry lettuce and salad ingredients before making the sandwich. Pack wet ingredients, such as tomatoes, cole slaw, or dressing, in separate containers or plastic bags and let your kids assemble them at lunchtime.

➤ Make sure containers don't leak and lids are on tight. Tell your kids to reseal the bottles.

➤ Wrap soft fruits, such as plums and peaches, in paper towels or napkins inside a plastic bag, plastic container, or recycled yogurt cup. Keep grapes in a plastic bag so they don't roll around and squish.

➤ Wrap vegetables in moistened paper towels and enclose them tightly in aluminum foil or resealable plastic bags.

➤ Wrap forks, straws, and knives in napkins or paper towels so they don't pierce foods.

➤ Enclose frozen juice packs and foods that might "sweat" in plastic bags.

What to Do When You're Tired of Sandwich Bread

Making the same old sandwich on white or wheat bread can get pretty boring. For an interesting and delicious change, try one of the following alternatives:

bagels	quick breads, such as cornbread, pumpkin bread, and raisin bread
flaky croissants	
deli minibreads	seeded breads
crusty Kaiser rolls	tortillas or sandwich wraps
hamburger, hot dog, or specialty rolls	crackers
pita pockets	toasted English muffins
	rice cakes

The Spiral Sandwich and Sandwich Wraps

A spiral or pinwheel sandwich is an easy-to-eat lunch with a different twist. To make one, take your sandwich bread and flatten it with a rolling pin. Spread cooked lunch meats, favorite spreads, and salads on the bread and then roll it tightly, jelly-roll style. Use a little spread or slightly moisten the edge of the bread with water to seal the roll. Cut it crosswise into several small rolls. Securing each with a fancy cocktail toothpick is always a treat. (You'll find a recipe for spiral sandwiches in Chapter 23, "Let's Wrap and Roll.")

Look in the bread or deli section of your supermarket for the latest in sandwich wrappers. These look like tortillas, but they are softer and more pliable and are specially designed for rolling sandwiches. They come in flavors ranging from sun-dried tomato to spinach. Follow package directions to fill and wrap them with meats, salads, spreads, hummus, cheese, and other lunchtime favorites. Seal the sandwich tightly with plastic wrap. Some people do use tortillas, but tortillas, if cold, tend to crack when rolled. Allow them to heat to room temperature before rolling.

Bento or Sushi, Anyone?

One alternative to a sandwich is sushi or a bento box of rice with fish or meats, vegetables, and salad. You can assemble your own ingredients or purchase these lunches as takeout. You'll find sushi chefs making fresh sushi daily at many supermarkets. You just pick up a prepackaged plastic container complete with soy sauce and ginger, and lunch is ready to go.

What my kids like about sushi, besides the taste, is the idea of popping miniature rolls of rice and vegetables into their mouths. It's different and fun for a change—not to mention low-fat and healthy. The kids get some grains and vegetables all in one bite. The nori (dried seaweed) used to wrap the sushi has a crisp, unusual taste that seems to appeal to kids. It also is rich in protein, calcium, vitamins, iron, and other minerals.

Reusable plastic bento boxes (miniature Japanese lunch boxes with tiny stacking compartments) are available at Asian stores. These cute boxes will be the hit of the lunchroom. With both sushi and bento, be sure to pack them inside an insulated bag or box so foods don't spoil.

Kid Quiz

What vegetables would make good containers for tuna, egg, or chicken salad?

Try using cherry tomatoes, cucumbers, raw or partially cooked zucchini, scooped-out cucumbers, bell peppers, and celery sticks.

Let's Hear It for Leftovers

Some of our best lunches come from leftovers. In fact, making extra at dinner is an old trick for easing the next day's lunch-making scene. Remember the old meat loaf sandwich?

Heads Up!

If you plan to freeze leftovers, keep in mind that mayonnaise, eggs, raw vegetables, and sour cream don't freeze well and tend to break down as they thaw.

Here are some ideas for lunches from leftovers:

➤ Make extra rice and pasta at the beginning of the week. They keep well and can be transformed daily by adding different ingredients and sauces. We like to cook extra pasta for emergency dinners and for lunches. Pasta and rice keep well in the refrigerator for about five days.

➤ Toss leftover vegetables with pasta or rice or add them to lettuce greens for a salad.

➤ Make leftover rice into rice balls and fill them with surprises ranging from a raisin to a small piece of meat or fish.

➤ Buy a roast chicken or cook your own and use the meat for salads and sandwiches during the week. Make a quick chicken stock with the bones and carcass. Strain and add vegetables, chicken, and rice or pasta for a quick soup.

➤ Liven up leftover vegetable stir-fry with some soy sauce.

➤ A leftover piece of pie or cake or an extra cookie is a welcome end-of-the-meal treat.

Bringing Back the Family Meal

These days, with parents' work responsibilities and kids' sport schedules, night meetings, and other commitments, the traditional family meal seems to have gone the way of the black and white television set. But because eating as a family plays such a vital role in children's lives, groups across the country have been encouraging families to make time to eat together.

Why Eat Together?

Here's the late humor columnist Erma Bombeck's take on her family's shared meals: "We argued. We sulked. We laughed. We pitched for favors. We shouted. We listened. It is still our family's finest hour."

Most families, including my own, can find truth in her humor. But what do kids really get out of a family sitting down to meals together?

➤ Kids learn about food preparation when they help put a meal on the table.

➤ People eat a wider variety of foods and more balanced meals when they eat jointly with family and friends.

➤ Sitting at the table teaches children manners and skills they'll use all their lives.

➤ Sharing a meal with others fosters communication. Kids learn to converse and share the news of their day.

➤ Family mealtime fosters food memories and traditions that kids will retain their entire lives.

Finding Time to Sit Down as a Family

The reality is, it's hard to find the time to eat together. If you want a family meal, you have to make a commitment to carving the time out for one. Sometimes that means creating a social opportunity, like a potluck meal with friends, to get your family together at the table. Other times it means turning down another commitment in favor of family time.

Here are some tips to make a family meal happen:

➤ Compare schedules at the beginning of the week and find a time that works for a meal.

➤ Get everyone involved to make it happen.

➤ Prepare a favorite dish. Everyone will be more excited about coming to the table.

➤ Keep meals simple.

➤ Sometimes you have to think beyond a homemade dinner at home. Plan for take-out meals or consider going out.

➤ Try meeting for lunch. I'll occasionally take my kids out to lunch or meet them at the school cafeteria. I got the idea from a recently divorced dad who used to have lunch with his daughter to get in more quality time and have the opportunity to meet her friends.

Kitchen Clue

The family meal doesn't always have to mean a home-cooked dinner at your own table. Look for other opportunities to share a meal together including a Sunday brunch, a weekday lunch, or an impromptu dinner at a local ethnic restaurant.

Playing Pretend Restaurant

Just get your kids thinking about it, and they'll probably come up with creative ways to get the family together at the dinner table. Our friends, the Nicholsons, have for years had dinner in a restaurant—their home. The kids call it Fratelli's (*fratelli* is

Italian for brothers). Zachary and Luke, the two brothers, team up with their sister, Kate, to plan a menu. Because their restaurant is Italian, they offer lots of choices from pizza to pasta. They'll plan a menu, shop with their mom, help prepare the meal, and then serve it (complete with the white cloth over the forearm). Everyone leaves the table happy and well fed and they get the time to catch up with one another. Think about creating your own restaurant and design your own theme dinners.

The Least You Need to Know

➤ Let kids make their own lunches as a way of familiarizing them with handling foods safely, expanding their palate, and ensuring that they have lunches they like and will eat.

➤ Break up lunchtime boredom with lunch box surprises and different sandwich alternatives.

➤ Packing foods safely and carefully can prevent them from spoiling or being crushed.

➤ Leftovers and ethnic foods, such as bento, tortilla wraps, and sushi, make great lunch meals.

➤ Sharing family meals helps develop your children's social and communication skills.

➤ Get the whole family involved in finding out when you can carve out time for family meals.

Part 3
Kid-Proofing Your Kitchen

Okay, you've set the stage for cooking with your kids. Now let's face facts. All parents worry about their kids' safety in the kitchen. My biggest fears when I taught my kids to cook were that they'd cut or burn themselves or start a fire. But don't let these concerns become stumbling blocks. Let's take a careful look at the potential hazards lurking behind the kitchen door and talk about ways to keep your kids safe at the counters, oven, and stove.

This section is designed for you to read with your kids so they can develop good, safe habits. We'll start with learning the safety rules of the kitchen and then move on to a complete rundown of kitchen appliances and the right way to operate them. We'll then get familiar with basic utensils and equipment, and we'll focus in on one of the most important and scary utensils for kids: the sharp knife. We'll end with a look at the latest in food safety, and I'll provide tips for how to protect your family from foodborne illness.

Chapter 7

The Golden Rules of Kitchen Safety

In This Chapter

➤ Understanding kitchen-safety rules

➤ Practicing good food-safety habits

➤ Preparing for and handling emergencies

➤ Using knives, stoves, and ovens safely

➤ Learning to clean as you go

What are your biggest fears about cooking with your kids? Chances are, you worry that they'll cut or burn themselves, leave your kitchen looking like a disaster area, or even set the house on fire. You're not alone. We can prevent these problems, however, when we teach kids the safety rules of the kitchen.

Explain to your kids that, when they learn to play soccer or any other sport, the first step is to understand the rules for safe play. Cooking is no different.

Before you start reading recipes and pulling out pots and pans, go over this chapter with your kids. Safety in the kitchen is just a matter of developing good habits. If you teach these safety rules to your kids when they're young, they'll have good skills for the rest of their lives. And remember, they're watching you as a role model. If you practice good safety habits, they'll do the same.

Kid Quiz

What are three top safety rules in the kitchen?

1. Always wash your hands before starting to cook.

2. Never cook without permission or supervision.

3. Don't play with knives or fire.

Read this chapter to find more safety rules. Write your own list and put it on the refrigerator door to remind yourself to be a safe cook.

Teaching Kids to Ask for Adult Help

Kids need to know that cooking is a lot of fun but that it's also serious business. Kids can cause accidents, cut or burn themselves, and at the extreme, cause a fire or electrocute themselves if they're not careful. Teach them to ask for and accept adult help at certain points, such as when getting hot plates out of the oven, dicing an onion, or emptying the boiling water from a pasta pot.

Kids like to be more independent as they gain confidence in the kitchen. You'll find you're constantly balancing making sure your kids are safe with giving them more responsibility. Keep the following points in mind as you're thinking about kitchen safety:

1. Never assume anything about your kids' safety IQ and never take their safe habits for granted. Always check in with them to be sure they're using safe techniques.

2. Supervise them carefully and get to know their strong and weak points. Practice positive reinforcement and praise and encourage them when they show safe kitchen skills.

3. Give them more and more responsibility as you go along. If you think they can handle getting the casserole out of the oven, let them do it with your supervision. After a few times, they might be ready to do it on their own.

4. You know your children best and will recognize at what point they can do certain tasks on their own. Kids may surprise you, though. They may not want certain responsibilities, or at the other end of the spectrum, they may show you more responsibility than you expected.

Follow the Golden Rules

Safety rules are simple and are a matter of common sense. Impress upon your kids their importance and, as you go over the rules, help your kids anticipate problems. Get them thinking about these rules by asking them what they think are safe kitchen practices.

Dress for Success

Cooking can be a messy business. You and your children should wear comfortable clothing protected by an apron. Roll up your sleeves and tie back or tuck in any baggy clothing that could catch on fire or get in your way. If you have long hair, be sure it's pulled back.

Scrub-a-Dub-Dub

Washing your hands thoroughly is the first step to kitchen safety. It prevents the spread of bacteria and germs. Wash your hands with soap and warm water, counting to 20 seconds as you scrub between your fingers, under your fingernails, and up to your wrists.

Show kids how to lift their arm and cough into the crook of their elbow when they're cooking. Remind them that touching their nose, mouth, or face and then handling food can spread their germs. If they blow their nose or wipe sniffles, they should wash their hands again.

Build Good Food Safety Habits

With the rise in incidents of food-borne illness, food safety has taken on tremendous importance. Although proper hand washing is key, it is only the start of good food-safety habits. Kids need to know to wash their hands after handling raw meat, poultry, fish, and eggs. Wash any surfaces and utensils that come in contact with these raw products before using them for any other foods. Your children will learn by your example. Be sure to read Chapter 10, "What You Need to Know About Food Safety," for more details about safe kitchen practices.

Heads Up!

Wash your hands before you start cooking and, when necessary, during cooking. Immediately wash cutting boards, knives, and surfaces that have come into contact with raw fish, poultry, meat, or eggs to prevent spreading any germs. Don't forget to wash your hands after handling these foods, too.

Kitchen Clue

Your local fire department can help you plan for fire emergencies. Request literature about developing your family emergency plan. In some communities, fire marshals will come to your home to help you with the plan and to spot problems. Check your phone book for the department nearest you.

Be Ready for an Emergency

Help your kids become confident cooks by talking to them about what can go wrong in the kitchen. Ask them how they would handle a situation, such as a cut, a burn, or a fire.

Fire-safety experts recommend that families sit down and plan out what they would do in an emergency, including figuring out escape routes and rendezvous points. Kids also should be aware of who else is in the house when they cook, just in case a fire does occur.

Help prepare kids for an emergency with these simple steps:

1. Post an easy-to-read list of emergency numbers in a visible spot right by the phone. Include numbers for the local police, fire department, and poison-control center; your doctor; and neighbors, relatives, and friends who live near-by. Update the list periodically. If you have programmed numbers into your phone, be sure everyone in the family knows how to access them.

2. Keep a first-aid kit and a fire extinguisher in or near the kitchen. Show your kids what's in the kit and how to use it and the extinguisher.

3. Make a fire emergency plan and practice it with the whole family. Your local fire department has information to help you plan.

Bigger Bites

Find out more about how you should handle emergencies, especially medical situations, by checking with your pediatrician and emergency service organizations. Request free brochures that detail emergency medical procedures or go to your local bookstore and select a good book on first aid.

Preventing and Handling Burns and Fires

Go over these fire-safety rules with your kids so everyone knows how to prevent burns and handle fires:

1. Never handle hot foods or equipment with your bare hands. Let foods cool or use dry pot holders to handle them.

2. Don't use or leave metal spoons or utensils, which can heat up, in a hot pot. If you forget and leave a spoon in a pot, use a pot holder to remove it.

3. Don't stick your head in the oven or reach your arm into the oven to remove pans. Always pull racks out and handle hot pots and pans with thick, dry pot holders. Never use kitchen towels as pot holders.

4. Keep pot holders and towels away from heat sources, and be sure nothing flammable is near the stove, oven, toaster oven, or toaster.

5. Never use flammable sprays, such as a vegetable oil spray, near a heat source.

6. Keep an open box of baking soda by the stove. Teach your kids to throw the baking soda, not water, on flames. Tell them to close the oven door if flames flare up in the oven or a microwave oven. For a pan fire, put the lid on the pan.

7. If your clothes catch on fire, "Stop, Drop, and Roll." That is, stop running, drop to the floor, and roll to put out the flames.

8. Treat burns by holding the affected area under cold, running water, not by putting butter or grease on the burn. Kids should show the burn to an adult so the person can evaluate how serious it is and seek medical attention if necessary.

Learn the Lingo

Burns are classified into three categories of seriousness. **First-degree** burns are those which cause reddening of the skin. With **second-degree** burns, the skin blisters. The most serious burns are **third-degree** burns, which involve the destruction of the skin and the tissues beneath it.

Kid Quiz

If you burn your finger, what should you do?

Put your finger immediately under cold, running water and show the burn to an adult. Do not put butter or grease on it.

Handling Knives

Handling knives can be scary business for kids and adults alike. Kids need to know the number one rule: Don't handle a knife without an adult's permission and supervision.

Adults also need to check knife blades to be sure they are sharp. A dull blade is dangerous because it requires more pressure and can result in slips or dropping the knife.

If your children cut themselves, they should stop cooking immediately and wash the cut with soap and water. Remove the soap with running water and cleanse the wound with hydrogen peroxide. If bleeding persists, apply gentle pressure to the cut with a sterile gauze pad or a clean cloth and elevate the wound. If you choose, apply an antiseptic ointment or cream.

Bandage the cut to keep it clean. Check to see if any blood has gotten into the food and discard it if it has. Also, check to see if blood has gotten on any utensils and clean them with hot, soapy water. If bleeding persists or if the wound looks deep or serious, seek medical advice.

Knife-Safety Rules

Go over these top knife-safety rules with everyone in the family:

➤ Always hold a knife by its handle, never by its blade.

➤ Never cut any food in your hand. Cut on a stable surface with a clean cutting board. The board will keep the food safe from germs and will protect the counter and the sharp blade of the knife.

➤ When cutting, hold food steady with your fingertips tucked underneath your knuckles.

➤ Stay focused on using the knife. Letting yourself get distracted can result in an accident.

➤ Don't walk or play with knives. If kids have permission to bring a knife from a drawer to the cutting board or to the sink, they should hold it by the handle, parallel to the body, with the point down and the sharp edge facing away from the body.

➤ When you finish using a knife, lay it on its flat side on top of the cutting board. Be sure it's not close to the edge; otherwise, it could slip or fall to the floor.

➤ Keep a knife visible. You could grab it accidentally and cut yourself if it's covered by a dish towel, a pot holder, or other utensils.

Heads Up!

Keep knife blades sharp for safety. A dull knife is more dangerous because it can slip or drop as you exert more pressure to cut.

➤ Never throw a knife into a tub or sink full of soapy water. You won't be able to see it when you put your hand in, and you might cut yourself.

Power Up Appliances Properly

Kids love to handle electric appliances. It gives them a sense of power to whir the blender, pulse the food processor, or operate the electric mixer. When it comes to handling this equipment, the following basic rules apply. (Check out Chapter 8, "A Kid's-Eye View of Appliances," for more detailed information about operating individual appliances.)

1. Ask an adult for permission before operating any appliance.

2. Never plug in appliances or handle them with wet hands. Be sure surfaces are dry and are not sticky. Never stand in a puddle or a wet spot while using an electric appliance.

3. Check to make sure appliances are turned off before you plug them in.

4. Don't touch appliance blades to see how sharp they are. Always keep your fingers away from blades in blenders or food processors and beaters.

5. Never put your hands or a utensil, such as a scraper, in an appliance until it has stopped moving.

6. Always unplug a toaster before attempting to remove stuck food.

Kitchen Clue

Keep a fire extinguisher and a first-aid kit in or near the kitchen and post emergency numbers by the phone. Keep an open box of baking soda by the stove to sprinkle on flames.

Stovetop and Oven Savvy

Learn these safety tips for handling pots and pans. For stovetop safety:

1. Turn pot handles away from you and toward the center of the stove so they don't get bumped, catch on anything, or spill over.

2. When you want to check what's inside a covered pan or casserole, lift the lid carefully away from you. Otherwise, you could be burned by a burst of steam.

3. Always use a thick, dry pot holder to pick up hot pots and pans.

4. Put hot pots on a heat-proof surface or one protected by a trivet or wire cooling rack. Be sure the surface is dry; otherwise, the pot could slip.

5. Turn off burners as soon as you're finished cooking.

For the oven, follow these rules:

1. Stand back when opening the door. Never put your head into the oven to check food.

2. Kids should ask for adult help to remove food from the oven. Pull the racks out with thick, dry pot holders or oven mitts and use them to remove the food.

3. Close the oven door and turn off the oven immediately when finished cooking.

Kid Quiz

How should you position pots on the stove?

Put pots on burners so their handles are away from you and are facing the inside of the stovetop. This will prevent them from catching on your clothes or being tipped over by a younger brother or sister.

Steady Stools and Good Tools

Height often is a problem with youngsters when they cook. Buy them a sturdy kitchen stool and never let them stand on chairs. You also could set them up at a small table in the corner of the kitchen. Reevaluate their height needs as they grow. Be sure your kids are using tools that feel comfortable, are safe, and are age appropriate.

Cleaning as You Go

Most cooks agree that clean-up is one of the least enjoyable parts of cooking. Successful cooks, however, have mastered the clean-as-you-go system. Teach kids that being a good cook means leaving the kitchen clean.

Two clean-up tips that have worked in our family are to make it fun with music and to make it equal by sharing tasks. We'll turn up the music and dance around as we put things away. We also divide up tasks. Sometimes one person will do all the cutting and prep work, and another will put things away and wash dishes.

Here are some tips for keeping clean-up under control:

➤ Put away ingredients as soon as you've used them. This cuts down on kitchen clutter. For perishable foods, it also prevents spoilage and eliminates food-safety problems.

➤ Contain the flour mess by putting a sheet of waxed paper down on the counter and measuring the flour over it. Excess flour can be funneled right back into the storage container.

➤ Spread parchment paper, waxed paper, or newspapers on the counters. When you're finished, just scoop up the paper and throw away the mess. Try using an inexpensive plastic drop cloth or newspapers on the floor in the area where the kids will be mixing.

➤ Clean and reuse bowls and utensils to avoid extra equipment around the kitchen.

➤ Unplug electric appliances first and then wipe them down with a clean, damp sponge. This prevents food spills from caking on the appliances and becoming more difficult to remove.

➤ Rinse off dishes and utensils and put them in the dishwasher as you use them. Fill a sink full of hot, soapy water to soak equipment with hard-to-remove stains.

➤ Take advantage of cooking and waiting times in a recipe to clean up.

➤ Throw trash right into the waste bucket instead of onto the counter. If you're using a cake mix, put the eggshells, butter wrappers, and other trash right into the box and throw it out at the end of cooking.

➤ When you're finished, wipe down the stove and countertops. Be sure the stove is cool before you start.

Kitchen Clue

Cut down on clutter and clean-up by putting ingredients away as soon as you finish using them. Put dishes and utensils right into the dishwasher and keep a sink full of soapy water for hard-to-remove stains. Throw used boxes and containers and other trash away immediately.

The Least You Need to Know

➤ Teach kids to ask for permission and help when handling electric appliances, using sharp knives, and cooking at the stove or oven.

➤ A good emergency plan and a list of emergency numbers helps kids feel safe in the kitchen.

➤ Washing your hands, using clean utensils, and practicing safe food handling are keys to kitchen safety.

➤ Handling pots properly and keeping flammable items away from the stovetop will help prevent fires and burns.

➤ Clean as you go to keep kitchen clutter under control.

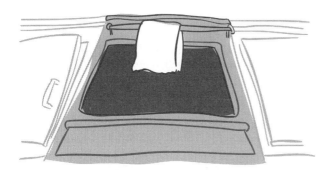

A Kid's-Eye View of Appliances

Kitchens look different when you view them from a kid's perspective. To them, appliances that whiz up smoothies and zap food are quite magical. To a kid, the kitchen can be one big playpen and appliances the toys.

Cooking should be fun for kids, but they need to know how to operate appliances cautiously and safely. Step back and take a kid's-eye view of the kitchen. This chapter does just that, as well as offering your kids a primer on using appliances. You'll find basic descriptions of appliances and tips for their safe use. Let your children read about the different appliances and go over these details as you demonstrate how to use the appliance.

Get Appliance Savvy

When it comes to operating kitchen equipment, don't assume anything about what your kids know. Stand by their side and make sure they operate the appliance properly. We know, for instance, that the button on the hand mixer needs to be off before it's plugged in. Kids might forget such things in their zeal to cook.

How often have you bought a new appliance, figured out the basics, and then shoved the instructions in a drawer to read later? Now is the time to pull out that booklet and make sure you're operating the appliance safely and getting the most out of your investment.

You're the Role Model

Kids learn by watching what you do and then doing it themselves. Rule number one: You're the role model, so be sure you always operate appliances safely. If you toss the blade of the food processor in the sink, your kids will do the same.

Heads Up!

Never handle electric appliances with wet hands. Be sure appliances are turned off before you plug and unplug them. Keep appliances away from water, especially the motor.

Kitchen Clue

Talk to your kids about why you use appliances and show them how to use them properly. Let them practice with you so they can gain confidence in using them.

It's equally important to supervise your kids and go easy at first. Know your child and how much responsibility you can give him or her around appliances. Some kids are very careful in the kitchen. Others will pulse the food processor or turn on the blender just to hear it whirl. Adjust your rules according to your particular child.

Let kids learn one appliance at a time and let them practice using it with you. Then add others as you use them while cooking. A blender is a good place to start because kids use it often to make drinks and smoothies. You also can cover lots of bases and teach your kids good safety habits that they'll carry over to other appliances.

Playing It Safe

Start by reviewing the basic safety rules for handling electric kitchen appliances:

➤ Never touch appliances with wet hands. A dish towel kept nearby will help you dry your hands and other surfaces that might get wet.

➤ Keep appliances away from water. Don't submerge the motor in water when cleaning.

➤ Be sure appliances are off and already assembled before plugging them into the outlet.

➤ Unplug appliances with dry hands after use.

➤ Clean up with a damp sponge or cloth immediately after use to prevent caked-on food.

Things That Go "Whiz!" in the Night

Appliances like blenders and food processors are among the most appealing to kids. They get a real sense of power when they use them, and they love to see how ingredients blend and change. The following sections provide basic safety rules and descriptions for common blade-driven appliances.

Blenders

Blenders are one of the first appliances kids use. These electric appliances use short, rotating blades to purée, blend, liquefy, and chop foods. A tall container sits atop the motor that spins the blades.

Blenders come with many speeds, and their airtight, narrow containers make them better for liquids than the food processor. Blenders cannot whip foods like cream or egg whites, however, because the shape doesn't allow much air to combine with the food, as happens with an egg beater.

> **Learn the Lingo**
>
> When you **purée** a food, you mash it to a thick and smooth consistency. Use a blender or a food processor to purée foods.

Kids will use blenders to make shakes and smoothies, to blend sauces and dressings, or to chop foods such as herbs and spices, nuts, or bread crumbs.

Follow these rules when operating a blender:

➤ Keep hands and utensils out of the container while operating.

➤ Before you turn on the motor, always cover the container with the lid and keep your hand on it to prevent it from popping off.

➤ Fill the blender only halfway for hot or very thick liquids. They could shoot up when you turn the blender on. Start on low and gradually increase the speed. With hot liquids, remove the center top to let steam escape.

➤ Be sure the blades come to a complete stop before adding other foods, opening the lid, removing the container, or scraping down the sides. If food gets stuck, make sure the motor is off and the blades are not moving. Then use the handle of a wooden spoon or a rubber spatula to dislodge the foods.

➤ Never put a utensil in the blender while the blades are moving.

➤ Clean the blender by pouring warm water and dish detergent into the container. Cover it and turn it on briefly. Remove it from the base and rinse it well. Parents also can take apart the bottom of the container to clean out any food.

➤ For small jobs, look for 1-cup containers that fit directly into the blender base. These are especially good for blending dressings or chopping nuts or bread crumbs.

Kitchen Clue

Manufacturers sell small containers that fit directly onto the motor base of an electric blender. Use these for blending salad dressings and small amounts of sauces, nuts, or bread crumbs. They come with lids so you can store the food right in the container.

Immersion Blenders

Immersion blenders have rotary blades at the end of a long, narrow handle, and they sometimes come with whisk attachments that allow for whipping foods. These blenders can go right into a glass or another container, and are easier to clean than stand-up blenders.

Follow these rules when using immersion blenders:

➤ Always keep your hands away from the blades.

➤ Remove pots from the stove before putting in the blender.

➤ Start on a low speed and work your way up if the blender has variable speeds.

➤ Wear oven mitts to protect yourself from hot foods.

➤ Clean by unplugging and running the blade tip of the blender under hot water.

Mixers

Mixers are electric appliances used to whip, mix, or beat foods such as batters, cream, egg whites, or cookie dough.

Mixers come in two types: stationary (standing) or portable (held by hand). Both have beaters that fit into holes in the top of the mixer. Stationary mixers, which have more powerful motors and can handle heavier batters and bigger jobs, also have other attachments, such as whisks, hooks, or paddle-type beaters.

The biggest concern with mixers is that kids will get their fingers or other articles caught in the beaters while they are moving. Remember these safety guidelines:

➤ Keep your hands out of the bowl while the mixer is on. If you're using a hand mixer, hold the bowl steady with your free hand.

➤ Add ingredients slowly.

➤ If the sides of the bowl need to be scraped down, turn off the motor and wait for the beaters to stop before doing so.

➤ Don't try to remove beaters while the motor is running. Turn off the machine and unplug it first.

Food Processors

Kids love the pulsing action and power of a food processor. These products can be tricky to handle, though. For one thing, they work so quickly they can turn food into mush. Mashed potatoes, for instance, can turn into a gluey mess in seconds. They also have razor-sharp blades and disks and require special care and supervision.

Heads Up!

Kids enjoy pulsing food in the food processor, but be careful not to let them over-process. Foods can easily turn to mush, and you'll wind up with ruined ingredients.

This electric appliance has a work bowl with a cover and a feed tube. The bowl sits atop a powerful motor with a shaft sticking up into the center of the bowl. A steel blade or dough hook fits atop the shaft inside the bowl. The blade can chop, blend, purée, or mix, and the dough blade is a whiz at kneading breads. Disks, such as ones that shred and slice, can be placed at the top of the bowl. Food is fed with a gentle but steady pressure through the tube and drops down into the bowl. Oils or liquids can also be drizzled through the hole in the feed tube.

Remember these safety guidelines when using a food processor:

➤ Always hold the blade by its plastic center when inserting or removing it from the bowl.

➤ Blades and disks are extremely sharp. Keep your fingers away from the sharp edges and take care when handling.

➤ Ingredients are either placed directly into the work bowl or added through the feed tube. The lid must be locked in place; otherwise, the motor will not start.

➤ Don't overfill the bowl when processing liquids. They can leak out between the blade and shaft and the rim of the work bowl.

➤ Use quick on/off pulses when chopping foods with the metal blade. It keeps them in the path of the blade but prevents them from turning to mush.

➤ When finished, wait for the blades to stop. Unplug the appliance, turn the cover to the left, and then push the bowl to the left to detach it from the motor. To empty the ingredients, put your finger in the hole on the bottom of the processor to hold the blade as you pour them out of the bowl. You also can lift up the blade by its center and scrape ingredients off the blade and out of the bowl.

Mini Food Processors

These small food processors operate the same way large processors do. Use them for small jobs, such as grinding nuts or mincing herbs.

Operating Ovens and Stoves

Ovens and stoves are powered by either electricity or gas. Refer to the information in Chapter 7, "The Golden Rules of Kitchen Safety," to review safety habits while at the stove or oven.

Go over the features of your oven with your kids. Note how many racks you have inside the oven and what the temperature settings mean. Practice opening and closing the oven door with pot holders, resetting the racks, and getting pans into the oven. If your kids can do this when the oven is off, it won't be so intimidating when they're really cooking.

Other things to review include the following:

➤ Make it a habit to turn off the oven or stove as soon as the food is cooked.

➤ Don't lean against or touch the stove or oven when it's on. These appliances get hot and you can get burned.

➤ Close the door immediately when you have to check on food or get something in or out of the oven. Not only can you burn yourself, but also the temperature will drop, which will affect your recipe.

➤ Use an oven thermometer and put it in a visible place. The temperature inside the oven can vary as much as 25 degrees from the setting on the dial.

How Hot Is It?

When cookbooks refer to a slow oven, what do they mean? Here's a list of oven temperatures and terminology. Refer to it when cooking recipes or trying to gauge temperatures.

Oven Temperature Chart

Type of Heat	Fahrenheit	Celsius
Very slow	250 to 300 degrees	121 to 149 degrees
Slow	300 to 325 degrees	149 to 163 degrees
Moderate	350 to 375 degrees	177 to 190 degrees
Very hot	450 to 475 degrees	233 to 246 degrees
Extremely hot	500 to 525 degrees	260 to 274 degrees

Electric and Gas Stoves

If you've cooked with both electric and gas stoves, you know there is a big difference between the two. You have to adjust your cooking habits depending on which you are using.

I've had both, and I much prefer gas because of its immediacy and the ease of regulating heat. When you're cooking with gas, you can see how high or low the flame is. You turn the burner on, and the heat starts immediately. If you've got too much heat, you turn the gas off and the heat is gone. If you turn it down, the heat is instantly reduced.

This is not the case with an electric stove. The heat depends on how quickly the coils heat up or cool down. This means you have to wait for the coils to heat up. When you're following recipes, you have to take this into account with timing. When something is burning and you turn down the heat, it takes time for the coils to cool down. If your heat is too high, you'll have to take the pan off the stove until the coils cool down.

This can present a problem for kids unless they know how to handle the heat. If you have an electric stove, show your kids how to transfer their pots safely to a trivet or an unlit burner while they're waiting for the coils to cool down. One visual cue is the color of the coils. The redder the coils, the higher the heat.

Heads Up!

Hot coils on an electric stove can spark a fire just as easily as the flame on a gas burner. Never touch the coils or put anything on them other than the pots you're using for cooking.

With both electric and gas stoves, the danger of burns and fires is clear to us but not necessarily to kids. Kids might not realize how hot the coils get or that they can spark a fire. Teach kids never to touch coils and to check the stove dial for the temperature range.

Numbers on the Electric Range Dial

The dials on an electric stove regulate the temperature. Turn the dial to the appropriate number to get the amount of heat you need.

Electric Stove Temperature Range

Dial Setting	Temperature Description
Low to 2	Low heat for barely simmering
3	Medium-to-low heat for more vigorous simmering
4 and 5	Medium heat for gentle boiling
6	Hot for boiling and sautéing
7 and up	Very hot for frying and rapid boiling

Kid Quiz

If a piece of toast gets stuck in the toaster, is it okay to use a fork or another metal utensil to get it out?

No. Never put a utensil into a toaster. If it's plugged in, you can electrocute yourself. You also can damage the coils. Unplug the toaster, bring it over to the sink or a plate, and invert it to try to dislodge the toast.

Toasters and Toaster Ovens

Kids might be tempted to stick a fork or a knife into a toaster to remove stuck toast. Teach them to never put their fingers near the coils or any utensils in the toaster. They should ask for help to remove stuck food.

Be sure to go over the features of your toaster oven. Kids need to know that it's different from a regular oven, in particular when it comes to broiling. Don't try to broil foods unless your appliance is specifically designed for that purpose.

Kid Quiz

Is it okay to turn on a microwave if there's nothing in it?

No. You can damage the microwave. Always make sure there's food in the microwave before you turn it on. Here's a handy trick: Leave a microwave-safe bowl or cup filled with water in the oven. This way, if you or a younger brother or sister turns on the oven by accident, it won't be empty.

The Magic of Microwaves

If there's one appliance kids use and like to operate, it's the microwave oven. It's fast and easy, and kids like the feeling that they're cooking when they're "nuking" their foods. Kids can get burned easily, however, if they're not careful. For one thing, microwaved foods get very hot, very quickly. That heat transfers to plates. When it comes to uncovering foods, the steam also can cause burns.

Microwaves use high-frequency electromagnetic waves to cook food. These waves cause the food molecules to vibrate very quickly, creating the friction that heats and cooks the food. Kids can picture this by rubbing their hands together quickly and seeing how hot they get.

Because the waves are short, they travel fast and cook the food quickly. The waves pass through containers holding the food and cook the food from the top, bottom, and sides all at once. (This is why you can't use metal containers, which deflect the waves.) The waves only penetrate about 1½ to 2 inches of the food, so the center usually is cooked by conducted heat. The food can cook unevenly because most ovens have spots where waves don't penetrate as well. That's why you'll see microwaves with built-in turntables and recipes that tell you to rotate or stir the food.

Bigger Bites

Appliance manufacturers often have recipes and additional information about preparing foods with their appliances. Many have produced their own cookbooks. Call their toll-free numbers to find out if you can receive additional information or offers for their appliances.

Go over the following list with your kids to make sure they're operating a microwave properly:

➤ Refer to your owner's manual to learn the wattage and features of your microwave and how to operate it. Be sure you're setting the controls properly.

➤ Be sure you can see the food inside and can properly reach the microwave. If kids have to reach up, they can spill food and burn themselves. They should never stand on a chair to try to get into the microwave.

➤ Never cook food in metal containers or use metal utensils or twist ties with metal strips while cooking. Check to be sure containers are microwave safe before cooking.

➤ Check recipe cooking times against the wattage of your microwave. Most recipes are written for 700-watt ovens. You might have to increase or decrease cooking times depending on your oven's power.

➤ Be aware that dishes can get hot. Have pot holders nearby to use. A dish might not seem hot at first, but the heat from the food transfers to the dish surface.

➤ To avoid steam burns, slowly lift the farthest corner of a lid or cover away from your face. Take special care when cooking microwave popcorn. Steam from the bag can cause a bad burn. Poke a hole in the bag to let the steam escape. If using plastic wrap, poke holes in the wrap or turn back an edge to allow steam to escape.

➤ Be sure foods are cooked thoroughly because they can cook unevenly in the microwave.

➤ Don't overcook foods. Dry foods, such as baked potatoes and cooked popcorn, can ignite.

➤ Pierce foods with a skin, such as potatoes, tomatoes, and squash, to prevent them from exploding while cooking. Never microwave peeled cooked eggs, egg yolks, or an egg in the shell because they can burst. Read your owner's manual or a microwave cookbook to find out about how foods react in the microwave.

➤ In the case of a fire, close the door and unplug the microwave. Make sure kids call an adult and follow general fire-safety rules.

Heads Up!

Be careful with hot plates and steam escaping from foods after they've been cooked in the microwave. Always handle plates with pot holders, and slowly lift the farthest corner of a cover away from you to avoid steam burns.

The Least You Need to Know

➤ Always supervise your children when they're using appliances. Show them how they work, what they're used for, and how to operate them safely.

➤ Teach children to keep their fingers away from the blades of blenders and foods processors and the beaters of mixers. Show them how to remove and clean these items safely.

➤ Teach kids never to stick utensils in appliances while they're operating.

➤ Have your kids practice getting foods in and out of the oven and the microwave when they're off and show them how to prevent burns from steam and hot plates.

➤ Go through your cupboards to determine which containers are safe for microwave use. Caution kids not to microwave certain foods that can burst, such as eggs in the shell and raw egg yolks.

Chapter 9

Getting Equipped

In This Chapter

➤ Tips for finding equipment

➤ A list of essential kitchen equipment

➤ Cool tools for young hands

Shopping for kitchen tools can be fun for you and your kids. You'll get a real education when you wander into a kitchen store and see all the gadgets that can fill your kitchen counters, cupboards, and drawers.

You don't need a lot of fancy equipment to cook. As you become more experienced, you'll no doubt add items to your kitchen. For now, however, look through this chapter to learn about the basic kitchen equipment used in the recipe section and where you can buy it. The section on cool tools for kids describes equipment I've found that's especially fun and well-suited for kids.

Buying Equipment

You can buy kitchen equipment in a variety of places with a variety of price tags. Department stores, discount outlet stores, specialty kitchen shops, warehouse clubs, discount chain stores, mail-order sources, and the Internet are a few possibilities.

My number one rule is to check the equipment for quality. If it's flimsy or cheaply made, it's not going to last and can affect your recipe. Heat, for example, will be conducted better in a better-made piece of equipment. Don't buy cheap just because you're cooking with the kids.

For standard items such as wooden spoons and Pyrex® measures and bowls, you'll do fine at discount chain stores.

When it comes to costlier items, I always shop the sales or look for outlet stores. Our local outlet mall has a kitchen store with name-brand equipment at hefty discounts. Here are some other ways to find kitchen equipment at lower prices:

➤ Check the phone book for restaurant-supply stores that carry specialty items or consult Appendix B, "The Resource Guide," at the back of this book.

➤ Order on the Web or through catalogs offering discounts.

➤ Call the manufacturer to find out the nearest outlet store.

➤ Shop at flea markets or school fairs. I picked up brand-new baking pans (the price stickers were still on them) at our school rummage sale.

➤ Check garage sales. I've found lots of interesting, older gadgets that are no longer produced today and that are made of better-quality materials. With electric equipment, such as old waffle irons, be sure they work or can be rewired.

Kitchen Clue

You can find interesting gadgets, kitchen equipment, and antique kitchen tools at garage sales and flea markets. If they're old, they're often made of sturdier materials than similar items you'd find today. Always wash them well in a bleach solution before you use them.

Tools to Measure and Prepare Food

Liquid measuring cups

Dry-ingredient measuring cups

Measuring spoons

Ruler

Small, medium, and large bowls

Small and large rubber spatulas

Wooden spoon

Wire whisks

Colander

Colander

Large strainer or sifter

Large strainer or sifter

Small strainer

Egg separator

Egg beater or hand-held mixer

Funnels

Blender

Food processor (optional)

Potato masher

Juicer or lemon reamer

Wooden skewers

Toothpicks

Vegetable brush

Ice cream scoops

Melon baller

Tools for Cutting

Cutting board

Paring knife

Small serrated knife

Chef's knife

Table knife

Long serrated bread knife

Vegetable peeler

Grater

Can opener

Kitchen scissors

Apple corer

Pizza cutter

Zester

Tools for Checking Temperature and Timing

Instant-read thermometer

Oven thermometer

Timer

Tools for Baking, Broiling, and Roasting

12-cup Bundt pan or fluted tube pan

Rolling pin

Pastry brush

Pastry blender with wire whisks

Biscuit and cookie cutters

Sifter or strainer

Cookie or baking sheets

Jelly roll pan (15½" × 10½" × 1")

Jelly roll pan (15½" × 10½" × 1")

Loaf pan (9" × 5" × 3")

Minimuffin and regular muffin tins

Rectangular baking pan (13" × 9" × 2")

Square baking pan (8" × 8" × 2")

Broiling pan

Roasting pan

9-inch pie pan

9-inch round cake pan

Rectangular 4-quart baking dish

Casserole dish

Cooling racks

Cupcake liners

Heads Up!

Don't skimp when it comes to buying cookware. You're better off buying equipment made from quality materials than picking up cheap, flimsy items. Good cookware usually is warranted, functions better, and lasts a long time. For the best price, shop the sales, discount catalogs, and outlet sources.

Pot holders or oven mitts

Cookie scoop

6-ounce custard cups or ramekins

Tools for Stovetop Cooking

Saucepans (1-, 2-, 3-, and 5-quart capacity) with lids

Steamer

Large nonstick skillets (8-, 10-, and 12-inch) with lids

Wooden spoons

Griddle

Spatula

Ladle

Tongs

Slotted spoon

Large pasta pot

Dutch oven with lid

Tea kettle

Kitchen Clue

Spatter screens, circular screens made of mesh that fit over pans, have multiple uses in the kitchen. They prevent hot oil from spattering out of the pan and causing burns. They also can be used as a strainer, a drainer, or a cooling rack. Look for them in kitchen stores or order them from one of the kitchen sources listed in Appendix B. A set of three screens costs about $20.

Dutch oven with lid

Finding the Best Knife

When you walk into a kitchen store, you'll get dizzy looking at all the different high-quality knives. Most home cooks really need only three basic knives: a chef's knife, a paring knife, and a serrated knife. Good-quality knives are expensive, but when you consider how long they last and how often you use them, I think you'll agree that they're a sound investment. Go to a reputable kitchen store and ask for help in selecting your knives. Ask how to use and hold them and how to clean and store them. Whatever you choose, make sure your knives are sturdy and the blades are made of high-carbon stainless steel.

A cooking essential: good knives. Pictured here are a chef's knife, a paring knife, and a serrated knife.

Kitchen Clue

We've found that soft-grip knives, vegetable peelers, and utensils are excellent for children's small hands. The cushioned handle gives them a comfortable and secure grip. The knives are affordable and come in various sizes and shapes. Take your kids knife shopping and try out different grips and sizes to see what works best for them. Look for OXO GOOD GRIPS® with its kid-friendly full line of kitchen knives and tools.

Chef's or Cook's Knife

This is an all-purpose knife that comes in sizes from about 6 to 12 inches long. Cooks use this knife to mince and chop everything from parsley to onions. This knife has a recessed handle to prevent the cook's knuckles from striking the work surface.

Paring Knife

The smallest of the special knives with blade sizes ranging from about 1½ to 4 inches long, this is used for a variety of chores including peeling and seeding vegetables and fruits. Its small and triangular shape and sharp point make it distinctive to pick out among knives. When your kids move into sharp knives, they'll probably start with this one.

Serrated Knife

This knife comes in long and short sizes. The jagged, serrated surface grabs slippery objects and crusty breads. The longer knives are great for cutting baguettes and thick-crusted, rustic breads, but you need to warn children that the teeth are very sharp. Shorter serrated knives are used to cut smooth-surfaced foods, such as tomatoes. These are good knives to start kids off with for cutting tomatoes and cucumbers because the knife has a round tip and doesn't slip.

Cool Tools for Kids

Over the years, I've found a number of kitchen gadgets that are not only fun, but educational for kids to use. They improve kids' motor skills and act as substitutes for more dangerous equipment (such as knives or electric mixers). In some cases, you can let your kids use them to do a safe kitchen chore while you're working on another part of a recipe.

Discover your own favorites by looking at tools in your kitchen and imagining how your kids could use them in ways other than their intended use. An egg slicer, for example, can be used to cut soft fruits, such as bananas and strawberries, or vegetables like mushrooms. We discovered during recipe testing that something as simple as the clean bottom of a can or a pot made a great garlic smasher.

Learn the Lingo

A **cookie scoop** looks like a small version of an ice cream scoop. When you squeeze the handle, a spring attached to a metal scraper presses the dough out of the ball of the scoop. **Dishers** look like cookie scoops, but they come in different sizes and are used in the food service industry to dish out foods. We like to use small dishers to shape chocolate truffles or to make large scoops of melon or mini-scoops of ice cream.

➤ **Apple corer and slicer** This nifty device cores and sections apples in one motion. Kids can fit the center cylinder over the core and then use the weight of their body to push down and cut through the apple.

➤ **Bean masher** My kids like to see the beans come through the round circular holes at the bottom of the masher. Kids can use it to mash a variety of foods.

➤ **Blunt kitchen scissors** A new pair of kid's art scissors can be used to cut herbs, green onions, and dried fruit. Mark them for kitchen use and keep them with your children's other kitchen tools.

➤ **Citrus reamer** This is one of my favorite kitchen tools. It doesn't take up much room, and it does a great job of extracting juice from lemons and limes. You put the point of the reamer right into the citrus fruit half and then turn the reamer.

➤ **Cookie and ice cream scoops and dishers** You'll find standard cookie and ice cream scoops in grocery and kitchen stores. Scoops in a range of sizes are available at restaurant-supply and kitchen stores.

➤ **Egg beater**   Remember the old trick of filling up a bowl with water and liquid soap and letting kids improve their motor skills by making suds and cranking away on the egg beater? Now you can let kids use this old favorite to mix batters, make frothy drinks, and blend liquids.

➤ **Egg slicer**   This introduces kids to slicing without using a knife. Kids can fit a cooked potato, an egg, a banana, or another soft fruit or vegetable inside the slicer and then press down on it.

Bigger Bites

Find out more about different types of kitchen equipment by visiting a kitchen store, sending for free catalogs from kitchen supply companies, and checking the Internet for information. Catalogs often describe why and how a kitchen tool is used. Listings of catalog companies and Web sites are available in Appendix B at the back of this book.

➤ **Garlic press**   This tool makes preparing garlic for sauces or garlic bread a snap. You don't have to peel the garlic before pressing. Kids also can put dough or frosting in the press to make "hair" for cookies and other decorations for cakes.

➤ **Hand-crank apple corer and peeler**   You'll have to clamp this to a table and set the apple in the peeler—be careful, the point is sharp—but kids love to spin the crank and see the peel come off the apple.

➤ **Hand-crank cheese grater**   This was always my favorite tool as a kid. You put a hunk of hard cheese over the grating barrel, press down on the handle with one hand, and crank away with the other. Fluffy pieces of cheese magically emerge from the crank.

➤ **Horizontal cheese grater over a plastic container**   These are particularly useful for kids because the grate fits snugly over a container and the cheese collects right in the container. Kids can get good leverage and can make a pushing motion to grate. The grated cheese stays contained in the bowl.

➤ **Lemon zester**   Kids enjoy making curlicues from the skin of fruits and vegetables with this tool. It's also a great tool for decorating.

➤ **Melon baller**   Kids find this to be a great tool for coring apples or for scraping out seeds from zucchini, cucumbers, and other fruits and vegetables. They like making melon balls, too.

➤ **Minitools like small rubber spatulas, spoons, forks, and whisks**   These smaller tools are kid-size, are easier to handle, and are just plain cute. I bought each of my daughters their own set when they were young, I painted their names on the tools, and I put them in their Christmas stockings.

➤ **Mortar and pestle**   Kids can grind spices or make guacamole with these tools.

➤ **Pastry blender**   The handle and shape of this tool are easy for kids to work with. Avoid the type that has attached pieces of metal. They're hard to clean and the blades are sharp.

➤ **Pastry scraper**   Here's a handy tool for kids to use to cut into pastry dough and other foods, to scoop up ingredients, or to scrape dough from the counter. Use a sturdy, stainless-steel scraper as an alternative to a sharp knife when cutting soft fruits and vegetables.

Kitchen Clue

Store your children's kitchen tools in a see-through plastic box with their names on it. Give them each an apron with their name on it and assign a special place in the kitchen for the tools and aprons. This way, they always know where their tools are, and when they want to cook, they can just go and get them.

➤ **Pizza wheel**   Another alternative to a sharp knife, the wheel gives kids a sense of cutting without the sharp edge. They can use it to slice bread, sandwiches, peppers, and other soft or cooked fruits and vegetables.

➤ **Potato masher**   My daughter likes using the masher for making guacamole and mashed potatoes. It's much easier than mashing food with a fork.

➤ **Potato ricer**   This tool works like a giant garlic press. You put potatoes in the cup, press down the lid, and the potatoes come out in strands and make incredibly fluffy mashed potatoes. Kids also can put dough through the ricer to make spaghetti-like strands.

➤ **Pumpkin carving knife**   This plastic safety knife is great for kids to cut up lemons and limes and other fruits and vegetables. Look for it around Halloween in grocery stores and stock up. You won't find it at other times of the year.

➤ **Salad spinner**   If kids are big enough to hold down the spinner or hold it cupped against their body with one arm, they can spin with their free hand. It's magic to see how much water collects from the lettuce. The inside strainer and its base also are useful for washing vegetables. Just put them in the inside strainer, fill the base with water, and then lift out the strainer. It acts like a colander.

➤ **Vinyl roll garlic peeler**   Kids can put a piece of garlic inside this tube-like tool and then roll it with their hands to remove the papery outer skin of garlic.

The Least You Need to Know

➤ Invest in quality cookware. It will last longer and will function far better than cheaper equipment.

➤ Find the best prices through sales, outlet stores, discount stores, the Internet, and mail-order catalogs.

➤ Let kids use kitchen tools and gadgets as a way of improving their motor skills and coordination.

FRIDGE CLEANING SUIT

Chapter 10

What You Need to Know About Food Safety

In This Chapter

➤ Teaching kids about food safety

➤ Washing your hands and keeping things clean

➤ Cooking and storing foods at the right temperature

➤ Preventing germs from spreading

➤ Storing and keeping food safe

My kids are used to reminders about food safety. "Did you wash your hands?" I ask when they walk in the door from school or sporting events and go straight for the refrigerator. "Don't wait, refrigerate," I chant as they leave the kitchen with the milk or juice carton still out on the countertop. "Don't spread the germs," I caution when they're handling raw meat, fish, or eggs. Of course, they always groan at my reminders, but they're grateful for them after they hear the latest tale about food poisoning.

Everywhere we turn today, there seems to be some warning about the food we eat. Product recalls and media coverage about food-related deaths are all too familiar. The good news is that we can protect ourselves by taking a few simple precautions. In fact, the federal government has joined with other agencies in mounting a whole campaign called Fight BAC!™ (for bacteria) to help us take the reins of food safety. Read on to learn what you and your family can do to make sure you don't become ill from the food you handle and eat.

Kid Quiz

What one simple thing can you do that will protect you from germs?

Wash your hands often, especially after you go to the bathroom and before you eat or handle food. Wash them in hot, soapy water and count to 20 or sing your ABCs to make sure you're doing a thorough job.

Teaching Kids About Food Safety

Teaching our kids about food safety can help protect them from getting sick from the foods they eat. It also gives them a head start to becoming good cooks because so much of cooking involves the proper storage and handling of food. Knowing about food safety empowers them and gives them control over their environment.

Kids are often in situations in which germs spread easily. They're around portable foods and might think nothing of digging into perishable lunch leftovers on the afternoon school bus or eating a snack that was not properly refrigerated. They easily transfer germs when they pick up foods without washing their hands after playing or using the bathroom.

They also might be around relatives who are among the groups at high risk for food-borne illness. These groups include young children under the age of 3, pregnant women, older people, and people who are seriously ill, particularly with AIDS or cancer. In all these groups, the immune system is either not developed or is weakened by age or a physical condition.

The FIGHT BAC!™ logo and simple food-safety plan.

Four Easy Steps to Food Safety

When you teach your kids about food safety, have them remember the three C's and an S:

➤ Keep it **clean.** Wash hands and surfaces often and properly.

➤ **Separate** don't cross-contaminate. Keep raw meat, poultry, fish, and eggs separate in your refrigerator and on countertops and cutting surfaces. Don't reuse utensils used for raw foods, including plates, for other foods without washing them with soap and hot water first.

➤ **Cook** foods well. Cook meat, poultry, seafood, and eggs to proper temperatures and reheat leftovers to 165 degrees F if possible.

➤ **Chill** foods soon. Keep hot foods hot and cold foods cold. When you finish with foods from the refrigerator, put them right back in. Teach kids the two-hour rule. Perishable foods should sit at room temperature for no more than two hours; otherwise, harmful bacteria start to grow.

Sudsing Up

There's been a big emphasis lately on proper hand washing—and for good reason. Sudsing up is the basis for good food-safety habits. Teach kids to wash their hands after they go to the bathroom and before they eat or begin a kitchen task. Likewise, after they've handled raw eggs, meat, poultry, or fish, washing their hands and all utensils is a must. Here are some simple guidelines for hand washing:

1. Use hot water and plenty of soap to wash your hands.

2. Be sure to distribute the soap all over your hands including between your fingers, up to your wrists, and under your fingernails.

3. Wash your hands for 20 seconds. Encourage your kids to sing the ABC song or to count to 20 to be sure they're doing a thorough job.

4. Cut down on the spread of germs by using a paper towel or the back of your hand to close the tap. Use a paper towel to open the bathroom door after hand washing, especially in public washrooms. In your kitchen, use the back of your hand to close the tap and dry your hands with a paper towel or a clean dishcloth. Tell your kids to pretend they are doctors on television preparing for surgery.

Heads Up!

Change dishrags and dish towels frequently to cut down on the growth of germs in your kitchen. Be sure you're using clean linens to wash and dry your dishes.

Keep It Clean

Clean dishrags, sponges, towels, and countertops are essential to reducing the spread of germs. Changing the kitchen linen often and washing down the countertops with a bleach solution helps prevent contamination.

Kitchen Clue

Get in the habit of washing down countertops and cutting boards with a mild bleach or sanitizing solution. Several anti-bacterial and bleach products for the kitchen are now on the market. You also can make up your own solution with ¼ teaspoon chlorine bleach diluted in a quart of water. Put it in a squirt bottle so it's handy for wipe downs. The solution needs to be changed when the chlorine smell disappears.

If you want to show your kids a graphic demonstration of bacterial growth, just snip a piece of your favorite dish towel, sponge, or dishrag and let it sit for a few days in a petri dish. Put it under a microscope and you'll be grossed out by the bacterial growth.

To avoid problems, get in the habit of changing your dishrags and towels several times a week and as soon as they become soiled. Wash countertops with a mild bleach solution. Dip sponges and dishrags into a bleach solution (¼ teaspoon of chlorine bleach in a quart of water) to keep them sanitized. We keep a squirt bottle filled with bleach solution under the sink so it's handy for wipe downs.

What's That Growing in My Refrigerator?

How often have you found foods with past-due dates in your refrigerator? Do you ever wonder how long that bottle of spaghetti sauce has been lurking at the back of the bottom shelf? It happens to all of us. We get busy, and before we know it, we've got wilted lettuce, stale cream cheese, and soggy leftovers in the refrigerator. The shelves look like they haven't been cleaned in a year.

Here are some tips for keeping your refrigerator food safe:

➤ Don't overpack the refrigerator. Cool air needs to circulate for foods to stay chilled. Keep a thermometer in the refrigerator so you can check the temperature. (It should be under 40 degrees F.)

➤ Date stamp your foods. I keep a laundry marker and a packet of self-stick labels in a drawer next to the fridge. As soon as I open something I won't use up quickly, I mark the date on the jar label or on a self-stick label.

➤ Follow the principle of first in, first out. Use older foods first before digging into the newly purchased foods.

➤ Get in the habit of doing a weekly sweep of the refrigerator to discard old produce and to check items for expiration dates.

➤ Be sure to keep raw meats and fish covered and on plates to avoid drips onto other foods. Clean up spills immediately and wipe down shelves regularly.

Don't Mix Raw and Cooked Foods

When you cut meat or poultry or handle raw eggs, wash your hands and immediately sanitize the cutting board, knife, and other utensils in hot soapy water. Never reuse a cutting board, knife, or dish that contained raw products or eggs without washing it first.

Some families designate separate cutting boards for risky foods, such as meat and poultry. Whatever you decide to do in your own home, you should wash cutting boards after each use.

Check and Change Cutting Boards

There's been great debate about whether wooden or plastic cutting boards are better for minimizing the risk of germs. Two new kinds of boards, a plastic antibacterial board and a flexible plastic board, are now on the market. Contact the Food and Drug Administration (FDA) to see which boards experts are currently recommending. Whatever type of board you choose, be sure to examine and replace it frequently. The grooves created by continuous knife use can harbor germs.

Bigger Bites

Check out the latest news in food safety at the Web sites listed below. Always be sure to click the "What's New?" section to find out the current news about food-safety recalls and advances.

Log on to the FDA Web site at www.fda.gov. (Kids can go to the kids' page and play interactive food-safety games.) There's also the Food Safety Information Service at www.fsis.usda.gov or FightBAC!™ at www.fightbac.org. For one-stop shopping of food-safety information, log on to www.foodsafety.gov. The site also offers numerous links to other food-safety–related sites.

Temperature and Color Count

Much to the regret of fans of medium-rare hamburgers, the days of pink ground meat (and poultry) are over. Pink ground meat, sausages, and poultry indicate that the meat is undercooked and might not have reached high enough temperatures to kill bacteria. Teach your kids to make sure the inside of their chicken is white and any ground meat and sausages are gray throughout. Large pieces of meat, such as lamb chops and steaks, can be pink inside because the surfaces are heated and the inside meat has not been exposed to bacteria. (The exception might be in meats that have been tenderized.) Be sure the meats have reached recommended temperatures, though. Pork chops need to be cooked to 160 degrees F, but they can have a slight blush of pink inside.

Safe temperatures for cooking and storing food.

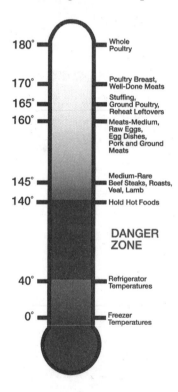

- 180° — Whole Poultry
- 170° — Poultry Breast, Well-Done Meats
- 165° — Stuffing, Ground Poultry, Reheat Leftovers
- 160° — Meats-Medium, Raw Eggs, Egg Dishes, Pork and Ground Meats
- 145° — Medium-Rare Beef Steaks, Roasts, Veal, Lamb
- 140° — Hold Hot Foods

DANGER ZONE

- 40° — Refrigerator Temperatures
- 0° — Freezer Temperatures

Use Food Thermometers

Food-safety experts are making a big push to get home cooks to use instant-read or digital thermometers to check meat temperatures. Use the thermometer along with visual clues to be sure meats are no longer pink and are properly cooked. Get kids involved by letting them help you read the thermometer. One caution: Thermometers may need to be calibrated before use. Put the thermometer in boiling water and set it to read 212 degrees F. Read the directions to learn how to make adjustments. (For an instant-read thermometer with a stem, you usually can adjust the nut underneath the dial and reset the dial.) You can also purchase thermometers with probes that extend outside the oven and enable you to constantly monitor the temperature.

Kid Quiz

You order a hamburger in a restaurant, and when you get it, the inside is pink. Should you eat it?

No, you shouldn't eat the hamburger. To be safe, hamburger meat needs to be cooked until it is gray. Don't be afraid to politely ask the waiter or waitress for a hamburger that is well-cooked.

Keep Bacteria at Bay

Has this ever happened to you? You go to a party and eat the buffet foods that have been sitting on the beautifully arranged table. They taste great, but the next day you feel like you're getting the flu. You have a little headache and your stomach feels funny. If the foods weren't kept at proper temperatures, you might be showing the symptoms of food-borne illness.

Eating foods kept at improper temperatures is one of the major causes of sickness from foods. Food experts call the temperature range from 40 to 140 degrees F the danger zone. At this temperature, harmful bacteria can multiply quickly. If foods are left in this range for more than two hours, they can become risky and cause illness. How can you avoid problems?

1. Don't leave perishable foods in the danger zone for more than two hours.

2. Get foods out of the danger zone as quickly as possible. Cooling takes time, and you might have to give foods a little help. If you've got a large pot of soup or chili, divide it into smaller portions and set the bowls in ice water up to the rim. Cut a roast or large pieces of meat into smaller pieces.

3. Always cook foods thoroughly. Remember, cooking foods to proper temperatures kills harmful bacteria.

4. Keep hot foods hot and cold foods cold. This means putting milk for coffee in the buffet line on ice and keeping hot foods in a chafing dish or a warm oven until they're ready to be served or eaten.

5. Refrigerate perishable foods immediately after they are used. Get kids in the habit of putting the juice, milk, or cheese right back into the fridge instead of on the countertop.

6. Keep foods that need to be hot at temperatures higher than 140 degrees F.

Food-Borne Illness

Unfortunately, my family has become sick from food on several occasions, and the symptoms have varied. One time, I swallowed one mouthful of tainted rice on an airplane and got sick within 15 minutes. The symptoms continued for a day and then luckily I was fine.

Another time, my husband became ill after eating in a restaurant. His symptoms mimicked a serious flu with 24 hours of stomach upset, headache, and other miserable symptoms. Fortunately, he recovered with no lingering ill effects.

Food experts say that the symptoms and the recovery from food-borne illness will vary depending on the bacteria, the person's susceptibility, and the amount of food eaten. Common symptoms include diarrhea, headache, and nausea—much like the flu.

If you suspect you have a food-borne illness, always call a doctor or an emergency hot line. Because children under age 3 are in a high-risk group, it's always a good idea to check with your pediatrician and monitor the symptoms. Review your activities and think of what you've eaten to help pinpoint the problem.

Kid Quiz

You're making brownies with your friend and the batter looks chocolatey and delicious. Can you lick the spoon?

No. You could get really sick. The batter contains raw eggs, which are not safe to eat even if they are hidden in chocolate batter.

Using Common Sense

There's no substitute for common sense when it comes to avoiding food-borne illness. Try to stay informed about the latest news regarding food-borne illness by listening to or reading the news, checking in with Web sites, or calling the toll-free government hot lines. Here are some tips my family has learned from experience:

1. If you or your children suspect a food has not been handled properly or is undercooked, don't buy it or eat it. We've sent back food at restaurants when it hasn't been hot enough or if the meat seemed undercooked.

2. Teach your kids to keep their eyes open to the sanitary conditions in the places you eat or buy food. If you or they have any doubts, don't purchase or eat the food. It's not worth the consequences. As the saying goes, "When in doubt, do without."

3. Teach your children not to be afraid to spit out or refuse questionable food. The ill-effects of eating bad food far outweigh any embarrassment they might suffer from discarding it. The tainted rice that made me sick on the airplane tasted a little funny. My mistake was not rejecting it immediately when I suspected a problem.

4. Never eat anything that tastes or smells bad to you, but don't rely only on taste or smell to determine if food is safe. Some foods might be contaminated but smell and taste fine.

5. Check expiration dates and don't purchase or eat foods with dates that are past due.

> ### Learn the Lingo
>
> **Fight BAC!**™ (for bacteria) is the name of a campaign to combat food-borne illness. A coalition of government and industry groups banded together in 1997 to educate the public about food-borne illness and to spread simple food-safety messages. Visit the group's Web site at www.fightbac.com to learn more about food-borne illness.

> ### Bigger Bites
>
> To hear recorded messages about food safety and the latest in food-safety issues, you can call the Food and Drug Administration and the USDA's toll-free help lines 24 hours a day. For the FDA Food Hot Line (including seafood information), call 1-800-332-4010. For the USDA Meat And Poultry Hot Line, call 1-800-535-4555.
>
> You also can speak to a consumer affairs specialist on weekdays from noon–4 P.M. Eastern time at these numbers.

The Least You Need to Know

➤ Children under 3 years of age are one of the four groups at greatest risk for food-borne illness. The other groups include pregnant women, seniors, and the seriously ill.

➤ Wash your hands thoroughly after using the bathroom and before eating and cooking to prevent the spread of germs.

➤ Cook foods to proper temperatures and rely on visual clues plus a thermometer to make sure they are properly cooked.

➤ Keep hot foods hot and cold foods cold to prevent harmful bacteria from multiplying. Beware of the "danger zone" between 40 and 140 degrees F.

➤ Separate utensils used for raw eggs, poultry, meat, and fish and wash them thoroughly in hot soapy water after each use. Keep dishrags, cloths, and countertops sanitized.

➤ Use common sense and follow your instincts when it comes to food safety.

Part 4

The Building Blocks of Cooking

Now that your kids know how to be safe in the kitchen, you're ready to cook with them. But wait. Do they know how to read a recipe? And what happens when the directions tell them to do something like sauté the onions or fold the nuts in a batter?

No problem. The following chapters take the mystery out of cooking techniques and are designed for you to read with your kids and use them as a reference guide. The chapter about recipes will show you and your kids how to tackle the toughest among them. Kids love to measure, and in the chapter about kitchen math, they'll learn how to do it right. With the cooking lessons your kids will get in the chapter on cooking techniques and handling tools, they'll be whipping up dinner in no time. Even if they make a mistake or get frustrated, you'll know how to handle it with the help of the chapter on kitchen mishaps. You'll even learn how to make substitutions when you run out of an ingredient. So relax, dig in, and discover the pleasures of cooking with your kids.

Chapter 11

Getting to Know Your Recipe

In This Chapter

➤ What makes a good recipe

➤ Reading through the recipe

➤ Anatomy of a recipe

➤ Handling recipe snags

Have you ever panicked in the middle of a recipe because you don't have an ingredient? Have you been stopped short by an unfamiliar cooking term or technique?

Pitfalls like these are frustrating enough for an adult cook, but they could spell disaster when you're cooking with kids. You risk losing face and their attention. Kids don't know that you've run into a temporary snag. All they know is you're not cooking. Learning how to read and follow a recipe can prevent these problems, and this chapter tells you how to do it. You'll learn what goes into a recipe, what to look for, and how to organize so you keep cooking with great efficiency. Be sure to go over the section on the anatomy of a recipe with your kids to give them a head start in the kitchen.

Recipe Reading and 'Rithmetic

Recipes are merely instructions that spell out what ingredients you need and how you must proceed to create a particular dish. A good recipe is like a foundation that builds a pleasurable cooking experience.

If you have a favorite cookbook author, you probably already know this. You might have found someone whose recipes always seem to work for you. You might like the personality he or she brings to them, the particular cuisine written about, or the fact that you are taken through the cooking steps clearly and with plenty of explanations. You know you can count on this person in the kitchen because all the steps add up.

Not All Recipes Are Created Equal

The fact is, some recipes don't work. They might be confusing and poorly written or simply contain mistakes. An ingredient might seem odd, the timing off, a method missing. You might want more detail about handling that sticky dough or understanding why the sauce seems too thick. One recipe might give it to you and another might not.

Heads Up!

It's fun to be creative in the kitchen, but when you first make a dish, stick to the recipe. With experience, you can add or subtract ingredients to give it your stamp. Or you might find you like it exactly as is.

Recipes as Scientific Formulas

Think of recipes as scientific formulas in which there are causes and effects. When you have a good recipe, the author takes you through the steps, tells you what to expect and in how much time, and anticipates and explains any problems that might develop. Unless you've picked a recipe that's written for very experienced cooks, you should not have any unanswered questions as you read a recipe and cook from it. If you do, it's important to get the answers to your questions before you start cooking.

Becoming a Recipe Expert

The more you cook from recipes, the better you'll be able to distinguish a good one from a bad one. As you read through the instructions, you'll naturally follow the steps and recognize any areas that might cause problems. You'll get good at detecting trouble spots in the ingredient list. Maybe the recipe seems heavy on an ingredient or flavoring, or the writer might list an ingredient that you know won't be available where you live. You'll know to figure out ahead of time whether you can make a substitution. (A good recipe will offer some suggestions.)

When you're not as familiar with cooking techniques, you'll want to stick to the directions and ingredients in the recipe. As you gain experience in the kitchen, you'll get ideas about improvising.

Good Recipes for Cooking with Kids

When you're cooking with kids, it's important to use recipes that are relatively simple and that work. This might mean cooking something you're already familiar with or trying a recipe on your own first to see if it's suitable for your kids.

Teach kids to read through the recipe first and to follow directions. This will develop their organizational skills and will show them how to work in sequence and follow instructions. They'll also sharpen their logical-thinking skills. Approaching recipes this way gives them a good foundation for tackling more challenging projects later.

How to Read a Recipe

Kids will think it's much more fun to just get out all the good stuff and start cooking. Resist the temptation. The basis for successful cooking is reading the recipe, start to finish, before you ever pick up a spoon.

Go over the recipe together with your child, first to get a general idea of where you're going. Then read it again for specifics. Start with the ingredient list and then read through the method and any notes that follow. Here are some questions to ask yourselves:

➤ Are you familiar with all the ingredients and how they should be prepared?

➤ Do you have all the ingredients and the necessary equipment?

➤ If you don't have an ingredient or a piece of equipment, will something in your cupboards work as a substitute? (See Chapter 14, "Dealing with Kitchen Mishaps," for suggested emergency substitutions or look through your cookbook to see what the author suggests.)

➤ Do you understand the method described in the recipe?

➤ Will this recipe satisfy your needs? Do you think you'll like the end result?

Kid Quiz

What is a recipe?

A recipe is the written list of ingredients and directions for preparing a dish. You should read the ingredient list and instructions all the way through before beginning to cook. Then you can assemble the ingredients and tools and begin.

Anatomy of a Recipe

Recipes are structured so the information flows naturally from one point to the next. In "talk" recipes, the writer just talks you through and sets up the recipe in paragraphs like a story. You'll see these in magazines or some of the recent food-related novels that include recipes. Most recipes, however, are set up with a separate list of ingredients at the beginning followed by instructions (sometimes numbered as in this book) and then notes. Recipes in this book also include notes regarding recipe difficulty and equipment needs.

Let's take a look at the parts that make up a typical recipe.

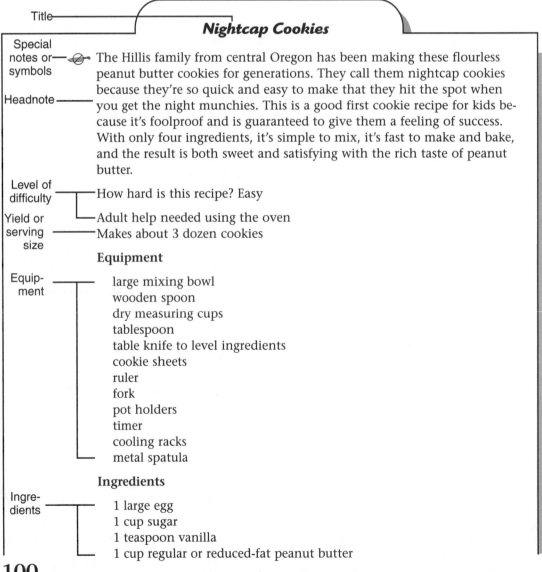

Title

Nightcap Cookies

Special notes or symbols

Headnote — The Hillis family from central Oregon has been making these flourless peanut butter cookies for generations. They call them nightcap cookies because they're so quick and easy to make that they hit the spot when you get the night munchies. This is a good first cookie recipe for kids because it's foolproof and is guaranteed to give them a feeling of success. With only four ingredients, it's simple to mix, it's fast to make and bake, and the result is both sweet and satisfying with the rich taste of peanut butter.

Level of difficulty — How hard is this recipe? Easy

Adult help needed using the oven

Yield or serving size — Makes about 3 dozen cookies

Equipment

Equip-ment
- large mixing bowl
- wooden spoon
- dry measuring cups
- tablespoon
- table knife to level ingredients
- cookie sheets
- ruler
- fork
- pot holders
- timer
- cooling racks
- metal spatula

Ingredients

Ingre-dients
- 1 large egg
- 1 cup sugar
- 1 teaspoon vanilla
- 1 cup regular or reduced-fat peanut butter

Instruc- 1. Position the rack in the middle of the oven and preheat the oven to 350 de-
tions   grees F.

2. Crack the egg into the mixing bowl and use the wooden spoon to beat the
   egg. Mix in the sugar and beat until well combined.

3. Mix in the vanilla, followed by the peanut butter.

4. Shape the dough into 1" balls. Place about 2 inches apart on ungreased cookie
   sheets. Press each cookie with a fork and then turn the fork and press again
icon   to make a crisscross pattern.
|
🌑 5. Bake, one cookie sheet at a time, for 10 to 12 minutes or until the cookies turn
      golden brown.

🌑 6. Use pot holders to remove the cookie sheet and place it on a cooling rack to
      cool for 5 minutes, or until the cookies can be easily lifted with the spatula.
      Use the spatula to transfer the cookies to the cooling racks.

Note
└   **Note:** These cookies are moist and chewy. If you prefer a crisper cookie, increase
         the baking time to 15 minutes.
Variation
└   **Variation:** Place a peanut in the center of each cookie before baking.

A good recipe should guide you easily in preparing food you like.

The Title and Headnote

A recipe starts with the title, which tells you what
you will be making. In the case of dishes from
foreign countries, it might be in the native lan-
guage. A title often will be followed by a headnote or a brief explanatory note about the recipe.
The author might tell you where the recipe came
from or what he or she particularly likes about it.

Special Notes and Symbols

Some recipes offer special notes and symbols.
Recipes in this book, for instance, tell readers

Learn the Lingo

A **headnote** is the introductory
note in a recipe that describes
some aspect of the dish or gives
a personal comment by the
author.

what kind of adult help is needed. Icons throughout the recipe alert readers to when
the help is needed. Icons at the top of the recipe indicate whether the recipe requires
cutting or cooking.

The Ingredient List

The ingredient list outlines what you will use to make the dish. A good recipe lists the ingredients in the order in which they will be used. Some lists tell you how the ingredients should be prepared—for example, ½ cup diced onions. Other recipes give you the whole ingredient and then tell you what to do with it later in the instructions. In this case, the list will say one small onion and then during the steps of the recipe tell you to dice it.

When you're looking at an ingredient, be sure you understand how it should be prepared. The success of your recipe will depend on it. For example, 1 cup sifted flour is different from 1 cup flour, sifted. In the former, you'll need to sift the flour and then measure it. In the latter, you'll need to measure out a cup of flour and then sift it afterward. Although it might seem the same, the quantities actually are different.

The Instructions

Directly following the ingredient list is a set of instructions that tell you how to use the ingredients and put them together. These instructions might be numbered steps, as in the recipes in this book, or they might run together in a paragraph. Ask yourself if these instructions make sense and if you are familiar with all the techniques. If you don't understand a technique, consult Appendix A, "Kitchen Lingo Glossary," or Chapter 13, "Let's Take a Cooking Lesson," in this book or another basic cooking reference book. Whatever you do, don't leave it to chance that you'll somehow stumble through the recipe.

Kid Quiz

What does it mean when you see **yield** or **servings** in a recipe?

The *yield* is the total amount of food the recipe makes. The *servings* tell you how many portions the recipe will provide. You'll need to look at this to figure out if you'll be making enough or too much of the dish.

End Notes, Yields, and Serving Sizes

Some recipes contain notes at the end that give extra details or substitution suggestions. A well-written recipe will always tell you the amount of food (yield) or the number of servings in the finished dish. Ask yourself if this will be enough or if you will have to double or triple the recipe.

Don't Get Stumped by Ingredients and Equipment

If you find yourself dealing with too many unfamiliar ingredients or methods, the recipe probably is not right for your skill level. This can happen especially with ethnic dishes in which ingredients and methods might be unfamiliar. You're better off acquainting yourself with the foods before you attempt to make the recipe. Do some research in a cookbook or go to a store that carries the ingredients and ask someone about them. Sample the dish first in a restaurant so you know what it looks, smells, and tastes like before you try to make it at home.

When it comes to equipment, make sure the recipe specifies the kind of bowl or pan you'll need. Then make sure you have it or something that can be substituted for it. If a recipe tells you to steam vegetables but you don't have a steamer, for example, a colander set inside a pot with a small amount of water will work just as well. Remember that the size or type of pan might make a difference in how the ingredients cook.

When I developed the Ham and Cheese Pie recipe in this book, for example, I used a deep casserole dish. Ten-year-old tester Kayla Kirk and her mom, Diane, put their pie in a 10-inch pie pan, and it came out just fine.

Heads Up!

Unless you're an experienced cook, don't dive into making complicated dishes until you're familiar with the ingredients and methods of cooking. You'll wind up getting frustrated. Always look for easy-to-complete recipes when cooking with kids.

What Does It Mean?

What happens when you come across a recipe in which the author just glosses over a direction, leaves a step out, or calls for a technique you've never heard of? If the direction is not clear or is missing, you'll have to put on your thinking cap to determine what to do.

Check other cookbooks for a similar recipe to see what's missing. Keep in mind, though, that recipes for the same dish could have different methods for arriving at the end result.

As for unfamiliar techniques, check the glossary in this book or try to look it up in a basic kitchen reference book. Again, you might decide that the dish is too complicated for your skills. You also might want to try to make it the first time with a more experienced cook.

The Least You Need to Know

➤ Recipes are formulas that list ingredients and the methods needed to cook them.

➤ Read a recipe twice—once to get a sense of it and again to look for specific ingredients and to be sure you understand the cooking methods.

➤ Teaching children to read recipes gives them a head start as cooks and strengthens their organizational skills.

➤ Cooks often improvise, but when you're trying a new recipe or teaching your kids, it's best to follow the recipe at least once and then decide if you want to change it.

➤ If you find yourself dealing with too many unfamiliar ingredients or methods, the recipe probably is not right for your skill level. Acquaint yourself with the foods and the methods before you attempt to make the recipe.

Chapter 12

Kitchen Math and Measuring

In This Chapter

➤ Learning to measure liquid and solid ingredients

➤ Using the right tools for measuring

➤ Measuring as a math lesson and game for kids

➤ Tables of measurement equivalents

Once you decide on a recipe, it's time to get out all the ingredients. Do you really need to measure? Won't pulling a spoon from the cutlery drawer do just as well as measuring using your graduated measuring spoon set?

Accurate measurements are the basis for successful recipes, especially when it comes to baking. Using the right tools, and not your tableware or coffee cup, is essential. This chapter explains what tools you need for measuring and how to use them. For kids, measuring ingredients and pouring liquids is a safe way to start getting involved in cooking, and it often is their first introduction to working in the kitchen. It brings alive and puts into practice the math they're learning in school. We'll look at some ways to reinforce those math skills, including some kitchen math games.

Measuring Dry Ingredients with Cups and Spoons

A set of graduated measuring cups and spoons with handles should be used to measure dry ingredients. (The spoons also are used for liquid ingredients.) You'll find cups in plastic and metal varieties. Whether you choose plastic or metal, look for heavy-duty materials so the cups don't dent or crack.

Measuring cups come in a nested set of four to seven cups. Most common are the sets of four that include ¼-cup, ⅓-cup, ½-cup, and 1-cup measures. Larger sets include ⅛-, ⅔-, and ¾-cup measures. You can also find 1½- and 2-cup measures.

Graduated dry measuring cups.

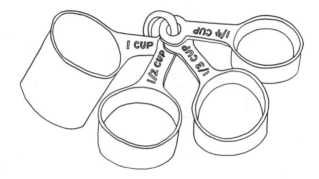

Measuring spoons also nest into sets of four to six spoons, and they are used for measuring liquids and solids that are less than ¼ cup. The most common four-spoon set includes ¼-teaspoon, ½-teaspoon, 1-teaspoon, and 1-tablespoon sizes. Additional spoons might include a ⅛-teaspoon and ½-tablespoon measures. I recently purchased a three-piece spoon set at Restoration Hardware with measures for a pinch, a dash, and a smidgen.

I recommend purchasing a heavy-duty metal set on a ring. Bright-colored plastic sets look nice, but you might find that they crack, accidentally melt in the dishwasher, or snap apart. The thin metal sets are less expensive, but they can bend or dent easily, resulting in inaccurate measurements.

Graduated measuring spoons for dry and liquid ingredients.

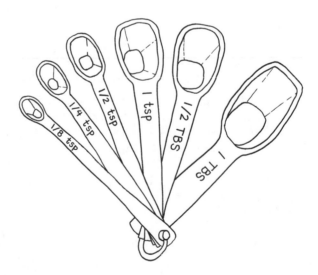

Check out Appendix B, "The Resource Guide, " for sources for purchasing this equipment.

How to Measure Dry Ingredients

When you're measuring dry ingredients, first find the cup or spoon size called for in the recipe. Because dry ingredients can become compacted when stored, lightly stir them to give them some air. Then, depending on the ingredient, either spoon it into the cup or use the cup to scoop out the ingredient from the container. It's very important to level your measurement by scraping the straight edge of a table knife or a metal spatula across the top of the cup or spoon. You can do this over a piece of waxed paper or a paper plate and then just pour the excess back into the canister. Never do it above the bowl you're using to mix the ingredients. Any excess might fall into the bowl and throw off your measurements.

Heads Up!

Resist the temptation to substitute a coffee cup or table cutlery for measuring tools. The measures might not be accurate. Accuracy counts, especially in baking where exact measurements are the key to success.

Bigger Bites

Look for visual aids listing measurement equivalents and post them in the kitchen for handy reference. Kitchen supply stores or cookbook stores with gadgets often carry these items. My kids bought me a magnet in the shape of a liquid measuring cup. The face of the magnet has a chart with liquid measurements.

Flour

When measuring flour, pass a spoon through the flour to give it some air. Then lightly spoon it into the measuring cup and scrape the flat side of a knife or a metal spatula across the top of the cup to level it. When the recipe calls for a heaping cup, you can let the flour mound up on top of the cup. Don't be tempted to tap the cup. This will pack the flour and throw off the measurement.

Brown Sugar and Solid Shortening

Brown sugar and solid shortening are two ingredients for which packing is important to get rid of air pockets. Spoon the sugar or shortening into a graduated measuring cup or spoon and then use the backside of a spoon to pack it into the measure. Use the straight edge of a table knife or spatula to level the amount. Unlike white sugar, packed brown sugar will keep its shape when turned out of the cup or spoon.

Heads Up!

Never level or measure ingredients directly over the bowl in which you are mixing your ingredients. You might overpour or scrape extra ingredients into the bowl and throw off your measurement. Instead, measure over a piece of waxed paper or a paper plate and then just pour the runover right back into the canister.

What's "Rounded" or "Heaping"?

Some recipes call for a rounded or heaping spoon or cupful. In this case, don't use a straight edge to level the measure. Simply leave a mound slightly higher than the measure on top.

What's a "Pinch"?

You might see an instruction in a recipe for a pinch of an ingredient. You literally pinch or squeeze the ingredient between your thumb and forefinger and then add that amount to your ingredients. If you measure a pinch, you'll find it equals less than ⅛ teaspoon.

Measuring Liquids

Liquid measuring cups are clear with pouring spouts and handles and come in plastic or glass. I like using the plastic kind with kids so you don't have to worry about chips or breaks. A good way to remember the difference between dry and liquid cups is to remember that you *pour* liquids, and the liquid measure looks like a small pitcher.

Liquid measures come in many sizes including 1-cup, 2-cup, 4-cup, and 8-cup capacities. You'll see markings on the side that indicate breakdowns of measurements such as ounces, milliliters, and fractions of a cup. Measuring spoons also are used for liquids.

Liquid measuring cups have spouts and handles for easy pouring.

Kid Quiz

What's the difference between liquid and dry measuring cups? Can you think of an easy way to remember the difference?

The dry measuring cups look like regular cups and have handles. The liquid cups have spouts and handles and look like a small pitcher. Just remember the Ps. You pour liquids from a pitcher.

How to Measure Liquids

When you're measuring liquids, place the liquid measure on a level surface and pour the liquid into it to the level required in the recipe. The most important thing to remember is to look at the liquid at eye level—you might have to squat down to see this—to make sure the liquid comes exactly to the correct line on the side of the cup. Pour out any excess liquid or add some if necessary to reach the correct line.

Some recipes call for a dash of an ingredient. Simply sprinkle two or three drops of the ingredient into the recipe ingredients.

Common liquid equivalents

> 8 ounces = 1 cup
>
> 2 cups = 1 pint
>
> 2 pints = 1 quart
>
> 4 quarts = 1 gallon

Learn the Lingo

The recipe term **pinch** refers to measuring a dry ingredient by pinching it between your thumb and forefinger. A pinch measures less than $\frac{1}{8}$ teaspoon.

The term **dash** means to sprinkle two or three drops of liquid into a recipe. The measurement is equivalent to about $\frac{1}{16}$ teaspoon.

Drawing measurement equivalents helps kids visualize measurements.

Butter Basics

If you look at the paper covering a stick of butter, you'll see markings that show how many teaspoons, tablespoons, and fractions of a cup are in the stick of butter. When a recipe calls for a tablespoon of butter, just use a table knife to cut the butter at the marking for a tablespoon. You can buy butter by the stick or in half-pound and one-pound packages. Here are the tablespoon and cup equivalent measures for butter:

1 stick butter	8 tablespoons, ½ cup, or ¼ pound
2 sticks butter	1 cup or ½ pound
4 sticks butter	2 cups or 1 pound

Stick butter is easy to use in cooking because measurements are written on the package. Here's a handy measurement reminder.

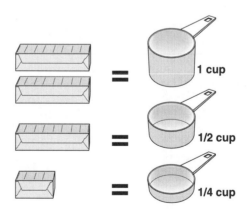

Kitchen Math Games

A fun way for kids to understand kitchen math and to practice measuring and pouring skills is to make up kitchen math games. Work from the measurement information in this chapter and the tearout card at the front of the book. Have kids measure out equivalents, using measuring cups, spoons, and liquid measures. See which amounts are equal. Kids can use regular table salt and water to make their measurements.

For another game, take out tableware, such as glasses, cups, bowls, and silverware and see how much they hold in liquid and dry measures. If you have a kitchen scale, you can compare volume to weight measurements.

Kids can record their results. They also can create and personalize their own chart of measurements and post it in the kitchen where it's easy to read. Writing out the measurements helps them to understand and remember them.

Visual reminders also are helpful. Instead of using numbers to note that 3 teaspoons equal 1 tablespoon, for instance, they can draw a picture of 3 teaspoons and a picture of 1 tablespoon and put an equal sign in between. They can draw sticks of butter with tablespoons and cups to show equivalents or cups and milk cartons to show equivalent measures for liquids.

Kitchen Clue

Use the measurement-equivalent tables to give your kids some kitchen math challenges. They can work out equivalents on paper, or they can use sugar, salt, or water to figure out equivalents with measuring spoons and cups. Kids can make their own measuring charts and post them near their work surface for easy reference. Writing or drawing pictures of equivalents also will help them remember and understand the equivalent amounts.

Finally, make your kids aware of measures by having them look in kitchen cupboards to check can and bottle sizes of their favorite foods and figure out how much they equal.

The Least You Need to Know

➤ Careful and accurate measuring is the key to creating successful recipes.

➤ Measuring ingredients can provide kids with valuable math lessons.

➤ Use graduated measuring cups and spoons for solids and dry ingredients and use clear liquid measures with spouts and measuring spoons for liquid ingredients.

➤ Level ingredients with a straight edge, but not above the bowl in which you're mixing ingredients. A spill or an overflow could add extra ingredients and result in inaccurate measurements.

➤ Kids can play measuring and math games to learn and reinforce math skills.

Chapter 13

Let's Take a Cooking Lesson

In This Chapter

➤ Commonly used kitchen techniques

➤ Handling eggs

➤ Teaching kids how to use knives

➤ Common methods of stovetop cooking

The Jansa family in my neighborhood has the dinnertime routine down pat. Each of the three children has the responsibility for a meal during the week. They decide during the weekend what they'll cook that week. Their mom buys the ingredients. Come the appointed nights, each one cooks a meal and serves it.

Incredible, you say? The fact is, kids are very capable cooks. If you give them some instructions regarding the building blocks of the kitchen, they'll take off.

This chapter covers some of the basic techniques kids can use when they're cooking. Teach them how to get around in the kitchen and you'll be amazed at what they will do!

Look Mom, It's All in the Wrist

Virtually everything kids have to learn in the kitchen involves wrist movements. Kids might feel awkward learning some techniques at first. But with practice, they'll get

Heads Up!

Kids love to beat and mix, but be careful that they don't over-beat. It can affect the outcome of the recipe, in particular with batters and baked goods.

movements down and will gain confidence. Kids can get frustrated easily, so you'll want to give them kitchen jobs according to their ability and age.

One way of teaching is to do it kinesthetically—for example, you stand behind them and hold their wrist and hand to show them how they should be cutting or whisking. They also can watch you and try to mimic your movements.

However you decide to approach kitchen techniques, be sure you encourage your children by noticing improvements and praising efforts. Keep encouraging them and reminding them that practice makes perfect.

How to Beat

Hand beating can be difficult for smaller children because the bowls are big and the batter can be too heavy for them. Explain why foods are beaten—to incorporate ingredients so they make a smooth batter or to lighten them by adding air. Show your kids how to use a circular movement to mix ingredients with a wire whisk or a wooden spoon. Find a bowl that's comfortable for them and be sure they're at the right height. Either stand them at a short table or have them stand on a sturdy stool.

Kids like to overbeat, so show them how to beat eggs lightly, just enough to incorporate the white and yellow colors. They also tend to splatter food everywhere if the bowl isn't big enough, so be sure to check the size of your bowl.

What's the Difference Between Simmer and Boil?

You know the old joke about someone who can't cook? They don't even know how to boil water. In fact, many adults, let alone kids, have difficulty distinguishing between a boil and a simmer. Here's the difference: With a boil, the liquid reaches a temperature of 212 degrees F. The liquid will be in constant motion, and the bubbles will rise rapidly to the surface and break. With a rolling boil, the surface will be bubbling continuously and vigorously. With a simmer, tiny bubbles form but barely break, and you'll see bubbles around the edge of the pan. The liquid is just below the boiling point.

To bring liquids to a boil quickly, put the pot of liquid on high heat. Keep it at the high heat if the recipe calls for a rolling boil. Lower the heat to medium to maintain a simmer. This slow method of cooking is frequently used to prepare soups and stews.

Stirring and Pouring Hot Liquids

When stirring hot liquids, hold the pot with a pot holder over the handle. Keep your face and body away from the pot. Stir slowly to prevent liquids from splashing and causing burns.

Kids need to ask for adult help when they have to pour or drain hot liquids, such as pasta water. If they are old enough to handle the pasta pot, have them take the pot firmly by the handles with pot holders and bring it to the sink. Rest it on the side of the sink and slowly pour the steaming liquid into the sink and away from their body. They should stop once or twice to let the steam evaporate. Be sure they know to arch their body back so they don't burn their face with steam.

Learn the Lingo

A **simmer** is when liquids are heated to just below the 212-degree F. boiling point. Simmering liquids form bubbles around the edges of the pot. Tiny bubbles rise to the surface but barely break.

When serving hot foods, such as soup or chili, never attempt to pour from the pot. Hold the pot firmly with a pot holder and ladle the food into serving bowls.

Kid Quiz

How do you get hot soup out of a pot?

Don't pour it, use a ladle. If you pour, you could splash the hot soup and burn yourself, or you could drop the hot pot. Instead, fill a ladle about three-quarters full and pour from the ladle into soup bowls or a serving bowl.

Cracking, Separating, and Handling Eggs

If your kids watch cooking shows, they'll be impressed with chefs who crack several eggs right into the bowl with the flick of a wrist. Let them know this is risky business. It is better to crack into a separate small bowl and then add the egg to the rest of your ingredients. Otherwise, you might wind up with a lot of shells mixed in with your eggs.

Heads Up!

When you crack an egg and you need to separate the white from the yolk, don't pass the egg from shell half to shell half. You risk spreading harmful bacteria from the shell. Use an inexpensive egg separator, pass it through a small strainer, or put the whole egg in a bowl and remove the yolk with a spoon.

To crack an egg: Tap the fat middle part of the egg with a firm, quick stroke against the side of a small bowl. Empty the inside of the egg into the bowl and immediately throw the shells into the garbage. You also can hold the egg in one hand and use the blade of a table knife with the other hand to crack the egg.

To separate an egg: Some recipes call for just egg whites or yolks, and you'll have to separate the egg yolk from the white. One old method was to pass the yolk from shell to shell and let the white fall into a bowl. Because of food-safety concerns, this is no longer recommended.

An inexpensive egg separator will do the job quickly and is fun for kids to use. Another method my mom swears by is using a small strainer with holes large enough to let the white pass through. You also can crack the egg, let the whole egg fall into the bowl, and use a large spoon to fish out the yolk. One trick: Separating eggs is easier when they are cold.

Making Egg Sense

When I was a kid, you could lick the batter when you were finished making cakes or cookies with raw eggs. Not anymore. Food-safety experts, concerned about harmful bacteria, advise against eating raw or undercooked eggs, even the small amount in an egg batter. Experts and the American Egg Board offer several guidelines for the safe handling of eggs:

➤ Use eggs directly from the refrigerator. If a recipe calls for room-temperature eggs, put them in a bowl of warm water while putting together other ingredients or leave them at room temperature for up to 30 minutes.

➤ Be sure to wash your hands before and immediately after handling raw eggs. Wash any equipment or surfaces that have come into contact with the raw egg with hot, soapy water. This helps prevent the spread of bacteria. Do not reuse utensils that have touched raw eggs without washing them.

➤ Use only clean and fresh A or AA grade eggs that have been properly refrigerated.

➤ Do not use eggs if they have cracks in their shells.

➤ Do not buy eggs from a carton with a cracked egg.

➤ Store eggs in their carton in the refrigerator (at 40 degrees F.) on a middle shelf, not in the door.

➤ If some shell drops into the egg, use a clean utensil to fish it out immediately.

➤ Be sure eggs are cooked properly. In basic dishes, the whites should be set, and the yolks should begin to thicken. (They needn't be hard.) No visible liquid should remain in scrambled eggs, omelets, and frittatas.

Cutting, Chopping, Dicing, Slicing, and Mincing

Kids should learn to handle knives by practicing with you at their side. It's a gradual process that starts with learning about the knife, developing skills using table knives, and then moving on to sharp knives.

Playing Knife Show and Tell

One of the best ways to acquaint kids with knives is to start them off with a butter or dull table knife. Have them play a game of show and tell. Let children show you where the handle and the blade is located. Bring out other knives, such as those with sharp points and serrated blades, and let the kids hold them and touch them gently while you talk about the dangers of sharp instruments and the differences between knives.

Have your kids show you what they think a good hand grip is for a knife. Ask them how they should pick up a knife and emphasize that you never pick a knife up by its blade.

Working with a table knife can help strengthen your kids' motor coordination and can get them ready to handle a knife with a sharp blade. It also will let you know when they're ready to move on to a sharp knife.

Let your children practice cutting soft objects with a table knife before you attempt these tasks with anything sharper. Start with slicing a banana, for example, and then move on to something harder like butter or cheese. Have them cut and spread butter or cream cheese on some bread or crackers. Practicing small cutting and spreading tasks will give them some experience handling a knife. It's also a great way to improve hand-eye coordination and motor skills.

Ease kids into using sharp edges by having them use kitchen scissors for tasks, such as snipping herbs.

Kitchen Clue

A good way to foster knife safety is to let kids have their own knife. It increases their self-esteem, and it reassures you that they are always handling one knife they know how to use. Have them put their name on the knife with a special sticker and keep it in a safe place. Emphasize, however, that they need your permission to use it.

Little Hands, Little Knives

When kids are ready to move on to a sharp knife, start out with a small paring knife or a small serrated knife. These work well because they're small like a child's hand.

You can still teach them good cutting techniques using these knives. One advantage to a serrated knife is the rounded tip and the blade's gripping action. (You definitely want to use these for tomatoes and slippery-skinned foods.) Whatever knife you choose, be sure it is sturdy with a sharp blade of high-carbon stainless steel.

Kids seem to like the newer soft-grip knives. The cushiony handle makes it easy for kids to hold, and it feels secure in their hand. You'll find these knives in a variety of grips and blade lengths and height. OXO GOOD GRIPS® has a full line that includes a small version of a cook's knife with a 3-inch-wide blade that tapers to a point. Let your kids try different grips to see what suits them best.

Kid Quiz

When you're cutting with a sharp knife, what should you do with the fingers holding the food?

Always tuck your fingertips underneath your knuckles and tuck your thumb behind your fingers. Make like an animal that uses its claw to grab and pull something. This way, you won't cut your fingers with the sharp blade of the knife.

To protect your fingers when slicing celery or other food, tuck them under like an animal clenching its claw.

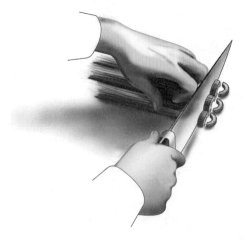

Watch Those Fingertips

If there's one thing you want to teach your kids about cutting technique, it's to keep the fingertips of the hand holding the food tucked under the knuckles. Tell your kids to pretend they are animals gripping the food with their claws. And don't forget about the thumb. It goes behind the fingers. My 12-year-old admits she has to constantly remind herself to pull it back.

Learning to Use a Larger Knife

As children become more proficient using knives, they will be able to use a long, serrated knife to cut rustic breads or a baguette. You also can teach them to use a small (8- or 10-inch) chef's knife. My oldest daughter, Julia, started using one when she was 11 years old. She took a summer cooking class with a local caterer who taught the kids the proper two-handed, rocking motion for chopping and mincing vegetables. Mastering that skill has given her confidence and speed in the kitchen.

Chef David Wasson, who has taught kids' cooking for 10 years in Seattle, says he starts kids right out with a 10-inch chef's knife. He compares it to a paper cutter at school, and he tells them to always keep the tip of the knife on the board and pull down the knife like the cutter. As for the grip, he tells kids to choke up on the handle the way they would a baseball bat. Not one child has gotten cut in his 10 years of classes, he says. In your home, you want to make sure your kids are using the proper technique. Check with a local culinary school about taking some knife-handling courses or look for videos demonstrating knife skills.

One-Hand or Two-Hand Knife Hold?

I start kids off with a one-hand knife hold. That means they hold the knife in the right hand if they're right-handed or in the left hand if they're left-handed. They hold down the food, fingertips tucked under and thumb back, with their other hand. The food hand acts as a guide to steady the food and to move it over the cutting board towards the knife.

A one-hand hold is used for slicing and paring, but when kids start out, they'll probably use it for chopping and dicing as well. Teach kids that food generally is cut into uniform pieces. The exceptions are rough cuts for stocks or food going in the blender or food processor. These equal sizes help food cook at the same rate and look nicer.

When you see chefs rotating a knife around the cutting board and chopping away madly, they're using a two-hand hold. The technique is used for mincing and chopping, and it's the one Chef David Wasson favors because kids have more control and their fingers are away from the blade.

A small chef's knife is a good knife for kids to use for this hold. Have kids shake hands with the knife handle using their dominant hand and then set the blade on the cutting board parallel to the body. The tip of the blade should always stay on the board, steadied by a gentle pressure from the palm of the free hand on top of the blade by the tip. The hand grasping the handle moves in an up-and-down motion like raising and lowering a paper cutter. The blade is worked across the food as if following the shape of a fan. Clump the food into piles to chop into finer pieces.

How to Peel, Core, and Chop an Apple

To peel with a swivel-bladed vegetable peeler: Start at the top of the apple, press the sharp blade of the peeler into the skin, and wind the peeler around the apple in a circle. You also can use long strokes from top to bottom or peel apple wedges.

To peel with a paring knife: Start at the top of the apple and wind the knife around the apple in a circle. (Some kids like to play a game to see if they can peel the apple in one continuous peel.) You also can cut the apple into wedges and peel the skin off each wedge.

To core using a cylindrical corer: Hold the apple firmly on a cutting board, center the corer, and press into the apple. Pull out the utensil containing the core.

To core with a melon baller: This is the most kid-friendly method I've used. Cut the apple in half and scoop out the core with the baller.

To core with a paring knife: Cut the apple in wedges and sweep the knife just below the core in a semicircle to cut out the core. You also can stand the whole apple on the cutting board and make one cut to one side of the core. Place the apple, cut side down, on the board and cut off the apple on each side of the core. Stand the apple up again and cut the last piece off the core. You'll be left with four chunks of apple and a rectangular piece holding the core.

To chop an apple: Cut the apple in half, place the flat side on the cutting board, and then slice lengthwise. Cut the apple wedges crosswise to make small chunks of apple.

Using an apple coring and slicing device: You'll see hand-held circular disks in stores that core and slice apples into wedges. Parents send kids to school with these so they can cut up their apples for lunch or snack. Kids have to use the weight of their body to push the slicer down the apple. They also need to be careful not to nick themselves while taking the wedges out of the slicer.

Learn the Lingo

An **apple corer** is a hand-held, cylindrical tool that can be positioned around the stem of the apple and then pressed into the entire apple. The edge cuts around the core. When you pull out the tool, the core comes with it.

How to Peel and Chop a Carrot

Use a swivel-bladed vegetable peeler to peel a carrot. Use a firm stroke to press the peeler against the carrot and run it down the side, away from you, from the root end to the tip. Chop off the root end and the tip and discard. Cut the carrot in half lengthwise. Place the flat side of each half on the cutting board and cut into lengthwise strips. Hold the strips together and cut across them to make small pieces.

To make carrot coins, peel the carrot and, keeping it whole, chop crosswise the entire length of the carrot.

How to Chop Celery

Take a rib of celery from the stalk and clean it thoroughly under cool running water. Pat it dry and place the rib on the cutting board. Cut off the white bottom and the leaves. Throw out the end piece and reserve the leaves if using the celery for stock or salads.

Place the celery on the curved or flat side (whatever is more comfortable) on the cutting board. Use the tip of a paring knife to make three or four lengthwise cuts completely down the celery rib. Hold these lengthwise pieces together with your free hand and cut crosswise across them to make small pieces.

Kid Quiz

Do you know why onions make you cry?

Chopping into an onion releases a gas that reacts with the water in your eyes to form sulfuric acid. Your body protects itself and creates tears to wash away the irritant.

How to Peel and Cut an Onion

Onions always are easier to peel when they're cut in half. Use a one-hand hold for the following techniques. Cut the onion in half lengthwise on a cutting board. Peel the papery skin off both halves. Throw away the skin.

Put the onion halves flat side down on the board. Cut off the stem end and throw it away. If you're dicing, wait to cut off and discard the root end until you're finished. The root will help keep the onion together.

To slice the onion, simply cut the onion widthwise into semicircles, or lengthwise for long thin slices. This will be the cut you'll use for recipes calling for sliced onions.

To dice the onion:

1. Take half the onion, cut side down, and curve the fingertips of your free hand on the top to hold it down. Use the knife to cut into the onion, parallel to the cutting board. You'll be cutting toward the root end of the onion, and the number of cuts will determine how big the dice will be. Don't cut through to the end because the root will keep the onion together.

2. Next, grip the curved top side of the onion with your fingertips and thumb. Your hand will look like a claw holding the onion together. Put the point of the knife just below the root end and make several side by side cuts into the onion lengthwise. Again, don't cut through the root.

3. Finally, make cuts perpendicular to the last cut. In other words, cut crosswise through the width of the onion. The diced pieces will fall onto the cutting board.

4. Repeat the procedure with the other half of the onion.

How to Clean and Cut a Bell Pepper

Pass the pepper under cool running water, making sure to clean any dirt out of the creases. Dry the pepper and set it on its side on a cutting board. Use a paring knife to cut a hole in the top of the pepper around the stem. Pull out the stem and the core.

Cut the pepper in half and scrape out any inside white membranes and seeds with a knife. Place each pepper half on the cutting board and make long slices. To dice, bunch the slices together and cut crosswise to the desired size.

Heads Up!

Always wear plastic gloves when handling hot peppers and don't touch your eyes or other sensitive areas without first washing your hands. Protect surfaces from the volatile oils with waxed paper and be sure to wash down knives thoroughly.

Mincing Herbs and Garlic

You'll have to mince herbs and garlic for some recipes. Mincing basically means cutting these foods very finely so they'll blend well with ingredients. To mince herbs, bunch the herbs together and slice coarsely. Then gather the herbs together and set your knife above the pile. Keep the tip of the knife on the cutting board and raise and lower it (like a paper cutter), passing it along the herbs. Occasionally rebunch the herbs and continue cutting until you achieve the desired fineness. With garlic, peel the garlic, slice it into slivers, and then use the preceding method.

Cutting and Skinning Tomatoes

To cut or slice a tomato with its skin: Cut off the stem end and use a serrated knife to slice the tomato in ⅜-inch slices crosswise. You also can cut the tomatoes in half and then into wedges.

Kitchen Clue

To seed a tomato, simply cut it in half, hold the half over a bowl, and squeeze out the seeds.

To skin tomatoes: Cut Xs into the bottom of the tomatoes and plunge them, a few at a time, into a pot of boiling water. Remove them with a slotted spoon after 10 to 30 seconds (depending on the type of tomato) and plunge them into very cold or ice water. The skin should slip right off.

To seed and chop the tomato: Halve the tomato crosswise and squeeze it over a bowl. If using plum tomatoes, halve them lengthwise. The seeds will drop out. Place tomatoes on their flat side on a cutting board and chop.

Grating Cheese and Other Foods

When I was a kid, one of my jobs was to grate the cheese for the pasta. We had a metal hand-crank grater, and I would plunk a piece of Parmesan cheese into the container and grate away. It always was such fun to see the fluffy cheese falling out of the grater, not to mention sneaking pinches of the cheese.

Kids love to use these hand-held graters, and they're among the safest ways to grate hard cheese and other foods. They also enhance children's hand-eye coordination and motor skills.

In addition to rotary graters, graters and shredders come in two basic styles: the multisided box grater and the flat grater. Both should be positioned over a piece of waxed paper or a plate to catch the shreds. Kids seem to do better with the box grater. They can hold it down firmly by the handle on top. You also can find flat graters that come attached to a box or a bowl to catch the shreds.

Heads Up!

To avoid nicking your knuckles with a grater, be sure the pieces of food being grated are long enough. With round foods like citrus fruits, hold the food with your fingers as far away from the grater as possible.

The biggest problem with graters is catching or cutting knuckles and fingers on the sharp edges. Be sure the pieces of food being grated are long enough to prevent fingers from touching the grater. When grating citrus fruits, grip the fruit as far away from the grater as possible.

Kneading

Kneading and kids go hand in hand. Kids love to get their hands in dough and work it. It's exciting to see how the dough changes and develops just by moving it around on a floured board. The movements are relaxing and soothing, and both kids and adults can feel a great sense of accomplishment by creating a dough and the resulting bread.

Make sure, however, that the kids do not add too much flour to the dough while they're kneading. They tend to put too much on the board and then dump even more on the dough. To avoid this, keep a cup of flour next to the board and add flour only from the cup. This way, you know how much you're adding.

To knead, place the ball of dough on a lightly floured surface. Use the heel of your hand to press down onto the dough and, at the same time, push it away from you. Then fold the dough over toward yourself (as if you're folding a piece of paper), turn it a quarter of a turn, and press and push again.

Repeat the push, fold, and turn motion until the dough feels satiny and smooth and no longer sticks to the surface. Depending on the dough, this generally takes from 10 to 15 minutes.

Kid Quiz

When you're kneading dough, about how much flour do you scatter on the kneading board?

Sprinkle only a very small amount, one or two teaspoons, so the dough does not stick to the board. The dough will absorb the flour so you don't want to add too much.

Sautéing

To sauté is to rapidly cook food at high temperatures in dry heat on the stovetop. The heat from the pan is transferred through a small amount of fat to cook the food. Juices produced during cooking make a delicious sauce to serve with the food.

The key to sautéing is to have a hot pan and oil before adding the food. You want the food to start cooking as soon as it hits the pan. Put the sauté pan on the stove, turn the heat to high, and add just enough fat to cover the pan. (If you're using a nonstick or well-seasoned pan, you might not need any fat aside from what's in the food.)

As soon as the fat or pan is hot, add the food. Cook it until it is golden or brown on the side touching the pan and then turn it to brown the other side. For smaller foods, you might want to flip the food more often either by shaking the pan on the stove or by using a spatula or a wooden spoon. Vegetables and fruits should be turned and tossed frequently. Adjust the heat according to what you're cooking.

Here are some sauté tips:

➤ Use a sauté pan or skillet with low sides and a handle. High sides will steam the food.

➤ Don't use a pan that is too big. The drippings will scorch.

➤ Cut foods into uniform sizes so they all cook at the same rate. Thin, delicate, and moist foods will cook more quickly.

➤ Food should be as dry as possible before it goes into the pan. This will help the food brown nicely and will prevent splattering.

➤ Test whether the oil is hot enough to start cooking by dropping pieces of food into the pan. The oil is ready if the food sizzles.

➤ Cook foods in one layer and don't overcrowd the pan. The food must come into contact with the pan to get browning or a nice crust. Too much food will also cause the temperature of the pan to drop.

➤ Don't salt food until after cooking. The salt will hinder browning.

➤ Lower the heat so the outside doesn't burn while the inside cooks.

➤ Don't cover the pan while cooking.

➤ To deglaze the pan for a sauce, remove the sautéed food and add a small amount of liquid, such as stock. Heat the liquid while scraping the browned bits off the bottom of the pan. Let the sauce thicken and pour it over the food or use it as a base for other sauces.

Stir-Frying

Whenever my family doesn't know what to make for dinner, we make a stir-fry with whatever vegetables, meats, tofu, or fish we happen to have in the refrigerator. Stir-frying is one of the fastest ways to create flavorful meals quickly.

With a stir-fry, small pieces of food are fried quickly over very high heat in a large pan. Use a wooden spatula to dig between the food and the pan and to turn the food over rapidly. The idea is similar to sautéing. The key difference is that the food is constantly and briskly tossed and in motion while cooking.

Kitchen Clue

Help kids succeed at stir-frying by giving them small amounts of foods to cook at a time. They'll be less likely to flip the food out of the pan, and it will be easier for them to master the constant tossing motion.

Stir-frying is associated with Asian cooking and a wok, but you don't need a wok to stir-fry. Several manufacturers have come out with stir-fry pans. These resemble a wok with their deep sides and flat bottom, but they aren't quite as deep. Any large, deep skillet that has enough room to toss and stir the foods rapidly will work.

If you are using a wok, remember that the hottest part is at the bottom. Use the spatula to constantly distribute the food so it passes over the bottom and up onto the side. Dig down under the food to the bottom and toss it up against the sides.

Stir-frying presents a challenge for kids because of the constant motion and tossing technique. When my kids first tried it, we wound up with food flying out of the pan. To prevent this, start with small amounts of food. You'll have to cook the food in batches, but your kids will be less likely to spill any, and they won't get frustrated. Use a nonstick vegetable spray (this prevents spatters from hot oil) and be sure the kids are at the proper height. My daughter likes to be slightly higher than the pan so she can get some leverage when flipping the food. Woks get very hot, though, so make sure your kids are at a good distance so they don't burn themselves.

This is one of those techniques for which you should always be at their side to check safety, catch spills, and keep encouraging them. The constant motion and speedy results of stir-fry cooking are exciting and gratifying for kids.

Pan-Frying

Teach children that hot oil can spatter if they are pan-frying or sautéing onions, garlic, or other vegetables in hot oil. To avoid burns and fires:

➤ Never leave the stove when oil is heating. If it gets too hot, it can catch on fire.

➤ Stand back away from the skillet in case the oil spatters.

➤ Be sure that utensils and foods being cooked are dry. When moisture meets hot oil, the oil spatters.

➤ Always use utensils, not your hands, to get foods in and out of the pan.

The Least You Need to Know

➤ The more kids can practice their wrist movements, the more proficient they'll become at simple kitchen tasks.

➤ Handle eggs carefully, following food-safety guidelines, to prevent illness from harmful bacteria.

➤ Teach kids how to handle knives by practicing with them and by giving them different knife tasks.

➤ Sauté and stir-fry foods to make quick, delicious meals.

Chapter 14

Dealing with Kitchen Mishaps

In This Chapter

➤ Getting around messes and common mistakes

➤ Ways to organize and anticipate

➤ Dealing with the kids and your frustrations

➤ A list of emergency substitutions

➤ Heading off mixing and rolling problems

When you're cooking with kids, mishaps come with the territory. The batter gets over-beaten. An ingredient is left out, or too much of an ingredient gets poured in. Food gets spilled, dishes get broken, and the kitchen winds up a mess.

Take heart. Every good cook, even the most experienced, can make mistakes or run into problems in the kitchen. This chapter takes a look at some of the typical snafus that naturally occur in the kitchen—and also because kids will be kids. You'll find tips for how to head off kitchen mishaps and advice about what to do when they occur.

Help! My Kitchen Is a Mess!

One of the biggest hesitations people have about cooking with kids is that, at the end, the kitchen will look like a tornado just hit. There's no getting around it: Cooking with kids is messy. My best advice is to relax and check your worries about the mess at the kitchen door. You can try to minimize the mess, however, by following some of the clean-as-you-go tips in Chapter 7, "The Golden Rules of Kitchen Safety."

Kitchen Clue

Kitchen mistakes often can be the mother of invention. Be creative and think about how you can salvage your recipe or what else you can do with the food.

Heads Up!

Overzealous young cooks can get into trouble with their curiosity. Anticipate your children's actions, especially when it comes to touching and handling things. To this day, my daughter Lizzie remembers the time she touched the burner because she wasn't sure if it was hot. She'll never do that again.

Oops, I Made a Mistake!

Some of the best dishes were born of kitchen disasters. The cookies are overdone, but instead of throwing them out, you put them in ice cream or use them for pie crust. A cake crumbles, so you break it up and serve it in a pudding. The meat is overcooked, so you turn it into a stew or a curry.

Making a mistake is not the end of the world. In fact, it gives you a chance to exercise some of your creativity. Just watch how your kids will come up with unusual solutions for correcting mistakes.

If your kids do make a mistake with a recipe, don't panic or reprimand them for doing something the wrong way. Try to stay positive with words like, "It's okay. Let's just see what we can do here." You also can make a joke of it. Humor always works wonders to diffuse tension in the kitchen.

Another remedy is to turn the mistake into a chance to learn the science of cooking. When the Noto family was testing the recipe for my mom's 1-2-3-4 cake in Part 6 of this book, "Now You're Cooking: The Recipe File," they left out the baking powder. Eight-year-old Torben said he liked the cake anyway, but his mom, Peggy, told me the cake was greasy and hard. She said it turned into an interesting science lesson to see the effect of baking powder on the cake. The kids were anxious to rebake the cake to see how it would turn out. The experience left an impression. They'll never leave out the baking powder in a recipe again!

A Tray Can Head Off Problems

One way to make sure you don't leave out the baking powder or any other ingredient is to work from a tray. Here's what you do: As you read the recipe, get out all your ingredients and set them on the tray. As you use the ingredients, put them away. (This also helps with clean-up and teaches kids to be organized cooks.) When you're finished with the recipe, the tray should be empty. If it's not, you'll know exactly what you've left out and whether it's too late to add it. Then you can decide how to handle the problem.

Organize to Avoid Mistakes

The tray is just one step in being organized. Remember how we said to read the recipe not once but twice? More kitchen mishaps occur because you've misread the recipe or misunderstood an instruction. Maybe you don't have an ingredient and you decide to substitute something else, only you're not quite sure what that something else is going to do to the recipe. Resist the temptation to rush through the recipe; you'll pay for it later. If you're organized, read through the recipe, and set out equipment and ingredients in advance, you won't be fumbling around in the kitchen as you cook. You also won't exhaust your child's limited attention span.

Anticipate Problems

Anticipating problems also can be a lifesaver when cooking with kids. If you're using a hot oven or stove, be sure you have pot holders nearby. If you know your child can't mix ingredients without getting the food all over the floor, use a bigger bowl to help contain the spills. Have plenty of paper towels and washcloths on hand, too.

Think through the dynamics of making the recipe. If you're cooking with two kids, for example, set up the work so each gets to do a part of it. Give them different tasks to avoid competition and confusion. Set up stations in the kitchen that are away from the main line of traffic.

Anticipate distractions, which always seem to lead to kitchen mishaps. Make sure the answering machine is working so you won't have to pick up the phone; or turn off the ringer on the phone. Plan your cooking time so it doesn't coincide with other appointments or comings and goings in the house.

Heads Up!

Be sure to give kids tasks that are appropriate for their age and skill level. They'll succeed and will feel much better about what they are able to do instead of getting cranky and frustrated. And you won't lose your patience.

Know Your Little Cooks

Part of anticipating is knowing the strengths and weaknesses of your young cooks. Most kids love to operate the blender and the food processor. Be one step ahead so you're right there when the button gets pressed. The same goes for cutting. If you know your children have difficulty with this task, be right there to help and encourage them.

Always give kids tasks that are appropriate for their skills and age group. Don't expect them to be able to whip up a sauce when they haven't had much experience stirring. They'll just get frustrated, and you'll just get impatient.

Never ask your kids, for instance, to get breakable utensils out of the cabinet if they can't handle it. My neighbor learned this the hard way. Her 8-year-old insisted on getting a bowl out of the cupboard. She struggled with it and wound up not only breaking the bowl but also smashing the two that were beneath it.

Kid Quiz

Can you ever make substitutions for ingredients or cooking pans in recipes?

Sometimes, but you need to be careful. When it comes to baking, recipes are precise formulas and substituting ingredients and pan sizes could cause big problems. With other ingredients, you might find workable substitutions such as those listed in the chart later in this chapter.

First ask yourself what the function of the item is that you want to substitute. Then see if some other ingredient could do the same thing.

Substituting Ingredients

One of the easiest ways to get into trouble in the kitchen is by substituting an ingredient or a piece of equipment for what is stated in the recipe. Yes, you frequently can substitute ingredients successfully. When you're cooking with kids, however, it's important to emphasize that, even though two ingredients might look alike, they might not taste alike or do the same thing in a recipe.

Consider what the function of the ingredient is before you start finding a stand-in. Does it cause the batter to rise, add liquid, or give a particular flavor? Ask yourself what you think could do the same. Remember that baking recipes usually are very precise formulas. It's best not to fool with them unless you have some experience. You also might want to consult a list of acceptable baking substitutions, like the one here, before you attempt to make any changes.

When it comes to substituting equipment, find an equivalent size by measuring the volume. Measure the amount of water held by the piece of equipment you want to use and then see how it compares to the one called for in the recipe. Keep in mind you might have to compensate in cooking time for the increased or decreased depth or other variations in the size of the equipment.

Emergency Substitutions

If you need ...	You can substitute ...
1 whole large egg	2 egg yolks + 1 tablespoon water
2 egg yolks	1 whole large egg (for thickening)
1 ounce unsweetened chocolate	3 tablespoons unsweetened cocoa powder + 1 tablespoon melted butter or margarine
1 ounce semisweet baking chocolate	1 ounce unsweetened chocolate + 1 tablespoon sugar
1 cup honey	1¼ cups granulated sugar + ¼ cup liquid OR 1 cup molasses
1 cup corn syrup	1 cup granulated sugar + ¼ cup liquid
1 cup granulated sugar	1 cup brown sugar or 2 cups confectioners' sugar
1 cup fresh whole milk	½ cup evaporated milk + ½ cup water OR 1 cup reconstituted nonfat dry milk + 2 teaspoons butter or margarine
1 cup plain yogurt	1 cup sour cream
1 cup buttermilk	1 cup plain yogurt or sour cream OR 1 cup whole milk + 1 tablespoon white vinegar or lemon juice. Stir and let stand 2 minutes.
1 teaspoon baking powder	¼ teaspoon baking soda + ½ teaspoon cream of tartar
1 tablespoon cornstarch (for thickening)	2 tablespoons all-purpose flour
½ cup brown sugar	½ cup granulated sugar + 2 tablespoons molasses
1 cup all-purpose flour	1 cup + 2 tablespoons cake flour
1 cup cake flour	1 cup less 2 tablespoons all-purpose flour
1 cup raisins	1 cup currants or other dried fruits
1 tablespoon fresh herbs	1 teaspoon dried herbs
1 teaspoon dry mustard	1 teaspoon prepared mustard
½ teaspoon grated fresh ginger	¼ teaspoon ground ginger

Overbeating and Rolling

Kids naturally like to stir, mix, and measure ingredients and roll out dough. The only problem is that they get so into it, they tend to go overboard. And there are consequences. They might love to beat the batter, for instance, but overbeating causes the gluten protein in the flour to develop. That makes whatever you're baking tough.

Similarly, when I've made apple pies with kids, they go crazy with the rolling pin. I have to remind them that their pie crust will be tough if they keep up all that rolling.

Here are a few hints to give your kids:

➤ When making batters, stop mixing when the dry ingredients are moistened by the wet ingredients.

➤ Roll your pie pastry in one direction (from the center out) and don't overroll.

➤ Beat eggs lightly. Stop beating when the yellow and white are mixed. Unless your children have mastered egg cracking, don't break the egg directly into the batter. You'll wind up fishing out the shell.

➤ Mix, don't mash, ingredients together.

When Kids Get Frustrated and Hyper

When kids get overexcited in the kitchen, you wind up doing the same things you would in other kid-related situations. Try to get them focused on one thing and calm them down. Play some soothing music in the background. Stop for a break and have them take deep breaths. Check to see if they need a snack break. It's amazing what a little nourishment can do to lower the intensity level.

Kitchen Clue

When things get too high-pitched in the kitchen, calm things down by regrouping. Take a snack break and refocus everyone's energies or put on some soothing music.

When kids get frustrated in the kitchen, they're generally feeling either impatient or overwhelmed. Try to break down kitchen projects and give them doable pieces of the project. Stay flexible and try to find a task they enjoy doing. If they're losing interest and you're smack in the middle of the recipe, let them take a break. You might lose them completely, but sometimes that happens. Young kids in particular like to wander in and out of the kitchen. That's okay. Just be prepared and realize they have short attention spans.

When *You* Get Frazzled

What do you do when you feel like you're beginning to lose it in the kitchen? The best thing I think you can do is try to simplify the situation and regroup. How about taking a break and sitting down for a cup of tea? Maybe going to the kitchen door and taking a breath of fresh air will relieve some stress. Or you could get everybody up for a stretch and put on some calming music. Look for natural break points in your cooking like times when you're waiting for something to cook.

If you find yourself screaming at the kids, stop. Walk away for a minute, take some deep breaths, and evaluate how you can get back on track. Some of your frustration might come from the kids trying to do something beyond their ability. Or you might feel you've simply lost control of the situation. Maybe you need to give kids an easier chore in the recipe. You also could finish the recipe yourself and find another task for the kids to do, even if it doesn't necessarily fit in with the recipe of the moment. Washing vegetables, grating cheese with a hand-crank grater, or tearing up lettuce leaves are three relatively safe projects.

The Least You Need to Know

➤ Take a creative approach to recipe mistakes. Remember, some of the best dishes have come from kitchen disasters.

➤ Head off mistakes by being organized and by anticipating your child's actions.

➤ Organize ingredients on a tray to cut down on mistakes, such as leaving an ingredient out of the recipe.

➤ Get to know your little cooks' abilities and find tasks appropriate to their age and skill level.

➤ Rely primarily on proven ingredient substitutions unless you're familiar with ingredients.

➤ Calm hyper or frustrated kids by refocusing their energy and giving them a snack, if necessary. Taking a break is a way for you to stay focused and in control as well.

Part 5

Fun with Food

Did your parents ever tell you not to play with your food? Forget about it! This section breaks that rule big time and looks at food in a whole new light. You're in for a great adventure as you learn to see the kitchen as a place to discover new cultures, art, science, and cheesemaking.

This section shows you how to put some spice in your life with seasonings and herbs. In the chapter about kitchen science, you'll turn detective as you uncover the how's and why's behind chemical reactions with sugar crystals, yeast, baking soda, and color-changing vegetables. You'll discover your artistic side and new ways to get kids eating colorful and healthful foods in the chapter about turning food into edible creations. The final chapter offers ways you can experience other cultures through their foods. Your kids will even find out how they can uncover their culinary talents by creating a cookie exchange or a cooking club.

So who said food was only for eating?

Chapter 15

Adding Spice—and Herbs—to Your Life

In This Chapter

➤ Discovering the flavors of spices and herbs

➤ The difference between a spice and an herb

➤ Storing spices and herbs

➤ Spice and herb flavor combinations

When it comes to getting creative and exploring flavor combinations, start with discovering spices and herbs. You can change the taste of the same piece of meat or vegetable just by adding a different spice or herb. Herbs and spices come under the culinary umbrella called seasonings. Although there are classic seasoning combinations, much of how you season depends on your own taste buds. You might prefer foods with some zip or with more subtle flavor. This chapter introduces you and your kids to the world of herbs and spices and offers some guidelines for your own experimentation.

The Great Flavor Enhancers

These days, spices and herbs are culinary buzzwords. Although herbs and spices have been with us for centuries, they've gotten a lot of press only lately. They're not only favored for their taste but also for their health and curative powers. In particular, cooks everywhere are using them as flavor replacements for fat and cholesterol in foods. Part of the interest stems from increasing curiosity about ethnic cuisine. We're becoming more familiar with seasonings used in different countries, and we are incorporating them into our everyday cooking.

Kid Quiz

What spices go into making spiced apple cider?

Answer: cinnamon, cloves, and allspice. (Do a taste test to see if you can really notice the spices.)

Teaching Kids About Seasonings

I once brought some fresh herbs and spices into a grade-school cooking class. The kids were very excited with the smell and taste of them, and they all wanted to take some home. So we cut them up and put them in aluminum foil. They couldn't get their little herb packets into their jeans pockets fast enough!

Kids are curious cooks, and the fresh smell of herbs and the unusual aromas of spices fascinate them. Begin to introduce your kids to this vast world of seasonings by noticing which ones are in the food products you eat every day. Make a game of it and look at the ingredients to see if any spices and herbs are listed. Ask yourselves if you can taste the spice. Check favorite recipes and see what seasonings are used.

Go through your own seasoning drawer and smell the different herbs and spices. Rub the dried herbs between your fingers to release the scent. Ask kids what the aromas remind them of.

When you're at the supermarket, go down the spice aisle and see the many spices available. Check out the fresh herbs in the produce department. With the increasing public demand for fresh herbs, supermarkets are stocking more and better-quality herbs. Pick them up; see what they look like and smell like. Buy some and crush the leaves to release their aroma. Taste them and try them in different foods to see how they each react and change the flavor of the food. Compare them to the same herb in a dried form.

Spices and herbs have a rich history, and it's fun to discover how they were used and where they originated. When you use a spice, look it up in the dictionary, a cookbook, or an encyclopedia. The whole family can discover the historical importance of trade routes and the significance of the particular spice.

Kid Quiz

Do you know the difference between a spice and an herb?

Both come from fragrant plants. Herbs generally are the leaves, such as parsley, and sometimes the flowers of the plant. Spices are the dried bark, seeds, buds, berries (such as pepper), fruit, or roots of the plant.

What's the Difference Between a Spice and an Herb?

Both herbs and spices come from aromatic plants. Herbs generally are the leaves and sometimes the flowers of the plant. Spices are the dried bark, seeds, buds, berries, fruit, or roots of the plant. Herbs generally come from temperate regions, and spices often come from tropical regions. Both are considered to be condiments or flavor enhancers. They add to the taste and aroma of a dish, and they can either make a very robust or a subtle change in flavor.

How Do I Store and Use Spices and Herbs?

Here are some guidelines for the storage and use of herbs and spices:

➤ Store dried herbs in a tightly covered container away from heat, moisture, and direct sunlight. If they're fresh, they should have a bright color and should release aromas when crushed or rubbed in your hand.

➤ Spices do not spoil but they can become stale quickly, so check and replace yours often. Buy them in small quantities. Experts say ground spices last one to two years, but some can go longer. These include pepper

Heads Up!

Avoid using too many spices together at once. Use your spices sparingly until you get to know how powerful they are and the combinations that work well together. The general rule of thumb is to season a dish serving four people with ¼ teaspoon of a dried herb or spice.

and salt, onion or garlic salt. Whole spices last about five years. Let your taste buds and your nose be your guide.

➤ Fresh herbs generally last up to a week. They should smell fragrant, and leaves should be bright in color and crisp. Avoid leaves that are turning brown around the edges or are limp. When you get them home, keep leafy herbs, such as parsley, basil, and mint, fresh by first cutting off the bottom stem tips. Immediately place the stems in a glass with a small amount of water and then cover the leaves loosely with a plastic bag. Store them in the refrigerator and change the water after a few days.

➤ Use leftover fresh herbs for making flavored butters or pesto, an uncooked herb paste often used as a sauce for pasta and in other dishes. (The classic pesto is either crushed or blended and is made with fresh basil, oil, garlic, pine nuts, and grated pecorino or Parmesan cheese.)

➤ Preserve fresh herbs for later use by freezing or drying them. Wash and gently pat them dry and then lay them flat in a freezer bag for freezing. Air-dry them by hanging them upside down by their stems.

➤ Seasonings should be used selectively and in small amounts. Generally, they shouldn't overpower the flavor of a dish. Some exceptions are curry and chili dishes, which rely heavily on the seasoning for flavor. Here's a general rule of thumb: For every four servings, about ¼ teaspoon of a dried herb or spice should season the dish.

➤ When using a fresh herb, use at least twice the amount of the dried herb. (Drying intensifies the flavor.) Let your taste buds be your guide.

➤ Avoid using too many different herbs or spices at once. Before adding a dried herb or spice to a dish, crush it in your hand to release the flavor. Taste it to determine its freshness and to see if the flavor will complement your food.

➤ Add flavorings to cooked foods toward the end of cooking. When using seasonings for fruits, juices, marinades, and dressings, add them at the beginning to allow time for flavors to marry.

What seasonings go best with which types of food? The following table provides some of the more common pairings.

Some Classic Seasoning and Food Pairings

Basil or oregano with fresh tomatoes, tomato sauce, and pasta

Oregano, tarragon, or marjoram with chicken

Sage with butter for pasta or ravioli

Rosemary or thyme with lamb

Dill with fish

Mint with vegetables, such as zucchini and carrots, and fruits, such as melons and strawberries

Mint with lemonade and teas

Chives with sour cream on baked potatoes

Cilantro with fresh Vietnamese spring rolls and Mexican foods, such as guacamole, salsas, and fajitas

Ginger with Asian foods

Chile powder with chili, Mexican foods, and sauces

Curry powder with Indian dishes

Allspice, nutmeg, cinnamon, cloves, cardamom, anise, coriander, ginger, or mace with baked goods

Growing Herbs

Gardening is one of the best ways to give kids a connection to foods they eat. Growing herbs—and then using them to cook—is an easy and fun introduction to this world. In the spring and summer, most garden centers and some supermarkets sell small herb plants. Take them home and put them in a sunny spot in your yard or on your windowsill. Let your kids snip them when you want to add some flavor to a salad or soup. Try some of the combinations in the preceding chart. You also can consult cookbooks to turn your herbs into a pesto sauce for pasta or a spread.

You also can start your own herb plants from seeds. This gives kids a chance to see the planting process from beginning to end. Check with a local garden center or a gardening book for ideas and directions on how to start herb plants from scratch. Catalog companies also offer a wide selection of seeds. Appendix B, "The Resource Guide," offers several sources for gardening products and seeds.

Learn the Lingo

Pesto is an uncooked herb paste made from fresh herbs and seasonings. It frequently is used on pasta, with toasted rustic breads as an appetizer, or as a spread for pizza or sandwiches. The classic pesto is made with basil, garlic, oil, grated Parmesan or pecorino cheese, and pine nuts.

141

The Least You Need to Know

➤ Most spices and dried herbs last only about a year or two. Buy them in small quantities and check and replace them often. Fresh herbs last about a week.

➤ Spices and herbs are packed with flavor and are healthful replacements for high-cholesterol and high-fat flavors.

➤ Use seasonings sparingly and be careful not to combine too many at once.

➤ Teach children about the characteristics and effects of spices and herbs by trying different seasonings on the same food.

➤ A windowsill or container herb garden gives kids the excitement of growing their own herbs and then using them in their food.

Chapter 16

The Magic of Food

In This Chapter

➤ Making rock candy from a sugar–water solution

➤ Inflating a balloon with yeast and baking soda

➤ Creating a mini volcano with baking soda

➤ Seeing how heat changes the green color in vegetables

The kitchen can be one big science lab, and it's fun for both kids and adults to explore the possibilities. In everyday cooking, we can see how liquids, such as eggs, can turn to solids with heat. We also can see how simply cooking a food changes its texture, color, and taste.

Chemical reactions happen constantly when we cook and handle food. This chapter introduces kids to the science of food with fun kitchen-counter experiments that the whole family can do. Some experiments require adult supervision at the stove.

Making Rock Candy Crystals

My daughter Julia came home from school with a kitchen-related science challenge: to grow sugar crystals over the course of several weeks, track her progress, and create the largest crystal possible. She didn't win the prize for the biggest crystal, but she did see how sugar crystals form from a supersaturated or sugar-water solution. In the end, she had a deliciously sweet piece of rock candy to eat. You can, too, if you do just what she did.

Heads Up!

Always ask for adult supervision and take care to handle ingredients carefully when doing experiments in the kitchen. The same kitchen safety rules used for cooking apply when you're conducting experiments.

You'll need …

1 cup water

small saucepan

2 cups sugar plus a little extra

spoon

potholder

clean, 1-quart canning jar

unsharpened pencil or chopstick (longer than the width of the jar)

clean string (2 inches longer than the height of the jar)

clean paper clip

1. Ask an adult to help you set up this experiment. To make the sugar crystals, heat 1 cup water to a boil in the small saucepan. Add 2 cups sugar and use the spoon to stir the solution until the sugar is thoroughly dissolved.

2. With the help of an adult, carefully pour the solution into the clean, 1-quart canning jar and let it cool. The clear jar enables you to see how your experiment progresses.

3. Take the pencil or chopstick and tie the string around the center of it. Attach the clean paper clip to the other end of the string. (This weighs down the string.)

4. Dip the string into the cooled solution in the jar and then pull it out and roll it in the extra sugar. Prop the pencil across the top of the jar so the string hangs down into the sugar water. (If the paper clip touches the bottom, just wind the string around the pencil until it doesn't hit the bottom.)

5. Store the jar where it won't be disturbed. Be patient because it could take up to two weeks for crystals to form.

Julia brought the jar up to her room so she could keep an eye on it. Occasionally, she had to poke holes in the top of the solution where crystals formed. This allowed air to circulate and evaporation to continue.

So what happened? Crystals can form as a saturated solution cools and the water evaporates. Julia created a saturated solution by boiling the water and adding and dissolving sugar in it. Over time, the water evaporated and the sugar settled out of the solution in the form of crystals and grew on the string. The result was a nice chunk of candy!

You can try variations of this experiment. Make your solution with different kinds of sugar, such as brown or confectioners' sugar. Store your jar at different temperatures. Keep a log of your crystal growth and whether changes vary with the type of sugar or where you store the experiment jar.

A jar with a sugar solution to make rock candy.

Kid Quiz

Do you know why you can inflate a balloon with yeast?

When yeast is active, it gives off carbon dioxide, which inflates the balloon.

Inflating a Balloon with Yeast

When you bake the yeast bread recipe found later in this book, you'll see how the yeast makes the dough rise. Yeast is a living, one-celled organism that you can only see with a microscope. It belongs to the fungus family, the same family as mushrooms. You can buy yeast in packets or jars. This kind of yeast is sleeping. All you need to do to wake it up and get it growing is to give it moisture, sugar or starch, and a warm environment (70 to 85 degrees F).

Something magical happens as the yeast digests the sugar or starch. It gives off carbon dioxide and alcohol. The alcohol evaporates into the air. When yeast is in dough, however, the carbon dioxide gets trapped as bubbles in the dough. These gas pockets get bigger, and that's what makes the dough rise.

Here's an experiment to see how the yeast forms the carbon dioxide.

You'll need ...

> balloon
>
> 1 package active dry yeast
>
> ¼ cup sugar
>
> 1-cup liquid measure filled with very warm tap water
>
> spoon
>
> clean, 1-liter soda bottle
>
> small piece of string or rubber band
>
> 3-quart saucepan half filled with very warm tap water

1. Stretch the balloon by blowing it up once or twice and letting the air out. Set it aside.
2. Add the yeast and the sugar to the water in the measuring cup. Stir with the spoon to dissolve the yeast and water.
3. Pour the yeast mixture into the soda bottle. Put the neck of the balloon over the top of the bottle and secure it with the rubber band or by tying the string.
4. Place the bottle in the saucepan half filled with water and let it stand in a warm place.
5. Check the bottle after 10 minutes, half an hour, and 1 hour.

What happened? You could see the yeast starting to come alive within 10 minutes. The top of the water got foamy. After half an hour, the yeast had filled the surface of the liquid in the bottle with frothy bubbles. The balloon no longer was flopping on its side; it was standing straight up as it started to fill with air. After an hour, the balloon was inflated. Just as your lungs can fill a balloon with air, the carbon dioxide released from the yeast created the air bubbles to fill the balloon. Those same air bubbles are what make baked goods rise. When you finish with the experiment, remove the balloon and discard it along with the yeast solution. You can rinse out the bottle to use again.

A Baking Soda and Balloon Experiment

You also can inflate a balloon by combining baking soda with lemon or vinegar. Baking soda (a base) releases carbon dioxide when it comes in contact with lemon juice or vinegar (an acid).

Let's try to inflate a balloon and compare how quickly the soda blows up the balloon.

You'll need ...

balloon

small funnel

measuring spoons

2 teaspoons baking soda

clean, 1-liter plastic soda bottle

1 cup liquid measure filled with ¼ cup vinegar or lemon juice

1. Stretch out the balloon by blowing air into it and then releasing the air.

2. Fit the funnel into the neck of the balloon and drop the baking soda down the funnel into the balloon.

> **Learn the Lingo**
>
> **Baking soda,** or **sodium bi-carbonate,** is a leavening agent used in baked goods. When baking soda (a base) comes in contact with acids, such as vinegar or lemon juice, it creates carbon dioxide. That gas causes the baked goods to rise.

3. Fit the funnel over the bottle and pour in the vinegar.

4. Carefully stretch the balloon over the neck of the bottle and shake the baking soda into the bottle.

What happens to the balloon and how long does it take?

You'll see that the soda reacts instantly with the vinegar to produce bubbles that, in turn, inflate the balloon.

After the balloon is inflated, remove and discard it along with the contents of the bottle. You can rinse out the bottle to use again.

> **Bigger Bites**
>
> Food science is a fascinating area that can teach kids about the chemistry of food and ingredients, like baking soda and salt, commonly used in recipes. Ask your child's science teacher for samples of experiments you can do at home. Several kid-friendly books on kitchen science are readily available in bookstores. Don't forget to tune in to kids' science shows on television. They frequently feature experiments and information about the science behind food.

Creating a Baking-Soda Volcano

To see and touch the carbon dioxide bubbles, watch how baking soda reacts with red wine vinegar in a small glass. The bubbles create the "lava" of a pretend mini volcano.

You'll need …

> small drinking glass, less than 6 ounces
>
> 1 cup liquid measure filled with ½ cup red wine vinegar
>
> measuring spoon
>
> 1 tablespoon baking soda

1. Fill the glass with the vinegar and hold it over the sink.
2. Dump the baking soda into the glass.
3. Watch how the reaction between the acid in the vinegar and the baking soda creates carbon dioxide bubbles and causes the vinegar to foam into an imaginary volcano.

When the volcano starts to die down, stir the solution to produce a few more bubbles. Time how long the bubbles last.

Kitchen Clue

Keep the color and the vitamins in vegetables by steaming them briefly, just until they are tender. Place vegetables in a collapsible stainless-steel steaming basket and set it in a saucepan with water that just comes up to the bottom of the basket. Cover and let the water come to a boil. The steam cooks the vegetables. Cooking time will vary according to the amount and type of vegetable.

Watching Green Vegetables Change Color

Did you ever notice how the color of green vegetables changes the longer they cook? They go from a bright green to a dull, brownish yellow-green.

All green vegetables contain chlorophyll. That's what gives them their bright green color. When these vegetables are heated, however, their cells are damaged. The magnesium in the chlorophyll is lost and is replaced by hydrogen, which changes the color. With this, the vegetables lose their bright green color.

You can do a green-vegetable experiment to see how long it takes for different vegetables to turn color. Gather together some vegetables, such as asparagus, broccoli, and green beans.

Kid Quiz

If you want to keep the bright green color in vegetables, do you think you should cook them for a long or short time?

The shorter you cook them, the brighter their color will be. Heat damages the cells containing chlorophyll, and the vegetables lose their bright color as they cook.

You'll need …

saucepans

water

several kinds of green vegetables, such as asparagus, green beans, and broccoli florets

timer

notebook and pencil or pen

1. Fill the saucepans with water. With adult supervision, put the pans on the stovetop and turn the heat to medium high.

2. When the water begins to simmer, add different vegetables to different pans.

3. Start your timer. Watch what happens to the color. Record when the color starts to change. Taste the vegetables. Notice how their texture changes and becomes soft and then mushy the longer they cook.

149

The Least You Need to Know

➤ A supersaturated sugar solution can form sugar crystals and make rock candy.

➤ The carbon dioxide released from yeast can inflate a balloon.

➤ Baking soda combined with an acid releases carbon dioxide bubbles and can inflate a balloon or cause a bubbling solution.

➤ Bright green vegetables turn a dull, brownish yellow-green when exposed to prolonged heat.

Chapter 17

Playing with Your Food

In This Chapter

➤ Playing with food to interest kids in nutrition and new foods

➤ Creating art from familiar foods

➤ Seeing people, animals, and things in foods

➤ Making plate and food faces

➤ Making garnishes

Food is a great medium for creative play. If there's one way to get kids interested in food, it's to let them play with it. Whether they're making face cookies or potato people, kids can let their imaginations go. They come up with all kinds of edible pictures and crafts.

Our parents might have told us not to play with our food, but educators have come to realize that, when you make food fun, kids are more likely to eat it. You can turn food play into nutrition lessons and opportunities to taste new foods.

This chapter introduces kids to the art of garnishing and making edible people, objects, and landscapes from everyday foods. Let your imagination go!

Why Play with Food?

In addition to being just plain fun and creative, playing with food offers a great opportunity to introduce kids to new foods. The color and art excites their senses and draws their interest. You also can turn food play into a lesson about the senses, taste, and nutrition. Here are some ideas you can propose and questions you can ask your child:

➤ What do you think of the color and smell of the food?

➤ Use your senses to explore the food. Touch it and discover how it feels. What kind of a texture does it have when you eat it?

➤ How is the food used in our culture and other cultures?

➤ What kind of nutrients does the food supply?

➤ Look at a picture of the Food Guide Pyramid in Appendix C of this book. Where does the food fit on the pyramid and how much of it should you eat every day?

➤ How could you change the flavor of the food? What would you eat it with or what spices would you like to try with it?

➤ Pick foods that are the colors your kids like for activities in this chapter, such as playing tick-tack-toe and making edible faces.

Is a Banana Really an Octopus?

Take a look at any ordinary food. What do you see? If you think beyond the fruit or vegetable and imagine it reminds you of something else, you can have fun making that something else.

In the book *Play with Your Food*, Joost Elffers takes this concept to new heights. He has turned ordinary fruits and vegetables into playful critters just by giving them facial features or by positioning them to take on different poses of animals or creatures.

Take the banana he turned into an octopus, for instance. The next time you and your children eat a banana, stop and imagine that it's this sea creature. Cut off the stem tip and use kitchen scissors to slice the peel into thin strips. Stop the slices about 4 inches from the base of the banana.

Break off the banana at the point where the strips end. Now prop the banana, using the fleshy part as a base, on a plate and fan the peel around it. You have an octopus spreading its tentacles. (And the kids will have a reason to peel and then eat their fruit!)

Why not give the octopus some eyes? Elffers pushes dry black-eyed peas into the peel, but your kids could just as easily take two cloves from the spice jar and push the stems through the peel near the tip of the banana, the octopus's head. I like to let my octopus either stare straight ahead by lining up the cloves in a straight line or have a goofy, cross-eyed look by putting the "eyes" at different angles. Your kids can make a whole octopus family—and be eating their fruit in the process.

Kid Quiz

What are some of your favorite animals? Can you see them in any of the fruits and vegetables around you?

Seeing Animals, People, and Things in Food

Once you let your imagination go, you'll see all kinds of things in fruits and vegetables. My own perspective shifted several years ago after I wrote a story for the Associated Press about a novel approach to nutrition in the Portland public schools. As part of the Chef in the Classroom program, chefs teamed up with nutritionists to teach kids about healthful eating and how to play with nutritious foods. "We wanted to connect having fun with food and nutrition," said Robert Schierburg, the Portland public schools chef-manager who helped create the now-dormant program. Kids learned how to make typical food garnishes (like the ones at the end of this chapter) and edible landscapes. The concept was that handling nutritious foods familiarized them with the food and made them more likely to eat it.

I took that concept to fourth and fifth graders at the Arbor School of Arts and Sciences in Tualatin, Oregon, and I was amazed at the kids' clever approaches. I brought a bag full of produce into the classroom, emptied it onto a table, and challenged the kids to make whatever they wanted with it. The produce included potatoes, a pineapple, broccoli, baby carrots, and cucumbers. I prompted some ideas by suggesting that broccoli florets looked like trees.

The kids gathered around the table and created a tropical water scene. They sliced the potatoes in half to make small hills and snapped off the broccoli florets to make trees on the hills. The pineapple top became an island with a tree growing out of it. They sliced the cucumbers in half to make boats, scooped out the center, and put the carrots inside for people.

Kitchen Clue

Let the colors, textures, and shapes of foods act as magnets to draw your kids to new foods. When kids play with food, they see it in a new way, make new associations, and are more likely to pop it into their mouths. It's a lot more fun eating vegetables off a funny face than off your regular dinner plate!

Your kids can have the same kind of fun with food. Just take a trip through the produce section or look at what you have in your refrigerator. I'm sure you'll be impressed, as I was, with what youngsters can see in ordinary fruits and vegetables.

Pepper and Potato People

You only have to think about how kids love to play with plastic potato people to realize they can do the same in the kitchen. I've always thought fresh peppers and potatoes make great bases for people and animal combinations.

When my daughter Lizzie appeared with me on a local television show to talk about playing with your food, she created a funny-looking lady out of a red pepper. She sat the pepper on its base, stem side up, and then topped it with a mop of orange curly hair. She made the hair by taking a lemon zester and running it down a carrot stick to get curly carrot shavings.

A baby carrot became a nose, raisins were turned into eyes, and pepper pieces became eyebrows. She gave her lady buck teeth by sticking almond slivers out of an imaginary mouth. The features were attached with toothpicks. Potatoes also make great bases for building similar faces.

The accompanying chart will give you some ideas about what foods to use for hair, features, and ears. Your kids can "draw" with them on a plate, an English muffin, or a piece of bread, or they can attach them to potatoes and peppers as a base.

Kitchen Clue

Use cleaned, cooked potatoes and vegetables when making potato people. Keep a bowl of low-fat sour cream or a favorite dip nearby so your kids can dip and eat as they pull apart their creations.

Edible Faces

There's no better way to get your kids to eat their fruits and vegetables than to have them make the food into funny edible faces. They can make these on a base like a muffin or a burger or right on the plate. They can create the face and then watch it disappear as they eat it.

I've developed the following chart to give you some ideas for making edible people. Visualize how these foods would work. Then, look in your own cupboards or refrigerator for others you might use.

Foods to Use for Edible Faces

eyes	carrot coins, raisins or currants, cloves, grapes, small candies, pasta pieces, beans, cranberries, blueberries, peas, corn, sliced olive rounds, cherry tomatoes
eyebrows	pepper strips, almond slivers, cashews, beans, hard cheese slivers, jicama sticks, curly parsley, cornichons, mandarin oranges
noses	baby carrots, pasta pieces, walnut and pecan halves, cashews, pineapple slices, mandarin oranges, hard cheese slivers, ears of baby corn, jicama sticks, cornichons, pickle slices, melon triangles
cheeks	carrot coins, red pepper pieces, cherry tomatoes
teeth	corn, almond slivers, apple and pear pieces
smiles	apple slices, pepper strips, mandarin oranges, cheese, banana halves or rounds, cornichons, pickles, avocado wedges or strips
hair	zested or curled citrus peels, edible dough squeezed through a garlic press, curly or Italian parsley, grapes, strings of cheese, zested cheese, olive rings, zested veggies such as carrots, cucumbers, or zucchini
ears	carrot or zucchini coins sliced in half, sliced button mushrooms with stems sticking out from face, Brussels sprouts cut in half, mandarin oranges, cashews

Making Landscapes, Boats, and Animals

Next time you make tuna or chicken salad for lunch, try putting the salad into a little edible boat. Cut a green, yellow, or red pepper or a cucumber in half and scoop out the insides. You can also make a container out of a large tomato. Have your kids fill the container with the salad. Attach a sail by cutting a piece of cheese into a triangle and mounting it on a toothpick sticking out of the salad boat.

Let your kids arrange food on their plates to "draw" faces or landscapes. Look at the food chart to see what foods can become facial features. For landscapes, broccoli and cauliflower florets always make wonderful trees and bushes. Mashed potatoes or scoops of salad become mountains. A sauce can become a lake, and vegetables can be arranged as boats.

Heads Up!

Because of food-borne illness scares with sprouts, be sure not to use them when making your edible faces. Remember that basic food safety applies when you're eating edible creations. Be sure your hands and work surfaces are clean. Wash vegetables before using them. Don't leave perishable foods, such as baked potatoes, at room temperature for more than two hours.

As for animals, any round food, such as cherry tomatoes, a peach, or other fruit cut in half and placed down on the flat side, can make great bodies. Use baby carrots or sliced veggies for limbs and other small foods, such as olives, peas, or pieces of corn, to fashion feet and hands.

A Game of Tick-Tack-Toe

You can get kids eating all kinds of foods when you let them turn the food into the board and game pieces for tick-tack-toe.

Take a piece of bread and arrange a slice of cheese or a piece of meat on top of it. This is your game board.

Use slivers of vegetables, such as carrots or pepper slices, to make the lines. Pieces of fruit and vegetables become the moveable game pieces. Instead of collecting them, the kids can eat them. Next time you want to get your kids eating a new food, try using it as a game piece.

Cool Garnishes You Can Eat

A great way to get kids to eat their fruits and vegetables is to have them make the food into garnishes. These decorative art forms look pretty on the plate and can be eaten. If kids are going to peel an orange to make a rose, they're more likely to eat the orange, right?

Be sure you wash your hands and the fruits and vegetables before starting. A clean cutting board and a paring knife are all you need to make these beautiful garnishes. In some cases, small children can do the garnishes with a table knife, a plastic serrated knife, or kitchen scissors.

Kitchen Lingo

A **garnish** is an edible food used to decorate a plate. Garnishes add color and visual appeal to a dish. They can be as simple as a few sprigs of parsley or miniature vegetables arranged in an artful way. Like the garnishes described in this chapter, they also can be works of art created from everyday foods.

Radish Rose

1. Wash the radish and cut a small slice from the bottom and top of the radish. You will have two circles of white on the radish.

2. Place the flat-sided bottom of the radish on a cutting board. Cut a petal by slicing vertically down one side of the radish, positioning your knife just beyond the outside edge of the top white circle. Do not cut through to the bottom. Make three more petals by making the same vertical cuts evenly spaced around the other sides of the radish.

3. For more petals, hold the petals together and make four more vertical cuts diagonally across two petals at a time.

4. Soak the rose in a bowl of ice water for 15 to 20 minutes to allow the petals to open.

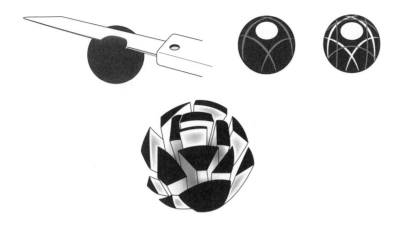

Careful cuts into a radish can turn it into a rose.

Spinners

These are fun and easy to make, and they look pretty on a plate.

Radish spinners are easy, but you also can make them out of other hard vegetables cut into coins like zucchini, carrots, or English cucumbers.

1. Wash the radish, trim off the root end, and slice crosswise into thin coins.

2. Use a small, sharp knife to cut from the center of each coin to the end.

3. Fit two coins together into a spinner by holding one in each hand and gently pushing them into one another on the line of the slits.

4. Continue with other slices to make more spinners.

Kitchen Clue

Use a cutting board and a small paring knife to turn everyday foods into lovely creations. A zester pressed and pulled down against citrus peels, carrots, cucumbers, and zucchini can make festive-looking curls to put on plates.

Veggie and Fruit Fans

These are really fun and easy for kids to make, and they don't always require sharp knives. Kids can make fans from strawberries, avocados, wedges of pears, and cucumbers.

157

1. Wash the fruit or vegetable and place it on a cutting board. Take the knife and insert it just below the base of the fruit or vegetable. Be sure to leave the fruit attached at the base.

2. Make a cut the length of the fruit. Next make several other parallel cuts the length of the fruit. The cuts should allow the fruits to be spread out like a fan, attached at the base.

3. Gently twist the fruit and fan out the cut pieces.

Vertical cuts into soft fruits, such as straw-berries, can turn them into decorative fans.

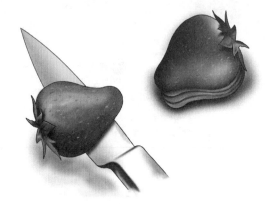

Baskets of Fruit

You can make lemons, limes, oranges, and melons into baskets and can fill them with edible things or use them as decorations. The basic technique is the same.

1. Wash the fruit and place it on a cutting board.

2. Place the citrus fruit on its side and, with a sharp knife, make two vertical side-by-side cuts a short distance apart on the top of the fruit to create the handle.

3. Position the knife in the middle of the fruit and make a horizontal cut from the outside edge of the fruit toward the center. Stop at the first cut (the base of the handle). This will create a wedge of fruit that you should remove.

4. Repeat on the other side.

5. Use the knife to cut out the flesh directly underneath the handle.

6. If filling a melon, scoop out the flesh with a large spoon or knife. Use a melon baller to shape the flesh into balls and fill the basket with these spheres of melon.

Green and White Scallion Brushes

Scallions, also called green onions, make decorative brushes.

1. Wash a scallion, slice off the root end, and trim the green tips about ½ inch. Separate the white bulb and the green leaves by cutting the scallion just where it turns green. The green leaves should be attached at the base.

2. To make a white brush, use a sharp knife to make parallel lengthwise cuts from the top of the white bulb toward the base. Leave about 1 inch of the base intact.

3. For green brushes, use scissors or a knife to make cuts from the tip toward the base where the green leaves are joined.

4. Place the brushes in cold water to curl the ends. For a fun experiment, drop the scallion into ice cold water and see how the ends frizz.

A Citrus Rose

Kids can do this with a plastic serrated knife or a small paring knife. The trick is to make a circular peel of the orange skin without breaking the peel. If you break the peel, simply layer the citrus skin pieces into one another for the rose.

1. Cut the top off an orange about 1 inch below the stem.

2. Slip the knife under the peel and start peeling the orange by holding the knife under the skin and rotating the orange in the hand without the knife.

3. When finished, take the peel and coil it into a circle. You might need a tooth-pick to hold it together.

Garnishes with Zesters and Vegetable Peelers

These curls made from the skins of brightly colored fruits and vegetables are always appealing on a plate. Make them by pulling a zester over the washed fruit or vegetable.

Bigger Bites

Learn more about the art of garnishing by taking a class at your local cooking school or culinary academy. You can purchase special tools, books, and videos on garnishing at kitchen supply stores. Be aware that tools are sharp and their use requires care and supervision.

You also can use a vegetable peeler, pulled along the side of a carrot, to make edible carrot curls. Press the blade of the peeler into the side of the carrot to remove thin strips. Roll each strip and press it together with others in a small cup or the compartment of an ice-cube tray. Cover with cold water and refrigerate for several hours. When fully chilled, the carrots will come out curled.

The Least You Need to Know

➤ Playing with food helps kids see food differently.

➤ Food art can become a vehicle for introducing kids to new foods, improving eating habits, and teaching nutrition.

➤ Follow basic food-safety rules when making edible creations.

➤ Let kids make food faces and then take them apart by eating them.

➤ Play a game of tick-tack-toe with food to make mealtime fun.

➤ Using a knife, kids can turn everyday fruits and vegetables into beautiful, edible garnishes.

Chapter 18

Do-It-Yourself Dairy Adventures

In This Chapter

➤ Making a soft lemon cheese

➤ Making a dessert topping

➤ Making your own butter

Since most kids love dairy products, just think about how exciting it would be for them to make these tasty treats in their own kitchen. You'd be surprised how easy it is to make yogurt cheese, soft lemon cheese, cool dessert toppings, and even butter. Your kids can have a food-related science lesson and end up with something delicious to eat. This chapter contains instructions for making these dairy products.

An added bonus to making these products is the calcium quotient. Dairy products are an excellent source of calcium, and kids need lots of calcium to build strong bones and healthy teeth. Kids ages 9 to 18 need four servings (a total of 1,300 milligrams) of calcium a day, and kids ages 4 to 8 need two to three servings a day (800 milligrams). One serving equals 300 milligrams. While you're experimenting in the kitchen, you can reinforce to your kids the importance of having calcium each day.

Curds and Whey

Have you ever accidentally put lemon in tea with milk or another milky liquid? The acid causes the milk to curdle or clump together and to separate into curds (a semi-solid) and whey (a watery liquid). This happens because the acid—the lemon juice or vinegar—reacts with the protein in the milk to form the curd. When you make cheese from acids, like the lemon cheese in this chapter, this is the process that occurs.

Kid Quiz

What, exactly, are the "curds" that Little Miss Muffet ate?

Curds are the semisolid and soft (coagulated) part of milk from which cheese is made. When you put an acid, like lemon, in milk it creates curds. Cheese that's made with acid is called acid-curd cheese.

Bigger Bites

Your local dairy council can supply information about dairy products, their nutritional benefits, and ways to cook them. Learn more about cheesemaking by requesting a free catalog from the New England Cheesemaking Supply Company. Write them at P.O. Box 85, Ashfield, MA 01330, call 413-628-3808, or access their Web site at www. cheesemaking.com. The company sells a kid-friendly 20-minute mozzarella and ricotta kit for around $20.

How to Make Lemon Cheese

This is a quick-and-easy cheese to make—it's ready in an hour—and it's exciting to actually make a cheese in your own kitchen. The taste is quite different and very lemony, and the texture reminds me of ricotta cheese. We found that we liked it better when we sprinkled some brown sugar on the cheese and spread it on a cracker. You also can use it in a sauce, or you can mince some fresh herbs and mix them in with the cheese. Try crumbling your cheese into a salad or experimenting by adding other flavorings.

How hard is this recipe? Easy/Intermediate

Adult help needed at the stove

Makes 3½ ounces of cheese

Equipment

double boiler or bowl in a saucepan	15-inch piece muslin or cheesecloth
liquid measuring cup	colander
candy or instant-read thermometer	perforated ladle or spoon
lemon reamer or juicer	container for reserved milk
wooden spoon	bowl or pot at least 4½ inches deep

Ingredients

1 quart pasteurized milk

juice of 2 medium lemons

1. In the double boiler or bowl within a saucepan, heat the milk to 100 degrees F. Take the bowl out of the water and add the lemon juice. Use the wooden spoon to stir the mixture well. You'll see the acid in the lemon cause the milk to immediately separate into stringy curds and liquid whey.

2. Let the milk sit for 15 minutes. Meanwhile, spread the cheesecloth or muslin inside the colander.

3. Use the perforated ladle or spoon to gently ladle the curds into the colander. Reserve the leftover milk and refrigerate it for use in baking or as a chilled drink with mint leaves.

4. When you've finished gathering all the curds, pick up the four corners of the cloth. Take the rinsed wooden spoon and tie the cloth into a knot over the handle of the spoon.

5. You're ready to drain the cheese. Hang the cheese over the bowl by propping the ends of the spoon over the rim of the bowl. Leave the cheese for an hour.

6. The whey will have dripped into the bowl. Gently squeeze any excess moisture by twisting the top of the cheese bag. Slip the bag off the wooden spoon, untie the cloth bag, and remove the cheese. Add salt to taste if desired.

7. Serve immediately or refrigerate for two to three days.

Experimenting with Yogurt

Yogurt can make a delicious base for many things:

➤ Mix it with ripe, fresh fruit for a healthy snack.

➤ Make a yogurt parfait by layering it with fresh or dried fruit, nuts, and granola.

➤ Use it as a low-calorie alternative to sour cream or mayonnaise.

➤ Mix it with spices, vanilla, or flavor extracts and use it as a dip for vegetables.

➤ Use it in sauces and salad dressings.

➤ Mix it with diced cucumbers or puréed, cooked eggplant for an interesting side dish.

➤ Turn your yogurt into a tangy drink by thinning with milk or water.

➤ Make it into cheese to spread on everything from a bagel to crackers.

Learn the Lingo

The **whey** is the liquid or thin, watery part of milk that separates from the **curd,** which is the semisolid and soft mass of the milk produced when cheese is made.

Kitchen Clue

Yogurt has been eaten by Middle Eastern cultures for centuries. It is believed to have been invented accidentally by nomadic Balkan tribes and later used as a way of preserving milk. Yogurt is rich in B vitamins, calcium, and protein. It is easily digested, and its "good" bacteria help keep your intestines healthy.

How to Make Yogurt Cheese

When you drain the liquid or whey out of yogurt, it becomes a solid, creamy cheese. Use it the way you would cream cheese or as a substitute for sour cream in baking. Mix it with spices, fresh fruit, or jam and spread it on a bagel or crackers.

To make yogurt cheese, you must start with a yogurt that's drainable. Some contain stabilizers such as vegetable gums, modified food starch, or gelatin. These enhance and maintain the yogurt's consistency and texture but do not allow for drainage. Check the label and choose yogurt without these stabilizers.

To make yogurt cheese, line a funnel, coffee filter, or strainer with a double layer of wet cheesecloth or a coffee filter liner.

Spoon yogurt into this container and prop it over a glass or a bowl. Cover the yogurt with plastic wrap and refrigerate. After an hour, remove the yogurt and stir gently. Re-cover and return to the refrigerator for several more hours. The longer the yogurt drains, the thicker the cheese will become.

Kid Quiz

What happens when you put lemon in milk?

The acid in the lemon causes the milk to curdle and form soft, gelatin-like masses in the milk.

Making a Cool Dessert Topping

A rich, thickened cream—called crème fraîche (French for fresh cheese)—can easily be made by simply mixing cream with buttermilk and letting the mixture stand for up to 24 hours. The result is a slightly nutty, tangy cream with a silky, smooth texture. Kids will like it spooned atop baked goods and desserts such as puddings, pies, scones, and cobblers. Use it in place of heavy cream or mix it with fresh fruit for a special treat. You can sweeten and flavor the cream with honey or confectioners' sugar or a favorite extract, such as vanilla. Add minced, fresh herbs and spices or even horseradish for a savory flavor. Experiment with different flavors or new tastes.

How hard is this recipe? Easy

Makes 1 cup of crème fraîche

Equipment

1-cup liquid measure

1-tablespoon measure

clean glass container with a screw-top lid

tablespoon for stirring

Ingredients

1 cup whipping cream (not ultrapasteurized)

2 tablespoons cultured buttermilk

1. In the glass container, combine the whipping cream and the buttermilk and shake well to combine. The cream and buttermilk should be at room temperature, or you can combine them in a saucepan and heat to 100 degrees F.

2. Set the covered container in an area outside the refrigerator where it will not be disturbed. (The acid in the buttermilk keeps it from spoiling outside the refrigerator.) Let the cream rest until it begins to thicken, which could take anywhere from 8 to 24 hours depending on how warm the room and the ingredients are. Be sure to keep tasting the cream so it does not become too acidic or take on an ammonia-like taste.

continues

well and add flavorings if desired. Cover and refrigerate for 8 hours before
...g. The cream will thicken in the refrigerator.

...re the cream in an airtight container in the refrigerator for about one week.
...heck the sell-by dates on ingredients to be sure they don't expire before the end
of the week.)

Kid Quiz

Do you know where butter comes from?

Butter is made from cream. When the cream is churned (stirred forcefully), it turns into a
solid (butter) plus the liquid (buttermilk) that is squeezed out. You can make your own
homemade butter by shaking very cold cream in a clean jar or "churning" it in the food
processor.

Learn the Lingo

Ultrapasteurized dairy products are heated at higher temperatures and for longer periods of time than regularly pasteurized products. With pasteurization, milk and other liquids are heated to moderately high temperatures for a short period to kill bacteria. Ultrapasteurizing gives the milk a longer refrigerator shelf life.

Make Your Own Butter

My friend Betty Shenberger told me what she jokingly
refers to as an "antique" story. Some 60 years ago,
when she was in kindergarten, she and her classmates
would make butter during story time. The teacher
would put heavy cream in a Mason canning jar and
cover it tightly, and the kids would pass it around. As
they sat cross-legged in a circle listening to the story,
each child would give the jar a couple of vigorous
shakes when it was his or her turn. By the end of the
story, the jar would be filled with butter and the liquid
buttermilk. The kids would get to spread the butter on
graham crackers and then head off for their nap.

You can make your own butter at home in this old-
fashioned and fun way or, for a speedy version, in the
food processor. You'll find it's far more delicious than
any prepackaged butter you'll buy in the supermarket.
It's also very satisfying to watch it turn from cream to
butter and know you've made your own.

Homemade Butter

Making butter in the food processor is a fast and fun project.

How hard is this recipe? Easy

Adult supervision needed handling the food processor workbowl and blade and operating the food processor

Makes 9 $\frac{1}{4}$ ounces of butter and $\frac{3}{4}$ cup of buttermilk

Equipment

food processor

covered jar for reserved buttermilk

rubber spatula

paper towels

covered container for butter

Ingredients

1 pint chilled heavy whipping cream, not ultrapasteurized

1. Chill the bowl and the metal blade of the food processor for 15 minutes in the refrigerator.

2. Pour the pint of chilled heavy cream into the bowl of the processor and process until the cream separates into solids (butter) and liquid (buttermilk.) At first, it won't seem like much is happening. Then, suddenly, after around 4 minutes, the cream will separate into solids and liquid. Soon after, the butter will clump into a large mass.

3. Remove the bowl of the food processor and pour off the buttermilk into the jar. Cover and refrigerate.

4. Run cold water over the butter in the food processor bowl until the water runs clear. Use the spatula to put the butter between sheets of paper towels. Press between the towels to remove as much moisture as possible. Change towels if necessary.

5. Transfer the butter to a container, cover, and refrigerate. The Oregon Dairy Council recommends using the butter within 4 to 5 days and the buttermilk within 2 to 3 days.

The Least You Need to Know

➤ Kids can learn about dairy products by making them from scratch at home.

➤ Making lemon cheese takes only an hour, and it introduces kids to the idea of cheesemaking.

➤ Homemade yogurt has a delicious taste and gives kids the satisfaction of making something from scratch.

➤ Yogurt cheese is easy to make and offers a healthy alternative to higher-fat cheeses.

➤ Mix buttermilk and cream to make crème fraîche as a topping for desserts and fruit.

➤ Try making butter from cream either by hand or in the food processor.

'Round the World in Your Kitchen

Kids can take a trip around the world right in their own home. Making and experimenting with foods from other cultures gives them a firsthand look at the way people eat in other countries. When you create opportunities for cooking, such as hosting an old-fashioned English tea party, a cookie exchange, or cooking clubs, you give kids a chance to explore cooking and new foods. This chapter tells you how to do it.

Exploring Other Cultures

The Children's Museum in Portland occasionally provides kids with a special way of experiencing other cultures. Kids can walk into a mini-environment based on a particular country's customs. They sit in a typical house, rummage through a trunk filled with typical costumes and daily dress, look at their foods, scan their magazines, and listen to their music.

Why not do something similar on your own? Pick a culture you would like to explore. Go to the library and see if you can find a cookbook, particularly a children's cookbook, for that country. Pick out a dish you would like to make and visit an ethnic store where you can buy the ingredients.

Explore the customs of the country and look in books to find out how the people dress. Check the music section at the library or a local music store and see what you can find. Then plan a family meal or a meal with friends based on that culture.

If you have friends from other countries, ask them if they'd like to share their customs with you. You can plan a similar gathering with them. Perhaps they'll take you to their favorite ethnic food shops and explain the various foods to you. You also can join them for a meal at a restaurant that specializes in their cuisine, and they can tell you about their native foods. Ask your friends if they'd be willing to teach you how to make one of their favorite dishes.

Bigger Bites

If you're thinking of starting a cooking club, send away for a teaching guide with recipes, activities, and organizational how-to's (the cost is $5) to the National Pork Producers Council, Kids Cooking Packet, PO Box 10383, Des Moines, IA 50306. Also check with your local cooperative extension service for tips from 4-H.

Forming Your Own Kids' Cooking Club

Gourmet groups, in which adults get together to cook foods with a particular theme, are big all over the country. But why should adults have all the fun? If your kids have any interest, help them put together a cooking club or try to do it with another family.

For a kids' club, all you need is a willing group of kids and some interested adults. Maybe a teacher would like to host the activity after school, or some parents could get together and plan to rotate meetings in their homes.

Make the cooking club like a playgroup in concept. Kids get together and each one has a role, only the play is replaced by a cooking activity. Parents can share the responsibility, and a different family can act as the host for each meeting. The host is responsible for getting the recipes and photocopying them for the kids to take home.

What about equipment and ingredients? One of the easiest ways to deal with equipment needs is to ask each child to bring his or her own. I've done this when I've taught and taken classes at Bob's Red Mill, millers and manufacturers of whole-grain natural foods in Milwaukie, Oregon. At classes at the mill outlet store, students learn and make a recipe, preparing it with their own equipment in class. If something needs to be baked or cooked, they bring it home and finish it off in their own kitchen. This system works beautifully for adults, so why not try it for kids? Just be sure to mark your child's name on the bottom of all his or her equipment with a laundry marker.

Another thing that's helpful is if the class leader has at least a picture and, if at all possible, a sample of what the kids will cook. (Be careful here so that some kids don't dampen others' interest. Tell the children that, if they don't like the food, they should keep their opinions to themselves.) This helps the kids visualize their project, it gives them a focus, and it builds enthusiasm. They get a nice snack in the process.

As for ingredients, you can decide whether the host should be in charge of purchasing them and then divide up the cost among the club members. Depending on what you're making, the kids could possibly bring their own ingredients. You also could rotate this responsibility among club members.

For starters, plan to meet once a month. If the club works out well, you might want to do it more often. Look through magazines or cookbooks to get ideas for projects. Start with small, simple projects that take less than a hour or two to prepare. Look through some of the recipes at the back of this book for ideas.

Another possibility is to consider a supper club. Kids can get together and make dishes that they can then take home for dinner. How proud and important they'll feel when they know they played a part in feeding the family that night. And what better way to build a child's self-esteem?

Kid Quiz

If you had a cooking party or a cooking club, what types of food would you like to cook?

Kids' Cooking Parties

Next time your child has a birthday party, consider hosting a cooking party. Whether it's make-your-own pizzas or twist-your-own soft pretzels, cooking parties offer great entertainment and a fun learning experience for kids.

If you don't feel up to cooking with the kids, hire a food professional to be in charge. Inquire at a local cooking school or culinary academy for names of cooking teachers or chefs in your area.

Kitchen Clue

Make a kids' cooking party enjoyable for you and the kids by hiring a food professional to plan and run the party. Or take the mess out of your home by holding it at a local cooking school. If the school doesn't offer parties, ask if they'd be willing to work with you to plan one.

Party favors also can take on the cooking theme. Kids can make their own chef's hat to take home, and goodie bags can be filled with kid-size cooking utensils, such as small whisks and rubber spatulas. Check at a local kitchen-supply store for aprons or chef's hats that kids can write their names on and decorate.

If you're doing the party yourself, be sure to do a trial run of the recipe and time it. You want to make sure it's doable in a one- to two-hour period. If something is going into the oven, plan to let the kids decorate aprons or hats while the food is cooking. You also could play some food-related games. Turn "Pin the Tail on the Donkey" into "Put the Pepperoni on the Pizza," for instance. Your kids will enjoy coming up with these activity ideas.

An Old-Fashioned Tea Party

We always love having a tea party. It's such a great excuse to spend some time together and to explore new teas and sweet and savory snacks. And although planning and preparing food for the party just seems like fun to your kids, they're also learning important kitchen, social, and life skills. They're exploring other foods, sharpening motor skills as they prepare sandwiches, and learning about other customs.

If you bake with your kids for the party, you're reinforcing math and measuring skills and teaching them how to organize and plan. Even setup and cleanup provide valuable lessons, and when you have a successful tea party, your child feels good about what he or she has accomplished.

The key element in a tea party, of course, is the tea. Try any decaffeinated herbal teas or fall back on my childhood favorite, milk tea. Just add hot water and sugar to milk.

Making the Menu

For an English-style tea party, shortbread, cookies, tea breads, and scones always go nicely with the tea. Try topping them with homemade crème frai[af]che. You also can add this dessert topping to some fresh fruit. As for sandwiches, we always like them delicate and small. Use thin sandwich bread (with the crusts cut off) and make them tiny by cutting them into four squares or by cutting a big X across the top to make four triangular sandwiches. Use miniature breads like deli party breads, and mini-rolls or cookie cutters to spruce up regular sandwiches.

When it comes to fillings, try some of our favorites:

➤ Salmon salad and cream cheese

➤ Cream cheese with or without jelly

➤ Thin rounds of English cucumber with butter

➤ Watercress with butter

➤ Butter sandwiches (try the honey butter in Chapter 29, "The Baker's Rack")

➤ Egg salad

Bigger Bites

Turn a tea party into an occasion to explore different tea customs around the world. Go to the library or a bookstore and find books about tea, tea party customs, and typical foods served with tea. Consider having a series of tea parties, each focusing on a different country and its use of tea.

A Kids' Cookie Exchange

During the Christmas holidays, we like to have a tea party/*cookie exchange*. We invite several families and ask each family to bring several dozen cookies on trays along with copies of the recipes for their cookies. We spread all the cookies out on the dining room table, and during the party, we drink tea and nibble on some of the cookies.

The idea of the party is for guests to take home cookies and exchange recipes. Everyone brings a tin and walks around the table, filling it with samples of each cookie. We ask guests to try to bring different cookies each year so we get to bake and taste new things every year.

Cookie exchanges are so much fun that there's no reason to limit them to the holiday season. Why not plan a weekend tea party that includes a cookie exchange? Ask guests to tell you the type of cookie they want to bake so you can be sure there are no repeats. Tally the number of guests and then ask everyone to bring that number of copies of their recipe. They should bring 6-12 cookies for each person plus an extra dozen for eating at the party. In other words, if there will be a total of six people, everyone will bring six copies of the recipe and a maximum of seven dozen cookies. Separate the dozen you'll be eating at the party so the host can include them in the party tray. Display the rest attractively on a tray or in a basket. One holiday exchange, one of our guests, Kay Carlisle, made large gingerbread people, wrapped them individually in colored cellophane, and displayed them in a basket.

Learn the Lingo

A **cookie exchange** is a gathering where cookies and recipes for the cookies are exchanged among the guests to take home. Exchanges are frequently held around the Christmas holidays as a way of enjoying a wide variety of seasonal cookies.

Heads Up!

Be sure to keep hot foods hot and cold foods cold during your potluck gatherings. Assign guests to bring hot plates, ice, and ice chests. Remind guests to pack perishable foods in insulated containers so that, if they have to be stored in the kitchen, they'll be safe.

For an educational experience, why not learn about different cultures by asking guests to choose a country and bring a cookie or confection typical of that culture? During the party, your guests can talk about what they learned about the meaning behind the cookie. They can discuss any special ingredients and can tell you what it was like to make the cookie.

Organizing Potluck Gatherings

Potluck brunches and suppers also are a good way to explore new foods and to encourage families to share their food experiences. A few years ago, we joined a group of neighborhood families who came together once a month for an ethnic potluck. We would always focus on a different country. The host would decide the theme and guests would make and bring a dish from the country. The host would find decorations and music from the country and guests would come dressed in clothing typical of the culture.

You can involve your children in the planning, decorating, and cooking for these potlucks. Let them help you decide on a theme, the number of guests, and the menu. Ask guests if they have any special favorites they'd like to prepare. Make a list of the food and who is making what so you don't get any repeat dishes. If one of your guests hates to cook, have him or her bring nonfood items, such as paper plates, cutlery, ice, or beverages.

Here are some tips for planning a potluck:

➤ Start several weeks ahead to give yourself enough time to plan the guest list and menu and to send out invitations.

➤ Make sure everyone brings something, even if it's only the ice or beverages.

➤ Be sure guests bring their own serving dishes and utensils and mark them. Marking your name on a piece of masking tape on the bottom of the dish works well.

➤ Find out which foods need heating or refrigerating so you're not left with space or timing problems.

➤ Set up a hot plate and an ice chest or ask one of the guests to bring an ice chest to cool beverages and foods.

➤ Suggest that your guests consider how their dish looks. Colorful and appealing dishes create curiosity and interest, especially important if you're trying to offer kids new foods.

Tapping into Ethnic Customs and Celebrations

Seasonal and yearly ethnic celebrations offer us an opportunity to look at the food customs of other cultures. Take a look at the calendar and plan to explore these foods when the celebration comes around. Search the Internet for Web sites that provide information about the holiday. Look through ethnic cookbooks and your local newspaper's food section just before the holiday. Newspapers usually cover the holidays and include recipes. Plan a family dinner centering around the foods of the culture and prepare some of these recipes with your kids.

A Calendar of Celebrations

To help you think ahead about planning some ethnic meals and foods from other cultures, here's a list of some major holidays celebrated in the United States.

Month	Type of Food	Holiday
January	African American Southern	Martin Luther King Day
Between Jan. 10 and Feb. 19	Chinese	Chinese New Year
February	Early American and colonial foods	President's Day
March/April	Irish	St. Patrick's Day
	Jewish Foods	Passover
	various Christian cultures, such as Italian, Greek, Russian	Easter

continues

continued

Month	Type of Food	Holiday
changes yearly	Islamic cultures	Islamic New Year
May	Mexican	Cinco de Mayo
July	American regional customs	Fourth of July
September	Sephardic and Jewish	Rosh Hashanah Yom Kippur
October	American/regional	Halloween
	Italian	Columbus Day
November	Native American, early American	Thanksgiving
December	Jewish	Hanukkah
	African American	Kwanzaa
	various Christian cultures: French, German, Greek, Irish, Italian, Russian, Scandinavian, South American, Spanish, Swiss	Christmas

The Least You Need to Know

➤ Explore new cultures by cooking foods from other countries with your family or with friends.

➤ Kids' cooking clubs give kids a chance to learn about cooking with their friends.

➤ A tea party teaches kids about tea customs from around the world.

➤ A cookie exchange encourages families to bake cookies from other countries and to share favorite cookie recipes.

➤ A themed potluck offers families the chance to get together and share new foods.

Part 6

Now You're Cooking: The Recipe File

Now it's time to get into the kitchen and cook. The recipes in this section give you lots of choices, including some family favorites, classic dishes, and foods from cultures around the world. Every recipe has been kid– or family–tested and is marked to tell you its difficulty level: Easy, Easy–Intermediate, Intermediate, or Advanced. Most recipes are written for four servings, although you'll find a few that serve more. Keep in mind that every oven and stove is different and cooking times may vary depending on your equipment.

The adult help warning line at the beginning of the recipe provides information about the need for help with appliances or a technique. Recipes are also marked with the following icons. 🔵 *means that adult help is required, usually because children have to cut, use appliances, or cook at the stove or oven.* ⊘ *means that the recipe does not involve any cooking.* ⌀ *denotes that the recipe does not require use of sharp knives.*

Reminders for Kid Cooks

➤ Always ask permission to cook. Ask an adult to help or supervise when handling knives, sharp equipment, or appliances, when pouring hot liquids, and when working at the stove or oven.

➤ Always use thick, dry pot holders when picking up hot pots, pans, and utensils.

➤ Stand back when adding any ingredients to hot oil or grease. Lift pot covers off away from you to prevent steam burns. Never stick your head in the oven to see if something is cooked. Pull the rack out carefully with pot holders.

➤ Turn off the stove or oven immediately when you're finished cooking.

➤ Use a timer so you know how long to cook foods.

Chapter 20

Breakfast Bonanzas

Recipes

➤ Crunchy Munchy Granola

➤ Breakfast Yogurt Crunch Parfait

➤ Tummy-Warmer Oatmeal

➤ Blueberry Buttermilk Pancakes

➤ Apple Puff-Up Pancake

➤ On-the-Run Fun Smoothie

➤ Morning Maple Syrup Corn Muffins

➤ Bubbly Broiled Grapefruit

➤ Cinnamon Toast

➤ Crêpe Faire's Orange French Toast with Orange Butter

➤ Ham and Cheese Pie

➤ Sleepover Huevos Rancheros

➤ Lizzie's Zucchini Frittata

Breakfast is one of the first and easiest meals that kids can learn to cook. Just think back to when you were young. Remember how much fun you had flipping pancakes and spreading cinnamon sugar on toast?

These breakfast standbys are just a few of the delicious meals you'll find in this section. I've included many old-time favorites along with several of our favorite recipes from the Pacific Northwest—Blueberry Buttermilk Pancakes, Orange French Toast with Orange Butter, and my own Ham and Cheese Pie.

Eating a nutritious breakfast helps kids do well in school and gives adults a jump-start for a busy workday. For those rushed mornings, I've included many quick-to-fix breakfasts. Try blending the power smoothie or making the breakfast yogurt crunch parfait, the broiled grapefruit, or a bowl of granola or oatmeal. And check out the "Breakfast for Dinner—or Lunch" section for great meal ideas that work any time of the day. Whether you're looking for a speedy start to your weekday or a special weekend brunch, you'll find lots of choices on the following pages.

Crunchy Munchy Granola

 Once you learn to make a basic granola, you can add different ingredients to create your own blend. Try adding other kinds of dried fruits, nuts, or seeds. This granola tastes great as a breakfast cereal or sprinkled on vanilla yogurt, ice cream, or frozen yogurt. You also can just munch on it plain for a snack like we do.

How hard is this recipe? Easy/Intermediate

Adult help needed using the oven

Makes 7 cups

Equipment	**Ingredients**
dry measuring cups	4 cups oats, quick cooking or regular
measuring spoons	½ cup toasted wheat germ flakes
large mixing bowl	2 tablespoons sesame seeds, hulled or unhulled
wooden spoon	½ cup sweetened flaked coconut
liquid measuring cup	½ cup blanched slivered almonds or chopped pecans,
large jelly roll pan	walnuts, or hazelnuts
pot holders	½ cup honey
timer	2 tablespoons canola oil
cooling rack	1 teaspoon vanilla
container with lid	½ cup sweetened dried cranberries
	½ cup raisins

1. Position the rack in the middle of the oven and preheat the oven to 325 degrees F.

2. In the large bowl, mix the oats, wheat germ flakes, sesame seeds, coconut, and nuts with the wooden spoon.

3. Add the honey, canola oil, and vanilla and mix well.

4. Spread the mixture onto the ungreased jelly roll pan and use pot holders to place the pan in the oven.

5. After 10 minutes, use pot holders to pull out the rack and stir the mixture carefully. Use pot holders to push back the rack and close the oven. Repeat, stirring every 5 minutes until all the mixture is crisp and lightly golden in color. The granola should be cooked in 25 to 30 minutes.

6. Use pot holders to remove the pan from the oven and place it on a cooling rack. When the granola is cool, put it in a container and add the cranberries and raisins. Stir to combine.

7. Serve immediately or store the granola in a tightly covered container outside the refrigerator for about 2 weeks.

Breakfast Yogurt Crunch Parfait

When you're in the mood for granola or cereal, why not try it with some yogurt and fresh berries? This recipe is really easy to make, and you start off your day with a delicious dose of needed nutrients, such as calcium, fiber, and vitamin C.

How easy is this? Easy

Makes 1 large serving

Equipment	Ingredients
spoon	1 (8-ounce) container vanilla yogurt
cereal bowl	¼ cup granola or your favorite crunchy cereal
dry measuring cups	½ cup berries

1. Spoon the yogurt into the bowl.

2. Sprinkle granola and berries on top of the yogurt.

Variation: Try different types of fruit alone or in combinations. Add more granola if you like more crunch.

Tummy-Warmer Oatmeal

 A warm bowl of creamy oatmeal with raisins or fruit is a nutritious, quick, and easy breakfast to make, especially in the microwave. This is one of our favorite breakfasts, especially on cold winter days. You can try maple or flavored fruit syrups instead of the sugar, or you can sprinkle dried fruit on top.

How hard is this recipe? Easy

Adult help needed at the stove

Makes 2 bowls oatmeal

Equipment	Ingredients
liquid measuring cup	1¾ cups water
small saucepan	1 cup oatmeal
dry measuring cups	4 tablespoons brown sugar
stirring spoon	2 heaping tablespoons raisins
timer	4 tablespoons half-and-half or milk
pot holder	
measuring spoons	
cooling rack	
serving bowl	

1. Bring the water to a boil in the saucepan. Add the oatmeal.
2. Cook 5 minutes, stirring occasionally, until the oatmeal has absorbed almost all the liquid. Use the pot holder to remove the pan from the heat to a cooling rack.
3. Spoon the oatmeal into a bowl and stir in the brown sugar, raisins, and half-and-half or milk.
4. Serve immediately.

Microwave: Mix the oatmeal and water in a microwave-safe bowl. Microwave on high for 2½ to 3 minutes, stirring after 1½ minutes. Use the pot holder to remove the bowl from the microwave. Stir in the brown sugar, raisins, and half-and-half or milk.

Blueberry Buttermilk Pancakes

Pancakes were one of the first breakfasts my kids cooked, so when I tasted these buttermilk pancakes, I knew they'd want this recipe. Shirley Thompson serves them at her McCoy Creek Inn in Diamond, Oregon. The recipe has been in her family for three generations. You also can make them without the blueberries and top them with a fruit syrup.

How hard is this recipe? Easy

Adult help needed at the stove

Makes 18 pancakes, about 3 inches each

Equipment	Ingredients
large mixing bowl	2 cups buttermilk
liquid measuring cup	2 large eggs
measuring spoons	1½ teaspoons baking powder
dry measuring cups	½ teaspoon baking soda
whisk	1 teaspoon salt
griddle or skillet	1 tablespoon sugar
spatula	2 cups all-purpose flour
pot holder	4 tablespoons vegetable oil or melted butter
serving plate	¾ cup fresh blueberries
	butter or cooking spray (to grease the griddle or skillet)
	maple or fruit syrup

1. In the large bowl, use the whisk to mix the buttermilk, eggs, baking powder, baking soda, salt, sugar, and flour.

2. Whisk in the oil or butter, just to combine. The batter will be thick like a soft fudge sauce. Gently fold in the blueberries, taking care not to crush them.

3. Preheat the griddle or skillet over medium-high heat. To tell if the griddle is hot enough, flick a few drops of water on it. If the water sizzles and jumps around, the griddle is ready.

4. Grease the griddle or skillet with a pat of butter or cooking spray. For each pancake, dip a ¼-cup measuring scoop into the batter, fill it, and pour the batter onto the griddle. Cook several pancakes at once, leaving some space between them.

5. When the pancakes get puffy and dry around the edges and the surface is covered with bubbles, they're ready to be flipped. Slip the spatula under the pancake and flip quickly. Cook the other side until it is golden brown.

6. Hold the skillet handle with a pot holder and use the spatula to lift the pancakes off the griddle and to put them on the serving plate. Serve the pancakes hot and with syrup.

Note: You don't have to use this batter right away. Just mix it and put it in the refrigerator, covered, to use it the next day. The batter might turn dark on the top, but just stir it and you're ready to cook.

Kid Comment

Christopher Wearn, 13: "These were nice and fluffy and light." Christopher made these for his parents and his three siblings for a weekend brunch. "Everyone wanted more," said his mother, Maureen.

Christopher Wearn, 13

Apple Puff-Up Pancake

When my neighbor, 9-year-old Megan Clarey, made this recipe, she said she was "amazed to see it puff up and then deflate." Peek through the glass window on your oven door to see what she means. The batter inflates while cooking and then, just like a balloon that loses air, falls down once it's out of the oven. How will you know when the pancake is ready? Your kitchen will smell wonderful from the aroma of the cooking apples and brown sugar.

How hard is this recipe? Easy/Intermediate

Adult help needed with cutting and at the oven and stove

Serves 4

Equipment
cutting board
small sharp knife
peeler
medium mixing bowl
liquid measuring cup

dry measuring cups
measuring spoons
whisk
8- to 10-inch oven-
  proof skillet
timer

metal spatula
rubber spatula
pot holder
cooling rack
serving plates

Ingredients
1 large apple (Granny Smith, Rome, or Red Delicious)
3 large eggs
½ cup whole milk
½ cup all-purpose flour

¼ teaspoon salt
¼ teaspoon vanilla
4 tablespoons unsalted butter
¼ cup dark brown sugar
¼ teaspoon cinnamon

1. Position the rack in the center of the oven and preheat the oven to 450 degrees F.

2. Core and peel the apple, cut it crosswise into ⅜-inch rounds, then cut the rounds in half.

3. In the mixing bowl, whisk together the eggs, milk, flour, salt, and vanilla to form a smooth batter. Do not overbeat.

4. Over medium heat, melt the butter in the skillet. Add the apples and cook, uncovered, for 4 minutes. Turn the apples with the metal spatula and cook for another 3 minutes.

5. Sprinkle the apples with the brown sugar and cinnamon and cook for another minute or until the sugar begins to melt. Stir lightly to coat the apples with the sugar and then, all at once, pour the batter over the apples and use the rubber spatula to scrape clean the bowl.

6. Use the pot holder to put the skillet in the oven and bake for about 15 minutes or until all the mixture puffs up and turns golden brown.

7. Use the pot holder to remove the pan from the oven and place it on a cooling rack. Watch how the pancake collapses within a minute or two.

8. Cut the pancake into four wedges and serve immediately.

Megan Clarey, 9

Kid Comment

Megan Clarey, 9: "My favorite ingredients were the apple and the brown sugar. It tasted really, really good. I asked for two pieces."

On-the-Run Fun Smoothie

 Try this breakfast smoothie when you're in a hurry but want a nutritious kick to get you going.

How hard is this recipe? Easy

Adult supervision needed using the blender

Makes 3 cups

Equipment	Ingredients
blender	1 large ripe banana
liquid measuring cup	1 cup nonfat milk
spoon	½ cup nonfat vanilla yogurt
measuring spoons	½ serving protein powder
glasses	4 ice cubes

1. Peel the banana, break it in half, and place it in the blender.
2. Add the milk, yogurt, and protein powder. Blend on low speed until combined.
3. Add the ice cubes and blend until smooth.
4. Pour into glasses and serve immediately.

Kid Comment

Sam Sadle, 13: "I had a fun time making this, even though I messed up the blender and the smoothie got everywhere. It was good. I enjoyed it a lot." Sam thought the full serving of protein powder I originally had in the recipe left a powdery taste, so I cut it back to half. He also added two strawberries for more zip.

Sam Sadle, 13

Heads Up!

"When you're going to make something in the blender, put the bottom on tight and make sure it's attached right to the blender," warns tester Sam Sadle. His smoothie leaked out of the blender bottom because the bottom was loose.

Morning Maple Syrup Corn Muffins

 The flavors of corn and maple syrup blend to make these a welcome breakfast treat. Poke holes in the muffins with a fork and drizzle extra maple syrup over the top for more maple flavor. Eat them warm or at room temperature and add your favorite jam or butter if you like.

How hard is this recipe? Easy

Adult help needed using the oven

Makes 12 muffins

Equipment

large mixing bowl	wooden spoon
dry measuring cups	12 paper or foil muffin cup liners
measuring spoons	2 (6-cup) muffin tins
whisk	timer
sifter or small strainer	pot holders
small mixing bowl	toothpick
rubber spatula	cooling rack
liquid measuring cup	fork
small saucepan or microwave-safe bowl to melt butter	serving plate

Ingredients

1½ cups all-purpose flour	¼ cup packed dark brown sugar
1½ cups yellow cornmeal	8 ounces fat-free plain yogurt
½ teaspoon salt	½ cup pure maple syrup
1 tablespoon baking powder	5 tablespoons unsalted butter, melted and cooled
2 large eggs	

continues

1. Position the rack in the center of the oven and preheat the oven to 350 degrees F.

2. In the large bowl, whisk together the flour, cornmeal, and salt. Sift in the baking powder and whisk to combine.

3. In the small mixing bowl, whisk the eggs, add the brown sugar, and whisk to combine. Use the rubber spatula to add the yogurt, maple syrup, and butter and combine.

4. Make a hole in the center of the dry ingredients by pushing the ingredients up onto the sides of the bowl. Pour the wet ingredients into the hole and stir with the wooden spoon in a circular motion just until all the ingredients are combined into a moist batter. Do not overbeat.

5. Place the cup liners in the muffin tins. Use the spatula to scrape the batter into the muffin cups. Fill evenly to the brim of the muffin cups.

6. Bake for 25 to 30 minutes. Check the muffins after 15 minutes and reverse the position of the tins in the oven if they are not cooking evenly. When baked, the muffins should turn golden and will spring back when touched. To test whether the muffins are done, insert and remove a toothpick from the center of a muffin. The toothpick should come out clean.

7. Use the pot holders to remove the muffin tins from the oven and place the tins on a cooling rack. Let them stand for 5 minutes and then transfer each muffin to the rack. Serve warm or at room temperature.

Kid Comment

Kayla Kirk, 10: "The maple syrup gave these a good flavor. I liked the taste of these muffins. These were really easy to make."

Bubbly Broiled Grapefruit

The contrast of a warm, sweet, bubbly topping and the cool, tart grapefruit makes this a wonderful pick-me-up in the morning. The raspberry jam blends with the grapefruit for a great sweet-tart taste. You also can try another favorite jam on top or brown sugar.

How hard is this recipe? Easy

Adult help needed cutting the grapefruit and using the broiler

Serves 4

Equipment	Ingredients
cutting board	2 cold medium grapefruit, pink or white
sharp knife	4 tablespoons raspberry jam
serrated grapefruit knife or spoon (optional)	
broiler pan or baking dish	
measuring spoons	
pot holders	
timer	
cooling rack	
tongs	
serving plates	

1. Position the rack in the upper half of the oven and preheat the broiler. Keep the oven door slightly open.

2. Cut each grapefruit in half crosswise. With the sharp knife or the serrated grapefruit knife or spoon, cut around and under the sections of the grapefruit, freeing them but leaving them in the grapefruit shell.

3. Place the grapefruits, cut side up, on the broiler pan or in the dish. Smooth the jam over the top of each grapefruit. Spread with your clean finger to coat the top evenly.

4. Use pot holders to set the broiler pan in the oven so the grapefruit tops are about 4 inches from the heat source. Keep the oven door slightly open. Broil for about 3 to 5 minutes or until the jam is evenly bubbly.

5. Use pot holders to remove the pan and place it on the cooling rack. Use the tongs to put each grapefruit half on a serving plate. Serve immediately.

Kid Comment

Hannah Albert, 12: "I like spreading the jam on the grapefruit and cutting it with a knife with edges. The grapefruit is a bit sour, but the jam or brown sugar makes it sweeter. I like it warm." Hannah's mom, Kathy, makes the whole grapefruit warm by cooking it longer. "It looks decorative, and it's nice to serve on special occasions," she said.

Hannah Albert, 12

Cinnamon Toast

 Cinnamon sugar on toast is always a welcome treat in the morning. We make this toast two different ways. The first way is to make the bread crisp in a toaster and then spread on the topping. The second way, my favorite ever since I learned it from my friend Gil Cavanagh, is to put the topping on untoasted bread then broil it to get a hot, almost-crunchy topping with soft, chewy bread on the bottom.

How hard is this recipe? Easy

Adult help needed using the broiler

Serves 1

Equipment	**Ingredients**
toaster	1 piece white or whole wheat bread
plate	½ or 1 tablespoon butter (depending on cooking method)
table knife	
measuring spoons	1 tablespoon cinnamon sugar (recipe follows)
cookie sheet if broiling	
pot holder	
timer	

Toaster method:

1. Toast the bread in the toaster. Remove it to the plate.

2. Spread ½ tablespoon butter on the toast. Sprinkle it with cinnamon sugar and serve immediately.

Broiler method:

1. Position the rack in the oven so the top of the cookie sheet is about 6 inches from the heat source. Preheat the broiler to medium. Keep the oven door slightly open.

2. Place the bread on the cookie sheet and evenly dot the bread with 1 tablespoon of butter, broken into small chunks. Sprinkle the tops of the bread with cinnamon sugar.

 3. Use potholders to set the cookie sheet in the oven. Keep the oven door slightly open. Broil for 1½ to 3 minutes or until the butter is melted and the sugar starts to get bubbly. Watch carefully to prevent burning. Use pot holders to remove the cookie sheet to a cooling rack. Serve the toast immediately. (For a moister topping, broil just until the butter melts, about 1 ½ minutes. For a crunchier topping, broil up to 3 minutes.)

Cinnamon Sugar

 Cinnamon sugar tastes great on toast, on fruit, sprinkled in yogurt, or on top of ice cream or hot chocolate. Make a double batch and keep it in a closed container to have on hand.

How hard is this recipe? Easy

Makes 2 tablespoons

Equipment

small bowl

measuring spoons

Ingredients

5 teaspoons sugar

1 teaspoon cinnamon

In the small bowl, mix the sugar with the cinnamon until the mixture is an even color. You can vary these proportions if you want more or less of a cinnamon taste.

Crêpe Faire's Orange French Toast with Orange Butter

This orange-flavored bread was a signature dish for 17 years at a Portland restaurant owned by our friend Helen Hazen. Helen sold Crêpe Faire nine years ago, but she continues to make the toast with her 11-year-old daughter, Inga. Serve it dusted with confectioners' sugar and a dab of orange butter or drizzle it with your favorite syrup.

How hard is this recipe? Easy

Adult help needed with grating and at the stove

Makes 6 pieces

Equipment	Ingredients
shallow bowl or pie pan	3 large eggs
whisk	2 teaspoons sugar
measuring spoons	¼ teaspoon salt
grater or zester	2 tablespoons milk
cutting board	2 tablespoons orange juice
sharp knife	zest of one orange
fork	6 slices challah, white, French, or Italian bread, preferably a day old
2 large plates	
large skillet or griddle	butter (for greasing the pan)
timer	confectioners' sugar (for sprinkling)
table knife	
pot holder	
spatula	
serving plates	
spoon	

1. Crack the eggs into the bowl or pie pan and beat with the sugar, salt, milk, orange juice, and orange zest.

2. Dip the bread, one slice at a time, in the egg mixture and turn the bread with a fork to soak both sides. Press it with a fork to moisten the bread thoroughly. Remove each slice to a large plate.

3. Heat the skillet for 1 minute over medium heat. Grease the skillet with a pat of butter and, when the butter starts foaming, cover the bottom of the skillet with a single layer of bread slices.

4. Cook for 3 to 4 minutes or until the bottom side of the bread is golden. Use the spatula to flip the bread to the other side. Cook for another 2 minutes or until golden. Use the pot holder to grasp the skillet handle and remove the bread with the spatula to a clean plate. Repeat the cooking procedure until all the bread is cooked.

5. Serve immediately, sprinkled with confectioners' sugar and a dab of Orange Butter (recipe follows).

Kid Comment

Inga Hazen, 11: "This is really good. The orange makes it smell and taste really good."

Orange Butter

Top the French toast with this butter or spread the butter on your favorite bread or rolls.

How hard is this recipe? Easy

Makes about ½ cup

Equipment	Ingredients
small bowl	4 tablespoons butter, softened
table knife	1 cup confectioners' sugar
dry measuring cup	2 teaspoons orange zest
grater or zester	2 tablespoons orange juice
measuring spoons	
wooden spoon	

1. Combine butter, sugar, orange zest, and orange juice in a small bowl.
2. Beat well with a wooden spoon until combined and smooth. Ingredients will come together slowly at first but will eventually make a smooth mixture.

Learn the Lingo

French toast is also known as **pain perdu,** which translates from French as "lost bread." This method of dipping day-old bread in an egg mixture and then pan-frying it was developed by industrious 15th-century cooks as a way of restoring dry bread that would have been lost or unusable otherwise.

193

Breakfast for Dinner—or Lunch

Some dishes are just too good to have only for breakfast. When you feel like having a light lunch or dinner, try one of our favorites.

Ham and Cheese Pie

Here's my twist on ham and cheese. Bake them together in a crustless, custard-like pie. It's so easy to put together, and it tastes delicious any time of day.

How hard is this recipe? Easy/Intermediate

Adult help needed with cutting, grating, and using the oven

Serves 4

Equipment

1½ quart casserole or baking
    dish or 10-inch pie pan
cutting board
small sharp knife
plate
grater
dry measuring cups
wooden spoon
small mixing bowl
whisk
liquid measuring cup
measuring spoons
small strainer
pot holders
timer
cooling rack
large spoon
serving plates

Ingredients

butter (for greasing the pan)

4 large pieces stale or dried-out white bread

3 ounces sliced ham (about 10 slices), cut into
    bite-size pieces

6 ounces Swiss cheese, divided and shredded
    (about 1½ cups total)

3 large eggs

1 cup milk

¼ teaspoon salt

¼ teaspoon dry mustard

1 medium tomato, sliced into 4 rounds

¼ teaspoon pepper, if desired

1. Position the rack in the center of the oven and preheat the oven to 350 degrees F.

2. Butter the baking dish. Tear the bread into large chunks and place them in the dish. Add the ham and 1 cup of the cheese and toss with the wooden spoon to mix.

3. In a small mixing bowl, beat the eggs with a whisk, add the milk and salt, and sift in the mustard through the strainer. Stir to mix.

4. Pour the egg mixture over the bread and lightly toss the ingredients with the wooden spoon to moisten.

5. Layer the tomatoes on top and sprinkle with the remaining cheese.

6. Bake, uncovered, for 35 to 40 minutes or until the cheese is melted and the pie is golden brown and bubbling.

7. Use pot holders to remove the pie to a cooling rack and sprinkle it with pepper if desired. Serve immediately.

Variations: Use other grated cheeses, such as cheddar, muenster, or jack, or use a combination of cheeses. You also can make an all-cheese-and-tomato casserole by leaving out the ham. Get creative and sprinkle in some of your favorite chopped fresh herbs or add flavor with a tablespoon of green chilies.

Note about the bread: To dry out the bread, put it in a preheated 140 degree F oven for 30 minutes. You also can leave it out on a cooling rack on your counter for several hours.

Kayla Kirk, 10

Kid Comment

Kayla Kirk, 10: "This was excellent, quick, and easy. I had to make myself stop at three helpings."

Sleepover Huevos Rancheros

Whenever my daughter Lizzie has a sleepover at her friend Caitlin Goebel's house, they eat Huevos Rancheros. Caitlin learned how to make these delicious fried eggs with fixings when she lived with her family in Mexico. Fried tortillas are covered with black beans and fried eggs. Salsa and a sprinkling of cheese top the eggs, and avocado slices serve as a garnish on the side. Kids will have fun layering all the ingredients and will learn how to make a fried egg when they follow this recipe. Adult help is required throughout the recipe with the assembling, and especially with frying the tortillas and eggs at the beginning. Lizzie and Caitlin say these hearty eggs make a perfect light dinner or a fun sleepover breakfast.

How hard is this recipe? Intermediate

Adult help needed throughout the recipe, especially using the grater and can opener, and in frying at the stove.

Serves 2 to 4

Equipment

grater	can opener
plate for cheese	small rubber spatula for beans
large nonstick skillet with lid	liquid measuring cup
measuring spoons	serving spoon
tongs	timer
plate	2 small saucers
paper towels	2 to 4 dinner plates
aluminum foil	slotted spoon
pot holders	metal spatula
2 small saucepans or microwave-safe bowls	cutting board
	small sharp knife

Ingredients

4 (6-inch) corn tortillas	4 large eggs
1 (15-ounce) can black beans	4 tablespoons grated jack or cheddar cheese
½ cup tomato salsa	½ avocado, sliced into wedges
2–3 tablespoons vegetable oil	Salt and freshly ground black pepper to taste

1. Position the rack in the center of the oven and preheat to 200 degrees F. Prepare the tortillas. Heat 1 tablespoon of oil in the skillet over medium high heat. When the oil is hot enough to allow a drop of water to sizzle, have an adult add tortillas, one at a time, to quick fry on each side for 30 seconds. Use the tongs to turn the tortillas and add more oil, if necessary. Drain between paper towels on the plate.

Turn off the heat under the skillet. Blot the tortillas with paper towels to remove excess oil and then discard the towels. Stack the tortillas and wrap them in aluminum foil. Use pot holders to place them on the rack in the oven to keep warm.

2. In separate small saucepans, heat the black beans and the salsa over medium heat for 3 to 6 minutes, or until hot. If heating in the microwave, place in separate microwave-safe bowls and heat for 1 to 3 minutes on high or until hot.

3. Meanwhile, fry the eggs. Add 1 tablespoon oil to the skillet and heat on medium high until a drop of water sizzles. Crack 2 eggs into each saucer and slip the eggs into the pan. Immediately reduce the heat to low. Cook for 4 to 6 minutes (you'll hear the eggs begin to sizzle) or until the whites are set and the yolks begin to thicken. The eggs should not look runny. Cover the pan after 3 minutes to allow even cooking.

4. Meanwhile, set out the dinner plates and put two tortillas on each plate. Using the slotted spoon, spoon the beans on top of the tortillas. When the eggs are ready, use the pot holder to hold the pan handle and remove the eggs with the spatula. Place an egg on each tortilla.

5. Spoon the salsa on top of the eggs, distributing the salsa evenly. Sprinkle 1 tablespoon of cheese over each egg and divide the avocado slices between the plates, setting them beside the eggs. Season with salt and pepper, if desired.

6. Serve immediately.

Caitlin Goebel, 13

Kid Comment

Caitlin Goebel, 13: "This is easy, and it's lots of little things put on one tortilla. It's fun to layer all the ingredients. It tastes really good because all the flavors fit together."

Lizzie's Zucchini Frittata

We were at a party one Saturday night when the host ran out of appetizers. Our friend Catherine Whims, the chef/owner of Genoa restaurant in Portland, stepped into the kitchen to make this puffy Italian omelet. Somehow our daughter Lizzie, who was 9 years old at the time, wound up at Cathy's side, assisting her in making the frittatas. Early the next morning, we heard clanking in the kitchen and found Lizzie re-creating her kitchen adventure and making us a frittata for our Sunday breakfast. She's been making frittatas ever since. In this version, she's added zucchini.

How hard is this recipe? Intermediate

Adult help needed with cutting and at the stove and broiler

Serves 4

Equipment	Ingredients
large mixing bowl	6 large eggs
whisk	½ cup grated Parmesan cheese
dry measuring cups	¼ teaspoon salt
measuring spoons	⅛ teaspoon freshly ground pepper
cutting board	¼ teaspoon chopped fresh rosemary
sharp knife	3 tablespoons extra virgin olive oil, divided
10-inch oven- and broiler-proof skillet, preferably nonstick	1 medium onion, cut into thin slices lengthwise
wooden spoon	1 medium zucchini, unpeeled, trimmed, and cut into ¼-inch rounds
pot holders	
timer	
cooling rack	
metal spatula	
large serving plate	

1. Position the rack in the middle of the oven and preheat the oven to high broil. Keep the oven door slightly open.

2. In the large bowl, crack the eggs and lightly beat them with the whisk. Add the cheese, salt, pepper, and rosemary.

3. Put 2 tablespoons of oil in the skillet, lifting and tilting the pan to spread the oil evenly on the bottom. Heat the oil over medium heat for 1 to 2 minutes. Add the onion slices and zucchini. Cook, stirring occasionally, for 8 to 10 minutes or until the onions are translucent and golden. The onions and the zucchini should be soft.

4. Use pot holders to remove the skillet from the heat and add the onions and zucchini to the bowl with the egg mixture. Stir to combine well.

5. Use pot holders to return the skillet to the stove, add the remaining oil, tilt the skillet to coat the bottom, and heat for 1 minute. Add the egg mixture. Use the wooden spoon to distribute the zucchini rounds evenly around the mixture.

6. Cook until the frittata is set on the bottom. This should take about 5 minutes. When the oil starts to come over the edges and the rim of the omelet looks dry and set, gently start lifting up the edges to allow some of the runny eggs to seep underneath and cook.

7. When only the center of the frittata appears loose, use pot holders to remove the skillet from the stove and place it in the oven for 1 to 3 minutes or until the eggs are no longer runny and the frittata sets and lightly puffs. Keep the oven door slightly open.

8. Use pot holders to remove the pan to a cooling rack. Loosen the bottom of the frittata by gently running the spatula around the edges and underneath the eggs. Use pot holders to lift up the skillet and slide the frittata onto the serving plate.

9. Use the sharp knife to cut the frittata into wedges, like a pie, and serve immediately.

Lizzie Cooke, 12

Kid Comment

Lizzie Cooke, 12: "This is a fun and inventive recipe that kids can do. This tastes like a morning omelet but it's good all day around. Watch out because the onions will make you cry!"

Chef Catherine Whims: "The flavor of this is really good. It's a great appetizer or would be good on a picnic between two slices of bread or toast."

Chapter 21

Delicious Drinks

Recipes

➤ Hot Spiced Cider

➤ Hot Honey Milk

➤ Mexican Hot Chocolate

➤ Is It Chocolate Pudding or a Thick Mexican Hot Chocolate?

➤ Moroccan Mint Tea

➤ Fruity Soda Pop

➤ Apple-Lime Spritz

➤ Blazing Sunset

➤ Lorinda's Summer Water

➤ Lemon Velvet

Maybe it's because they feel like mad scientists concocting elaborate potions, but kids just love mixing drinks. They like the measuring, pouring, and inventing involved in coming up with their own special beverages. These days, with the popularity of smoothies, they're into drinks more than ever.

Hidden amidst all the play, though, are some valuable kitchen lessons. Kids gain experience pouring and handling hot and cold liquids, and learning to use the blender is a good first step to understanding safety with appliances. Drinks, such as smoothies and fruit-based sodas, also are a convenient way to pack in nutrition, fruits, and liquids.

Hot Spiced Cider

In the winter, this fragrant cider will warm you right up after a few hours in the chilly outdoors. Try a spice smelling game: Can you guess the spice that goes with each aroma?

How hard is this recipe? Easy

Adult help needed at stove and pouring hot cider into cups

Makes 4 1-cup servings

Equipment
4-cup liquid measuring cup
3-quart saucepan
measuring spoons
timer
pot holder
strainer
4 mugs

Ingredients
4 cups apple cider
5 whole cloves
2 cinnamon sticks, each about 3½ inches long
¼ teaspoon allspice

1. Pour the apple cider into the saucepan and add the spices. Bring the cider to a boil over medium-high heat.
2. Turn the heat down to low and simmer, uncovered, for 10 minutes.
3. Ask an adult to use pot holders and pour the cider through the strainer and into the 4-cup measure to remove the cinnamon and cloves.
4. Fill the mugs with cider and serve.

Hot Honey Milk

Whenever we're looking for a soothing drink, we reach for honey and milk. My kids often drink it just before bed or to wind down after a busy day. Try it in place of hot cocoa on a blustery, winter afternoon. Use clover honey or one of the many flavored honeys now showing up on supermarket shelves. We make it in the microwave for a quick and easy treat.

How hard is this recipe? Easy

Adult help needed heating and ladling the milk

Makes 1 serving

Equipment
microwave-safe liquid measuring cup or small saucepan
measuring spoons
spoon
pot holder
mug

Ingredients
8 ounces skim or low-fat milk
2 teaspoons clover or flavored honey (or to taste)

1. Pour the milk into the measuring cup and heat it in the microwave for 1 to 2 minutes.

 2. Use a pot holder to remove the cup from the microwave oven. Stir in the honey, pour the mixture into the mug, and serve.

 3. Alternatively, you can heat the milk in a small saucepan on the stove. Heat on medium until bubbles form around the rim of the milk. Stir in the honey, ladle the milk into the mug, and serve.

Learn the Lingo

Molinillo is the Mexican name for a hand beater used to make hot chocolate frothy. The wooden tool has a handle and a bulb–like base with loose rings around it. Mexicans put the base into the milk, the handle between their palms, and then rub their hands. The motion spins the base and froths the milk. Look for a molinillo in a Mexican or specialty foods store and try making hot chocolate this Mexican way.

Mexican Hot Chocolate

 Hot chocolate in Mexico is frothy with the taste of cinnamon and sugar accenting the chocolate. Mexicans use a *molinillo* (moh-lee-NEE-yoh), a wooden hand beater, to make the chocolate foamy. They rub the handle between their palms, and it turns the spinner on the other end to froth the milk.

You can find a molinillo and Mexican chocolate in specialty foods stores. The chocolate, particularly the Ibarra brand, also is widely available in supermarkets. It comes in round tablets containing a mixture of chocolate, cinnamon, and sugar. Whisking the chocolate milk in the pan or putting it in a blender will give you the froth.

How hard is this recipe? Easy

Adult help needed heating and ladling milk and using the blender

Serves 4

Equipment

1 (1-gallon) resealable plastic bag	whisk	paper towel
2- or 3-quart saucepan	timer	ladle
rolling pin (optional)	pot holders	4 large mugs
liquid measuring cup	blender	

continues

continued

Ingredients

1 (3-ounce) cake or tablet Mexican chocolate

4 cups nonfat milk

1. Put the chocolate in the plastic bag, place the bag on a sturdy surface, and use the back of the saucepan or the rolling pin to pound the chocolate and break it into small pieces.

2. Pour the milk into the saucepan, add the chocolate, and heat it over medium heat until the milk begins to simmer. This should take about 10 to 12 minutes. As the milk warms, occasionally whisk and press the chocolate to blend it with the milk.

3. Check the blender to make sure the bottom is screwed on properly and fits tightly.

4. Ask an adult to use pot holders and help you carefully pour the milk into the blender. Secure the lid tightly but leave a hole open on top to allow steam to escape. Cover the hole loosely with a paper towel to catch any splatters. Hold the lid firmly and blend on low for 2 minutes. Be careful not to get burned by milk that might splatter.

5. Remove the lid and ladle the milk into the mugs. Serve immediately.

Note: You can make this into a cold drink by allowing the milk to cool to room temperature and then adding ice cubes.

The directions on the Ibarra box call for proportionately less chocolate than we do, but we think it tastes better with the extra chocolate.

Kid Comment

Allie Hinckley, 9: "Pounding the chocolate was really fun. YUMmmm, this was really good but a little messy to make. I like licking the chocolate tablet, too." Allie said she liked the combination of chocolate, cinnamon, and sugar in the Mexican chocolate. Cooking something from Mexico also made her curious about the country and interested in learning Spanish.

Allie Hinckley, 9

Is It Chocolate Pudding or a Thick Mexican Hot Chocolate?

✐ When I went to Oaxaca with my daughters recently, the Mexican family we lived with served us a soothing but bland hot milk drink called atole (ah-toe-le). I mentioned it to my friend Claire Archibald, the chef-owner of the Portland restaurant Café Azul, and she told me how to make this rich chocolate version. Called champurrado (cham-poor-ra-do), it uses masa harina, the fine corn flour (found in many supermarkets) used to make tortillas.

My family tested the recipe, and when it came off the stove, my husband thought it looked too thick. He put some milk in his cup to thin it. Julia, Lizzie, and I liked it. As we tried to figure out what it tasted like, Lizzie declared: "It's yummy. It tastes like drinkable chocolate pudding." We looked at each other and wondered if it would turn into pudding when chilled. So we put some in the refrigerator and guess what happened? Within an hour, the champurrado had firmed up into a silky, light pudding. Have it as a drink or a pudding and decide which you like better.

How hard is this recipe? Easy/Intermediate

Adult help needed at the stove and ladling hot mixture

Makes 5½ cups

Equipment

4-cup liquid measure	Dutch oven or large, heavy 5-quart saucepan	cooling rack
dry measuring cups	whisk	tongs
small bowl	timer	ladle
fork	pot holders	serving cups or custard cups
rubber spatula		

Ingredients

2 cups whole milk	2 cinnamon sticks, each about 3½ inches long
1 cup half-and-half	⅓ cup packed dark brown sugar
⅓ cup masa harina	2 ounces bittersweet chocolate, broken into pieces
1½ cups water	

1. Assemble all the ingredients beside the stove. Combine the milk and the half-and-half in a 4-cup liquid measure so you can pour them easily.

2. Put the masa harina in the small bowl and slowly pour in ½ cup water, stirring with the fork to make it into a thick paste. Gradually add the remaining water, a little at a time, until you have a smooth paste.

3. Use the rubber spatula to scrape the masa harina into the saucepan. Add the cinnamon sticks and turn the heat to medium high. Cook, whisking constantly, for about 8 to 10 minutes. Watch how the mixture starts to thicken after about 6 minutes, and then it starts to bubble as it heats. Just continue to cook and constantly whisk.

4. Pour in the combined milk and half-and-half along with the brown sugar. Whisk immediately to combine. Add the chocolate and whisk once or twice. The chocolate will melt as the milk heats.

continues

continued

 5. Bring the uncovered mixture just to a boil, whisking occasionally to keep it from sticking to the bottom of the pan. (This takes about 10 to 12 minutes after you've added all the ingredients.)

 6. As soon as bubbles break the surface, turn down the heat to low and simmer for about 5 minutes, whisking occasionally.

7. Use pot holders to remove the pot from the heat and place it on the cooling rack. Use tongs to take out the cinnamon sticks and then ladle the champurrado into serving cups. The mixture will be very hot so let it cool slightly before drinking. If you are making it into a pudding, refrigerate for an hour before serving.

Note: Thickening and boiling times may vary depending on the brand of the masa harina and the thickness and size of the pot. Watch the mixture to be sure it doesn't burn.

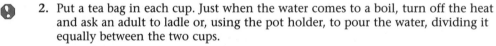

Moroccan Mint Tea

When I was a college student traveling in Morocco, we would drink this sweet, soothing tea several times a day. Our hosts poured the tea into short, thick glasses filled with sprigs of fresh mint and served it to us on large, stenciled bronze trays. Relax over a cup with a friend or your family.

How hard is this recipe? Easy

Adult help needed at the stove and pouring boiling water

Makes 2 8-ounce cups

Equipment		Ingredients
liquid measuring cup	ladle	16 ounces water
kettle or saucepan for boiling water	measuring spoons	2 herbal mint tea bags
2 tea cups	spoon	3 to 4 teaspoons sugar
pot holder		4 sprigs fresh mint

 1. Put the water in the large saucepan or the kettle and bring it to a boil over high heat.

2. Put a tea bag in each cup. Just when the water comes to a boil, turn off the heat and ask an adult to ladle or, using the pot holder, to pour the water, dividing it equally between the two cups.

3. Wait 5 minutes to let the tea steep.

4. Remove and discard the tea bag and stir 1½ to 2 teaspoons sugar into each cup. Add 2 sprigs mint per cup and serve.

Fruity Soda Pop

 Would you believe that you can make real soda pop out of fruit juice and seltzer? Try this combination or mix your own concoction by blending different juices and flavored seltzers. You'll make a delicious drink, get in some of your fruits for the day, and cut out the sugar and caffeine in bottled soda pop. You can adjust the amount of soda or juice to your own taste. (If you are making more than one glass, multiply the ingredients by the number of glasses.)

How hard is this recipe? Easy

Makes 1 drink

Equipment	Ingredients
liquid measuring cup	5 ounces fruit juice
large glass, at least 12 ounces	3 ounces lemon- or lime-flavored seltzer
spoon	2 ice cubes

1. Pour the juice into the glass. Add the seltzer and stir.
2. Add the ice cubes and serve.

Apple-Lime Spritz

 My niece, Sarah Flynn, used to make this drink after we went for summer afternoon jogs. It puts a refreshing new spin on a glass of apple juice. The lime adds a real punch to the flavor and adds eye-catching color to the glass.

How hard is this recipe? Easy

Adult help needed cutting

Makes 1 drink

Equipment		Ingredients
liquid measuring cup	cutting board	4 ounces apple juice
large glass, about 12-ounces	spoon	4 ounces seltzer
spoon	small resealable plastic bag	1 lime
serrated knife		2 ice cubes

1. Pour the apple juice into the glass. Add the seltzer and stir.
2. To remove residue or pesticides, wash and rinse the lime under lukewarm water. Dry thoroughly.
 3. Cut the lime in half, put one half in a plastic bag, seal well, and refrigerate. Cut a 1-inch wedge off the other half and set the wedge aside.
4. Squeeze the juice from the larger piece of lime into the glass and throw out the lime. Stir well.
5. Add the ice cubes, stir again, and drop in the lime wedge.

Kid Comment

Anna Wearn, 8: "This tastes like kid's champagne [bottled sparkling apple cider]. I liked it because it was bubbly. The lime put a little zest into it. I thought it tasted really good."

Anna Wearn, 8

Heads Up!

If you are concerned about residue on the limes or other fruits, wash fruits with a mild dishwashing liquid or fruit cleaner and then rinse them. Natural foods stores carry these cleaners.

Blazing Sunset

 This refreshing drink was inspired by the punches we've tasted on islands in the Caribbean. It's a refreshing cooler on hot summer afternoons, and it's a nutritious pick-me-up after-school or anytime of year. Garnish it with a slice of orange for added color and pizzazz. (If you are making more than one glass, multiply the ingredients by the number of glasses.)

How hard is this recipe? Easy

Makes 1 drink

Equipment

liquid measuring cup	cutting board
large glass, about 12-ounces	sharp knife
spoon	

Ingredients

4 ounces orange juice

4 ounces cranberry juice

pinch of nutmeg (optional)

3 ice cubes

¾-inch orange slice, slit crosswise halfway (optional)

1. Pour the orange and cranberry juices into the glass. Mix well with the spoon.

2. Stir in the nutmeg (if you are adding it). Add the ice cubes and stir again. If garnishing, push the orange slice through its slit onto the rim of the glass. Serve immediately.

Lorinda's Summer Water

 When it comes time for summer family gatherings, my friend Lorinda Moholt always makes big batches of this drink for all her children and grandchildren. Its refreshing and subtle fruity taste keeps kids coming back for more. Make a pitcher to quench your thirst on hot summer days. Garnish it with chunks of fresh fruit and eat them as you sip your drink.

How hard is this recipe? Easy

Adult help needed with cutting

Makes about 3 cups

Equipment	Ingredients
2- to 3-quart juice container or pitcher	1 teaspoon powdered, sweetened lemon-flavored iced tea mix
liquid measuring cup	6 cups water
serving spoon	2 tablespoons pink lemonade concentrate
measuring spoons	1 cup orange juice
cutting board	8 ounces lemon-flavored soda
sharp knife	5 cups ice cubes
	fresh mint for garnish
	1 cup cut-up fresh fruit

1. In a large pitcher or juice container, mix the powdered tea with the water. Add the lemonade, orange juice, and soda. Stir in the ice cubes.

 2. Pour into glasses and garnish with mint and chunks of fresh fruit.

Note: You can experiment with this punch by adding different types of juices or by using plain seltzer to vary the taste. Lorinda says the idea is to make a light drink that's bubbly with just a hint of fruity flavor.

Lemon Velvet

 When the Oregon Dairy Council introduced this smoothie at the state fair in Salem, so many people took home the recipe and made it that the city ran out of lemon yogurt! I made this with my daughter's fifth-grade class, and her classmates all agreed it was easy to make and definitely a winner.

How hard is this recipe? Easy

Adult help needed with the blender

Makes about 5 cups

Equipment	Ingredients
liquid measuring cup	1 (8-ounce) container lemon yogurt
small rubber spatula	6 ounces orange juice concentrate
blender	2½ cups low-fat or nonfat milk
measuring spoons	1 teaspoon vanilla
serving glasses	

1. Use the spatula to spoon the yogurt and orange juice into the blender.
2. Add the milk and vanilla.
3. Blend for 30 seconds on low speed.
4. Pour into glasses and serve immediately.

Variation: Add a few ice cubes and blend a little longer to make this drink into a frozen slurpie. You also can add 2 scoops vanilla frozen yogurt, blended or unblended, for a drinkable dessert.

Chapter 22

Super Soups and Salads

Recipes

➤ Pasta "Fazool"

➤ Build Your Own Potato-Corn Chowder

➤ Slurpin' Ramen Noodle Egg Drop Soup

➤ Nana's Elephant Soup

➤ Red, Green, and Orange Salad with Creamy Poppy Seed Dressing

➤ Greek Salad

➤ Terrific Trio of Salads: Tuna Fish Salad, Chicken and Grape Salad, Hard-Cooked Egg Salad

➤ Chewy Tabbouleh

➤ Sunny Day Salad

➤ Green-as-Your-Garden Salad

➤ Vinaigrette Dressing

➤ Creamy Pink Dressing

If you're looking to give your kids a safe and simple kitchen task they can call their own, get them started making salads and salad dressings. Young cooks will learn to wash and prepare greens and vegetables and to mix and measure ingredients. Not to mention how much fun they'll have shaking up the bottle of dressing and pouring the dressing on the greens. When it comes to making soups, they'll get good practice cutting up vegetables and some experience at the stove as they smell and stir the simmering soup.

Salads and soups are full of color, texture, and taste. You can add different ingredients to give kids a chance to try new foods and to experiment with new flavors.

I've included a mix of salads that our whole family has enjoyed over the years. Take off on a culinary journey with the salads from Greece and the Middle East. Get back to basics with classics like tuna, chicken, and egg salad. Discover how you can pair fruits and vegetables in dishes like carrot salad with pineapple and raisins and spinach salad with mandarin oranges and dried cranberries.

A steaming bowl of soup is among the best comfort foods I know, and you'll find plenty of good ones here. You can get creative with the Build Your Own Potato-Corn Chowder, or you can learn the magic of the egg drop in the Slurpin' Ramen Noodle Egg Drop Soup. Kids will enjoy making Nana's Elephant Soup, also. Watch as they come up with ideas for making their own homemade animal noodles. All of these dishes can be made ahead or fixed quickly on the spot.

Pasta "Fazool"

 This hearty pasta and bean soup was my dad's favorite. I can still see him sighing with contentment when he came home from work and smelled its garlic aroma. My kids must have their grandpa's genes because they do the same when a pot of this Italian comfort food is simmering on the stove. The kids also like the ring of the name— pronounced Pasta Fah-ZOOL. It's in our southern Italian dialect for Pasta e Fagioli (meaning pasta and beans). Although you'll see many versions with more vegetables and even the Italian bacon, pancetta, ours is a simple soup, easy for kids to make. I've even written the recipe so kids smash the garlic with a can and don't have to use a knife.

How hard is this recipe? Easy

Adult help needed at the stove, with can opener, and ladling hot soup

Makes 9½ cups

Equipment

cutting board	timer	pot holder
waxed paper	can opener	ladle
5-quart saucepan with lid	dry measuring cups	4 soup bowls
measuring spoons	wooden spoon	

Ingredients

2 large cloves garlic

2 tablespoons good-quality extra-virgin olive oil

1 (14½-ounce) can premium diced, peeled tomatoes in juice (unopened)

1 (48-ounce) can fat-free chicken broth

2 cups ditalini or ditali pasta or another short tube pasta, such as elbows

1 (15½-ounce) can chick peas

4 tablespoons Parmesan cheese

1. Place the garlic cloves on a cutting board and cover them with waxed paper. Clean the bottom of the tomato can and then smash the garlic cloves on the cutting board. Remove the papery skins from the garlic.

2. Heat the oil in the pot over medium-high heat for 2 minutes, add the garlic, and cook for 2 minutes.

3. Add the tomatoes and cook until small bubbles form and then continue to simmer for 3 minutes.

4. Pour in the chicken broth, pasta, and chick peas with their juice. Stir with the wooden spoon. Cover the pot and let the soup simmer for 30 to 35 minutes, stirring occasionally so the pasta doesn't stick to the pan. The soup is done when the flavors come together and the pasta is tender.

5. Remove the garlic cloves and ladle the soup into bowls. Serve hot and sprinkle a tablespoon of Parmesan cheese in each bowl.

6. Serve immediately.

Variation: For a slightly creamier soup, substitute 1 (19-ounce) can cannellini beans (Italian white beans) for the chick peas.

Kid Comment

Julia Cooke, 15: "This is a great soup on a cold day. The flavor is really good and comforting."

Kid Quiz

What are chick peas?

Chick peas are beans with a nutlike flavor. They are slightly larger than regular peas, tannish-yellow in color, and round but irregularly shaped. You'll also see them called garbanzo and ceci beans. These beans are used in Italian food, such as the Pasta "Fazool" soup, and in other Mediterranean, Indian, and Middle Eastern dishes. They are often added to greens in salads. Next time you go to a salad bar in a restaurant, look for these beans.

Build Your Own Potato-Corn Chowder

This soup is so much fun to eat because you can have it piping hot by itself or you can build it up with your favorite toppings. It's kind of like layering your favorite garnishes on chili or baked potatoes.

How hard is this? Intermediate

Adult help needed with cutting, using can opener, at the stove, and ladling hot soup

Makes 8 cups

Equipment

cutting board	dry measuring cups
sharp knife	liquid measuring cup
5½-quart pot or Dutch oven	pot holders
measuring spoons	ladle
wooden spoon	serving bowls
timer	serving bowls and spoons for toppings
can opener	

Ingredients

6 medium Yukon Gold potatoes (about 2½ pounds)	3½ cups chicken broth
1 medium onion, peeled and diced	2 teaspoons seasoning salt
1 tablespoon canola oil	2 cups frozen sweet corn
1 tablespoon unsalted butter	2 cups whole milk or half-and-half
	⅛ teaspoon black pepper

toppings

bits of ham or bacon	diced avocados
any kind of shredded cheese	shredded vegetables like zucchini, spinach, and carrots
crumbled blue cheese	tomatoes
sour cream	crunchy croutons
baby peas	chopped fresh herbs

1. Clean the potatoes but do not peel. Coarsely chop into bite-size pieces.

2. Put the oil and butter in the pot over medium heat until the butter is melted. Add the onions, use the wooden spoon to stir to coat them, and cook for 5 minutes. The onions should turn golden and should look shiny.

3. Add the potatoes and stir to coat them with the oil and onions. Stir in the chicken broth and seasoning salt.

4. Turn the heat down to medium-low and let the soup simmer until the potatoes are tender. This should take about 20 minutes. You can tell the potatoes are ready if you can mash them easily against the side of the pan.

5. Add the corn, milk, and black pepper. Mash one or two potato chunks against the side of the pan and stir them into the soup to add some texture. Cook until the soup simmers. This should take about 10 minutes.

6. Ladle the soup into bowls and serve it hot with toppings.

Note: Yukon Gold potatoes give this soup a rich flavor. If you can't find them, however, you can use red or white potatoes or the small red new potatoes. Just cut them into chunks. Do not use a russet or Idaho potato. These are baking potatoes, and they will break up in the soup.

Kid Comment

Kayla Kirk, 10: "This was a good soup. We tossed in some ham. I had fun cutting up the ingredients. It was fun having a choice about what to put into the soup." Kayla's family ate this soup for dinner with Morning Maple Syrup Corn Muffins (see Chapter 20, "Breakfast Bonanzas") and liked the combination.

Slurpin' Ramen Noodle Egg Drop Soup

Next time you pull out a package of ramen noodles, try making it with chicken broth and drizzling in a beaten egg. Watch what happens as the egg cooks in the soup. This quick and easy soup is as much fun to make as it is to eat. You're guaranteed to want to cook it over and over again, just like our testers did, to watch the magic of the egg drop.

How hard is this recipe? Easy

Adult help needed using can opener, at the stove, and ladling hot soup

Makes 3 cups

Equipment

liquid measuring cup	pot holder
small whisk	ladle
can opener	soup bowls
3-quart saucepan	cutting board
timer	sharp knife
wooden spoon	

Ingredients

1 large egg	salt and pepper to taste
3 cups fat-free chicken broth	fresh minced parsley for garnish
1 (3-ounce) package ramen noodles	

1. Crack the egg into the liquid measuring cup and whisk it to blend the yellow and white. (The handled cup will make it easier to pour the egg into the hot soup.)
2. In the saucepan, bring the chicken broth to a boil over medium-high heat.
3. Break the noodle cake in half with your hands, add it to the broth, and lower the heat to medium. If noodle package contained a seasoning pack, add the contents of the pack if you want. Cook for 4 minutes, stirring occasionally with the wooden spoon to separate the noodles.
4. Turn off the heat. Add the salt and pepper. Slowly drizzle a thin stream of the beaten egg into the soup in a circular motion like a whirlpool. Watch how the egg turns into white and yellow strands on the surface of the soup. Lightly stir with the spoon in a circle.
5. Ladle the soup into the bowls. Sprinkle some parsley over the soup.
6. Serve immediately.

Kid Comment

Mary Bishop, 6: "This is DEEEEElicious. My favorite part was eating it. My favorite part of making it was stirring in the egg and watching it cook." Mary's dad, John, who never eats any packaged soup, sat down with her and ate a whole bowl. "That was really good!" he said.

Kid Quiz

What's egg drop soup?

Egg drop soup is a soup in which a beaten egg is "dropped" or poured in a thin stream into the soup. The egg floats to the surface, and the hot liquid cooks the egg into thin strands and clumps.

Nana's Elephant Soup

My friend Lorinda Moholt made this homemade chicken noodle soup for lunch with her 3-year-old grandson, Austin, during his weekly visit to her home. It became an instant favorite. They rolled out the egg dough, pressed it with an elephant cookie cutter, and dropped the dough into a pot of hot broth to cook. They even went out to the garden to pick fresh chives to sprinkle in the soup to feed the elephants. Try making this soup as is or use your favorite animal cookie cutters to make an animal zoo soup. Use fresh herbs as "grass" for the animals.

How hard is this recipe? Intermediate

Adult help needed with cutting herbs, working and cutting the dough, using can opener, at the stove, and ladling hot soup

Serves 4

continues

continued

Equipment

dry measuring cups	paper towels	can opener
measuring spoons	cutting board	3-quart saucepan
medium mixing bowl	sharp knife	pot holder
wooden spoon	rolling pin	ladle
timer	3- to 5-inch elephant cookie cutter	soup bowls

Ingredients

1 large egg	1 teaspoon fresh chives or parsley
1 cup all-purpose flour plus extra for dusting	1 (48-ounce) can fat-free chicken broth
2 tablespoons 2-percent or whole milk	1 cup diced cooked chicken pieces (optional)
⅛ teaspoon salt	

1. Make a soft dough by mixing the egg, flour, milk, and salt in the mixing bowl with the wooden spoon. Let the dough rest, uncovered, for 15 minutes.

2. Meanwhile, rinse the chives or parsley under running water, pat them dry with the paper towels, and chop them into small pieces. Set them aside.

3. On a flat, floured surface, roll out the dough with a floured rolling pin to ¼-inch thickness. The dough will be very stiff. Use the cookie cutter to press out elephant shapes. Gather together any scraps as you go along and reroll so you can press with the cutter again.

4. In the saucepan, bring the chicken broth to a simmer over medium heat. Drop in the chicken and noodles and simmer for 7 minutes or until noodles are tender to the bite.

5. Ladle the soup into bowls and sprinkle with ¼ teaspoon chives or parsley.

6. Serve immediately. (If the elephants are big, cut them with your spoon as you eat the soup.)

Variation: Use other cookie cutters or cut the flat dough with a pizza wheel into long strips or different shapes.

You can make the dough as thick or thin as you like.

Adjust cooking time, if necessary, to size of the noodles.

Austin Moholt-Siebert, 3

Kid Comment

Austin Moholt-Siebert, 3: "I liked the trunk best. I ate it in one big bite." His nana was thrilled with this fun cooking project: "I re-member making noodles with my grandmother. Now it is my turn and I am delighted."

Salads

Red, Green, and Orange Salad with Creamy Poppy Seed Dressing

Whenever we can, we include fruits and vegetables in our salads. This colorful salad uses tender baby spinach leaves in place of lettuce and gives you a nutritional boost with oranges and dried cranberries. The juicy citrus and sweet, dried fruit combine with the creamy poppy seed dressing for a refreshing and flavorful blend. Kids will enjoy putting the greens on the plate, arranging the oranges on top, and then sprinkling on the cranberries.

How hard are these recipes? Easy

Adult help needed with the can opener and blender

Serves 4

Equipment

large salad bowl	blender
dry measuring cups	small jar or salad cruet
can opener	rubber spatula
measuring spoons	salad fork and spoon
liquid measuring cup	salad plates

Ingredients

8 ounces prewashed baby spinach leaves

1 (11-ounce) can mandarin oranges

4 teaspoons sweetened, dried cranberries

continues

continued

1. In the salad bowl, mix the spinach, oranges, and cranberries.
2. Dress with poppy seed dressing (the recipe follows). Toss lightly to prevent the oranges from breaking up.
3. Serve immediately.

Creamy Poppy Seed Dressing

Makes about 1¼ cups

1 cup canola or other vegetable oil

¼ cup sugar

1 teaspoon dry mustard

¼–½ teaspoon salt to taste

⅓ cup rice wine or white vinegar

2 teaspoons poppy seeds

1. Put the oil in a liquid measuring cup so it's easy to pour.
2. Place the sugar, mustard, salt, and vinegar in a blender and mix on low speed for 10 seconds, just to combine the ingredients.
3. Open the pour hole of the blender, turn the blender to low speed, and very slowly drizzle in the oil. (The dressing will start to get cloudy and thick.) Add the poppy seeds and blend just until combined with the dressing.
4. Pour the dressing into a small jar or salad cruet, scraping down the sides of the blender with a spatula.
5. Serve immediately or refrigerate for later use.

Kid Comment

William Bishop, 3: "These are my favorite things [mandarin oranges and cranberries]." William liked opening the can of oranges and sprinkling the cranberries on the salad. His mom, Suzanne, said he and his siblings "loved putting the salad together. It was a lot of fun."

Greek Salad

 This simple fruit and vegetable salad has a crisp, fresh taste with lots of flavor from the tangy, white Greek cheese (called feta) and the purple-black olives. Our friend Demetra Ariston frequently makes it with her kids. It reminds them of salads they have when they visit their relatives in Greece. This salad is colorful and offers kids lots of practice cutting vegetables.

How hard is this recipe? Easy/Intermediate

Adult help needed with peeling and cutting

Serves 4

Equipment

cutting board	measuring spoons	4 serving plates
paring knife	large salad bowl	2 salad cruets
vegetable peeler	salad fork and spoon	

Ingredients

½ red bell pepper, seeded and cut into lengthwise strips

½ green bell pepper, seeded and cut into lengthwise strips

1 small red onion, peeled, halved, and cut into semicircles

1 large cucumber, peeled, cut in half and seeded, and chopped into semicircles

3 medium tomatoes, cut into wedges

10 pitted kalamata olives

3 ounces feta cheese, crumbled

2 tablespoons minced parsley

cruet of extra-virgin olive oil

cruet of red wine vinegar

salt and pepper to taste

1. In the large salad bowl, combine all the ingredients except the oil, vinegar, salt, and pepper. Toss well to mix.

2. Bring the salad bowl, cruets, salt, and pepper to the table. Serve the salad family style and let each person dress his or her own individual salad to taste. Use about the same amount of dressing as you would for a regular green salad.

continues

Kid Comment

Lucy McVicker, 14: "This salad looks pretty." Lucy never had this combination of vegetables and lettuce before. Her favorite parts of the salad were the lettuce, olives, and cucumbers. Her mom, Yolanda, thought the salad of–fered a good presentation of dif–ferent ingredients.

Lucy McVicker, 14

Kid Quiz

Do you know what it means to eat "family style"?

Dining "family style" means you serve food from large platters right at the table, like the recipe says to do with this Greek salad. This kind of dining has a wonderful way of bring–ing together everyone sitting around the table as you share the experience of dishing out the food and passing around plates. Next time you eat with your family, try eating family style and volunteer to take responsibility for serving one of the dishes.

Heads Up!

Some food-safety officials have warned that certain fresh cheeses, like feta, should not be eaten by people at risk for food-borne illness. People at risk include pregnant women, infants and toddlers, senior adults, and people who are seriously ill. If you are in any of these risk groups, be sure to check current food-safety advisories before eating feta cheese.

Terrific Trio of Salads

You can't go wrong if you know how to make any of these salads. Serve them as the center of a mixed green salad garnished with tomatoes, cucumbers, and other chopped vegetables. You can also spread them between bread to make a sandwich or on crackers for a snack. You can vary the taste of each salad by adding fruits, such as diced apples, by mixing in fresh or dried herbs and seasonings, such as curry powder, or by garnishing them with chopped nuts.

Tuna Fish Salad

 This salad is a regular in lunch boxes across the country. Once you learn how to make it, you can fix your own lunch or use it for making tuna melts on English muffins. (You can find that recipe in Chapter 25, "Mealtime Magic.")

How hard is this recipe?

Adult help needed with cutting and using the can opener

Makes 2 sandwiches or small salads

Equipment

can opener	sharp knife
fork	measuring spoons
small mixing bowl	serving spoon
cutting board	serving plates

Ingredients

1 (6-ounce) can solid white tuna, packed in water

1 stalk celery, finely diced (about ⅓ cup)

3 tablespoons low-fat or regular mayonnaise

1 tablespoon lemon juice

⅛ teaspoon salt (optional)

continued

1. Open the can of tuna, drain the water, and place the tuna into the mixing bowl. Mash lightly with the fork. Add the celery, mayonnaise, lemon juice, and salt (if desired). Stir until well mixed.

2. Spread the mixture between pita or other sandwich bread or serve it as a salad. Serve immediately or cover and refrigerate.

Chicken and Grape Salad

The green grapes give this salad great color and add a sweet and juicy flavor. Toss in some nuts, if you like, for added crunch and flavor.

How hard is this recipe? Easy

Adult help needed with cutting and using the can opener

Makes 1½ cups salad

Equipment	Ingredients
can opener	1 (10-ounce) can premium chunk white chicken in water
fork	1 stalk celery, finely diced (about ⅓ cup)
small mixing bowl	3 tablespoons low-fat or regular mayonnaise
cutting board	14 green grapes, sliced lengthwise in half
sharp knife	1 tablespoon lemon juice
measuring spoons	¼ teaspoon salt
serving spoon	
serving plates	

1. Open the can of chicken, drain the water, and place the chicken into the mixing bowl. Mash the chicken with the fork. (It will become shredded.)

2. Add the celery, mayonnaise, grapes, lemon juice, and salt and mix well.

3. Spread the mixture on bread or crackers or serve it alone as a salad. Serve immediately or cover and refrigerate.

Note: You can make this salad using 6 to 10 ounces of cooked boneless chicken breasts, shredded or cut into chunks.

Hard-Cooked Egg Salad

Egg salad on toasted or soft white bread with some lettuce is a classic American sandwich. We like to add some curry powder to the egg salad for a change of pace.

How hard is this recipe? Easy

Adult help needed with cutting and at the stove

Makes 1 cup

Equipment	Ingredients
egg slicer (optional)	3 hard-cooked eggs, peeled and sliced (the recipe follows)
cutting board	
sharp knife	1 stalk celery, finely diced (about ⅓ cup)
small mixing bowl	3 tablespoons low-fat or regular mayonnaise
fork	1 teaspoon Dijon-style mustard
measuring spoons	⅛ teaspoon salt
serving spoon	¼ teaspoon curry powder (if desired)
serving plates	

 1. Slice the eggs with a knife or in the egg slicer. Place the eggs in the mixing bowl and mash them with a fork to break the whites into pieces and blend in the yolk.

2. Add the celery, mayonnaise, mustard, salt, and curry powder, if desired. Mix well with the fork to blend. Spread the mixture on bread or crackers or serve it as a salad. Serve immediately or cover and refrigerate.

Heads Up!

Alfalfa sprouts have joined the list of potentially unsafe foods to eat, according to health officials. Sprouts have been found to be contaminated with both salmonella and *E. coli* bacteria. Until the source of contamination can be determined, health officials are advising people in high-risk groups to avoid sprouts. These people include pregnant women, infants and toddlers, senior adults, and the seriously ill.

How to Hard Cook and Peel an Egg

Adult help needed at the stove

1. Put the eggs in a single layer in a sauce pan just large enough to hold the eggs. Fill the pan with water to about an inch above the top of the eggs. Cover the pan, place it over high heat, and bring the water quickly to a boil.

 2. Just as the water boils, use a pot holder to remove the pan of eggs from the heat to prevent further boiling. Let the pan stand, covered, for 15 minutes for large eggs. (For each size larger or smaller, adjust the time up or down about 3 minutes for each size.)

continues

continued

3. Meanwhile, place a colander in the sink under the faucet. When the eggs are ready, drain the water and eggs into the colander. Immediately run cold water over the eggs or place them in a bowl of water with ice.

4. When the eggs are cold, crack the shells by tapping the eggs gently on all sides against a flat surface. Loosen the shell by rolling the eggs between the palms of your hands. Peel the shell, starting at the large end of the egg, under cool running water. Grasping the filmy membrane beneath the shell as you peel makes it easier to remove the shell.

Bigger Bites

Want to know more about how you store, cook, and use eggs? Send away for free recipes and pamphlets to the American Egg Board or log on to the Web site at www.aeb.org to consult the *Eggcyclopedia*. Check Appendix B, "The Resource Guide," at the back of this book for further details.

Chewy Tabbouleh

Try eating this Middle Eastern bulgur wheat salad (pronounced tuh-BOO-luh) the traditional way. Just scoop it up with a romaine lettuce leaf and eat the leaf along with the salad. Romaine leaves are long and crispy, so they make the perfect scoopers. Ours is only one of many versions of this popular salad. Some have mostly parsley; others include cucumbers, red onions, or even a crumbly cheese called feta. My kids like the way our version balances the mint and parsley with the chewiness of the grains. What do you think?

How hard is this recipe? Easy

Adult help needed with chopping and at the stove

Makes 3½ cups

Equipment

liquid measuring cup	large strainer	small sharp knife
1-quart saucepan	pot holder	measuring spoons
lemon reamer or juicer	plate large enough to cover bowl	mixing spoon
small strainer	timer	plastic wrap
small cup	kitchen towel	small serving platter
dry measuring cups	cutting board	serving plates
large bowl		

Ingredients

2 cups water	1 small bunch mint (about 1 cup leaves), chopped
¼ cup extra-virgin olive oil	2 tablespoons chopped scallion (about 1 scallion) if desired
¼ cup fresh lemon juice (about that of 1 large lemon)	1 medium tomato, cut into wedges and then diced
1 cup fine-grained bulgur	⅛ teaspoon salt
1 cup parsley leaves, chopped	1 head romaine lettuce, leaves washed and separated

1. Fill a saucepan with the water and bring it to a boil over medium-high heat. Meanwhile, mix the oil and lemon juice in the liquid measuring cup.

2. Place the bulgur in the bowl, rinse it under running water, and strain it. Return the bulgur to the bowl. Use the pot holder to pour the boiling water over the bulgur to cover it. Turn a plate upside down and cover the bowl. Let it stand for 20 to 30 minutes or until the bulgur has softened and is tender.

3. Drain the bulgur in the strainer and shake it to remove extra water. Rinse and dry the bowl. Return the wheat to the bowl and add the parsley, mint, scallion, tomato, and salt. Stir to mix.

4. Drizzle the olive oil–lemon juice mixture over the salad and toss well to coat all the ingredients.

5. Cover the salad with plastic wrap and refrigerate it until chilled before serving. To serve, scoop the salad onto the center of a platter and surround it with the lettuce leaves.

Note: This salad tastes even better the next day after the flavors have had a chance to meld together. Make it the day before for an after-school snack or serve it as a side dish at dinner.

Kid Comment

Sammi McVicker, 8: "This is good. I like the flavor. You get to do chopping to make this salad." Her mom, Yolanda, noted that her kids were surprised by this ethnic recipe. "It's not macaroni and cheese. You're stretching the envelope for the kids and I like that," she said.

Sammi McVicker, 8

Learn the Lingo

Bulgur consists of wheat kernels that are first steamed, and then dried and crushed. Don't confuse this with cracked wheat, which has not been cooked. Bulgur (also spelled bulghur, bulgar and burghul) is a staple in the Middle East and has a chewy, tender texture. You can find bulgur with fine, medium, and course grains. Bulgur provides you with fiber, protein, complex carbohydrates, iron, calcium, niacin, and vitamins. You can buy bulgur in natural foods stores, in some large supermarkets, and in Middle Eastern stores.

Sunny Day Salad

This was one of the first salads I learned to make, and the bright orange and yellow have always reminded me of a sunny day. I like the slight crunch from the carrots combined with the juiciness of the pineapple and the sweetness of the raisins. This salad is always a family favorite at picnics and summertime gatherings because it's so easy to make. It always tastes as fresh and refreshing as it looks.

How hard is this salad? Easy

Adult help needed using grater and can opener

Serves 4

Equipment

grater or food processor with
    shredding disk
medium mixing bowl
dry measuring cups
can opener

measuring spoons
mixing spoons
serving plates
plastic wrap

Ingredients

4 medium carrots, shredded
    (about 2 cups shredded)
1 (8-ounce) can pineapple
    tidbits, drained

⅓ cup raisins
4 tablespoons reduced-fat mayonnaise

1. Combine the carrots, pineapple, raisins, and mayonnaise in the mixing bowl. Toss them well to distribute the dressing. The salad will get juicier as you toss the ingredients and as it sits.

2. Serve immediately at room temperature or cover and refrigerate to chill before serving.

Green-as-Your Garden Salad

In the summertime, we go to the farmers' market every week to select different kinds of lettuce to put in our salads. Some give a crunchier texture; others are softer and more buttery. We can make our salad colorful, too, by choosing leaves that are red or various shades of green.

Once you know how to make a basic green salad, you can get creative. Add some cherry tomatoes, cucumbers or radishes, chunks of cheese, or chopped nuts. Dried fruits, such as cranberries and apricots, or fresh fruits, such as oranges and grapes, add color, flavor, and texture. Try sprinkling your salad with beans, such as chick peas, to give yourself a protein boost.

How hard is this recipe? Easy

Makes 4 cups

continues

continued

Equipment

large pot or salad spinner

colander

paper towels or 2 clean kitchen towels

dry measuring cups

large salad bowl

salad forks

serving plates

Ingredients

3 to 4 different heads of lettuce to make 4 cups of salad greens

1. Fill a large pot with cool water. Set it in the sink.

2. Take each head of lettuce and remove and discard any bruised outside leaves. Pull several leaves off each head and place them in the pot of water. Use your clean hands to gently swish the leaves in the water. This will remove any dirt and sand. If the lettuce is very dirty, dump out the water, and put in fresh water to rinse again.

3. Set the colander in the sink and pour the water and the leaves from the pot into it. Lift up and shake the colander to remove excess water.

4. Place the kitchen towels or paper towels on a clean counter and put the leaves on them. Pat them dry. (If the leaves are wet, the salad dressing won't stick to them, and the water will make a big puddle in the bowl.) You can also just wash and dry the leaves right in the salad spinner.

5. Tear the leaves into bite-size pieces. Measure about 4 cups of leaves and put them in the salad bowl. Just before serving, pour the dressing on the salad and toss. (The leaves will get soggy if they sit in the dressing too long.)

6. Wrap up the remaining leaves and heads of lettuce in paper towels, put them in plastic bags, tie the bags, and store them in the refrigerator for later use.

Kitchen Clue

Dressings, toppings, and color are what attract young eaters to salad. For a no-cook and fun dinner, set up a salad bar and let your kids create their own meal. They'll like having the power to choose their own food and layering it on the plate. When you offer different choices, you encourage them to experiment with new flavors.

Set out plates buffet style and start with a big bowl of washed greens or tender baby spinach. Set out smaller bowls with bite-size vegetables, such as carrots, sliced artichokes, and broccoli florets; protein sources, such as beans, cheese, sliced meats, or hard-cooked eggs; and toppings, such as croutons, chopped nuts, dried fruits, and raisins. Offer a variety of dressings. Everyone gets a plate and fills it up, just like in a restaurant. This is a great meal in the summer when it's too hot to cook.

Vinaigrette Dressing

When you mix oil and vinegar together for a salad dressing, you make a classic French dressing called a *vinaigrette*. The oil in the dressing balances the acid in the vinegar. You'll see different proportions of oil to vinegar in recipes, but a classic ratio is 1 part vinegar to 3 parts oil. We like to add Dijon-style mustard, garlic, and dried herbs to give our dressing added flavor. Use these basic proportions and experiment with different flavored vinegars or oils to vary the taste. If your vinegar is particularly strong, add a little water to the dressing.

How hard is this recipe? Easy

Makes 1 cup

Equipment

liquid measuring cup   garlic press   salad cruet or jar with lid
measuring spoons   whisk

Ingredients

¼ cup red wine vinegar   1 small clove garlic, pressed
¾ cup extra-virgin olive oil   ¼ teaspoon dried fine herbs or Italian seasoning
1 to 2 teaspoons Dijon-style   ¼ teaspoon salt
     mustard   black pepper to taste

Combine all the ingredients in a liquid measuring cup and whisk vigorously. You also can combine the ingredients in a jar, cover the jar, and shake vigorously.

Learn the Lingo

Vinaigrette is the French word for a savory sauce or salad dressing used on salads and cold vegetables, meats, and fish. The most basic dressing includes oil, vinegar, salt, and pepper. Some versions can include shallots, garlic, mustard, onion, herbs, and other spices.

Creamy Pink Dressing

This simple dressing has few ingredients and is very versatile. Use it on salads, fruits (such as avocados), or meats and fish.

How hard is this recipe? Easy

Makes 2 cups

Equipment

small mixing bowl	measuring spoon
liquid measuring cup	whisk
dry measuring cups	plastic wrap

Ingredients

1 cup ketchup	dash Worcestershire sauce
1 cup mayonnaise	⅛ teaspoon salt

1. In a small mixing bowl, whisk together the ketchup, mayonnaise, Worcestershire sauce, and salt until well-blended.
2. Cover the bowl with plastic wrap and refrigerate until ready to use.

Kid Quiz

Do you know what Worcestershire sauce is and can you pronounce the word?

Sold in supermarkets, this sauce is very thin and dark and is used as a seasoning. It got its tongue-twisting name because it was originally bottled in Worcester, England, where words are pronounced differently than in the United States. Some of the ingredients in the sauce include vinegar, garlic, soy sauce, onions, molasses, lime, anchovies, and tamarind. Next time you're in the supermarket, see if you can find it. It's pronounced WOOS-thur-shir sauce.

Chapter 23

Let's Wrap and Roll

Recipes

➤ Sandwich Spirals

➤ Chicken Fajitas

➤ Helen Hazen's Sweet Crêpes

➤ Fresh Vietnamese-Style Spring Rolls

All around the world, cultures wrap and roll foods as a way to enclose ingredients. These foods often are eaten with your hands, which can be lots of fun for kids and adults alike. Whether you're making exotic fresh Vietnamese-style spring rolls or a big favorite—fajitas—wrapping your food is an adventurous way to cook and eat.

The recipes in this section include many of my family's favorites. Kids will enjoy an easy introduction to the art of rolling by making lunch time spiral sandwiches or by wrapping dinnertime fajitas.

I've found, and our testers have confirmed, that the key to making more involved dishes is to be organized. The Maletis family, for instance, had never attempted spring rolls. When they made them, however, they were pleasantly surprised to find them easy and doable because they read and understood the directions first. Be sure to assemble all your ingredients before you start to wrap. Then go ahead and have fun wrapping and eating. Welcome to the world of wrapped food!

Sandwich Spirals

 Wrapping different fillings in bread that has been pressed flat and then rolled gives a new twist to a lunch time favorite. When you cut the roll into small rounds, the fillings make colorful bite-size spirals. Try your favorite sandwich spreads or thinly sliced lunch meats for these sandwich rolls. They're also great for picnics, snacks, or tea parties.

How hard is this recipe? Easy

Makes 8 spiral bites

Equipment	Ingredients
cutting board	2 slices white or whole wheat sandwich bread
rolling pin	2 tablespoons peanut butter or cream cheese
3 table knives	2 tablespoons jelly
measuring spoons	
serving plate	

1. Place a slice of bread on the cutting board and use the rolling pin to roll over and flatten the bread. Slice off the crusts with the table knife.
2. Spread the peanut butter or cream cheese on the slice and cover it with the jelly. Leave ½-inch empty space at the edge of the bread to allow the filling to spread.
3. Start at the bottom end and tightly roll the piece of bread to the top. Press the end seam to secure.
4. Slice the bread roll into 4 crosswise rounds. Use your fingers to reshape the rounds. Place them flat side down on a plate.
5. Repeat with the remaining bread slice and fillings.

Variations: Fill the sandwiches with honey or orange butter, cheese spread, finely mashed tuna salad, or finely sliced deli meats spread with your favorite dressing, such as mayonnaise or mustard.

Chicken Fajitas

Fajitas are the ultimate quick-and-easy, wrap-and-roll meal. Stir-fried chicken or beef can be combined with colorful red and green bell peppers and onions and then wrapped in a warm tortilla. Top the fajitas with salsa and sour cream if you like. Serve this as a fix-it-yourself, family-style meal by putting the meat and vegetables on a large platter and the warm tortillas in a covered dish. You then can just pass both around.

How hard is this recipe? Easy

Adult help needed with cutting and at the stove and oven

Serves 4

Equipment

paper towels

aluminum foil

timer

cutting board

sharp knife

10-inch nonstick skillet or stir-fry pan

measuring spoons

wooden spoon or stir-fry utensil

2 large bowls for meat and vegetables

pot holder

large serving platter

microwave-safe plate (if using microwave)

covered dish for warm tortillas

4 dinner plates

serving spoons

Ingredients

8 large flour tortillas

3 tablespoons vegetable oil, divided

1 medium onion, sliced lengthwise

1 red bell pepper, sliced lengthwise into strips

1 green bell pepper, sliced lengthwise into strips

1¼ pounds chicken or beef, cut into strips

1 tablespoon chili powder or Mexican seasonings

salt and pepper to taste

1. If you are heating tortillas in the oven, position the rack in the center of the oven and preheat the oven to 350 degrees F. Stack the tortillas and wrap them in damp paper towels. Wrap them again in aluminum foil and heat them in the oven for 10 minutes. If you are heating tortillas in the microwave, wrap them in damp towels but not in foil and then set them aside.

2. In the skillet, heat 2 tablespoons of oil over medium-high heat for 2 minutes. Turn the heat to high and stir-fry the onions and peppers for 4 minutes, continually tossing with a wooden spoon or stir-fry tool. When cooked, transfer the vegetables to one of the large bowls.

3. Add 1 tablespoon oil and stir-fry the meat for 3 to 5 minutes or until the inside is no longer pink. Add the vegetables; sprinkle with the chili powder or Mexican seasonings, salt, and pepper; and toss to combine. Use the pot holder to grasp the handle and remove the meat from the heat to the serving platter.

4. If you are heating tortillas in the microwave, heat them on a microwave-safe plate for 30 to 45 seconds. Unwrap the tortillas, from either the microwave or the oven, and place them in a covered serving dish or a tortilla basket with a lid.

5. Serve immediately. Each person takes a tortilla and spoons a small amount of the meat and vegetables into the center. Fold both ends of the tortilla over the filling, roll, and eat by hand.

Build your own tortilla: You can eat tortillas plain or topped with a spoonful of tomato salsa, low-fat sour cream or yogurt, or guacamole.

Kid Comment

John Maletis, 12: "This is a good quick dinner on soccer, tennis, or track nights. You get good protein for energy; it's quick to make, eat, and clean up!"

Helen Hazen's Sweet Crêpes

Our friend Helen Hazen used to serve these easy-to-make blender crêpes in her French restaurant and bistro in Portland. She and her daughter, Inga, make them often for breakfast or dinner. Crêpes are delicious and are filled with sweet ingredients or savory foods, such as grated cheese and vegetables. You can eat them for dessert, as an appetizer, or as a whole meal. Just spread the fillings on the surface of the crêpes; fold, wrap, or roll them up; and they're ready to eat. Inga helps her mom put ingredients into the blender and strains the batter. She can even flip the crêpes on the griddle. Making the crêpes can be tricky, but you'll get better with practice.

How hard is this recipe? Intermediate

Adult help needed at the blender or food processor, stove, and flipping crepes

Makes 25 to 30 crêpes, depending on pan size

Equipment

small bowl

electric blender or food processor

liquid measuring cup

dry measuring cups

measuring spoons

rubber spatula

strainer

small pitcher or 4-cup liquid measuring cup

plastic wrap

timer

paper towels

6- to 8-inch heavy skillet, griddle, or crêpe pan, preferably nonstick

pot holder

metal or plastic spatula

serving platter

waxed paper

resealable plastic bag (for storing crêpes)

Ingredients

4 large eggs

2 cups whole milk

1 tablespoon sugar

2 cups all-purpose flour

1 teaspoon vanilla

salad oil for greasing the pan

Sweet Crêpe Fillings

sliced fresh fruits and berries

jams and preserves

granulated sugar

cream cheese with orange zest and confectioners' sugar

chocolate hazelnut spread

ice cream with chocolate sauce and sliced strawberries

blueberries and whipped cream

honey butter (see the recipe in Chapter 29, "The Baker's Rack")

1. Crack the eggs into a bowl and then put them in the container of the blender or food processor. Add the milk, sugar, flour, and vanilla. Blend on low speed until the ingredients are thoroughly mixed and the batter is smooth. Scrape down the sides of the blender with the rubber spatula. The batter should be the consistency of heavy cream. Add water or flour to thin or thicken the batter if necessary.

2. Pour the batter through a strainer into the small pitcher or 4-cup liquid measuring cup. If possible, refrigerate the batter, covered with plastic wrap, for 60 minutes.

3. Moisten a paper towel with salad oil and wipe the pan lightly with the oiled towel. Heat the pan over medium-high heat for several minutes or until a drop of water sizzles on pan's surface.

4. Pour a small amount of batter onto one end of the skillet. Use a pot holder to very quickly lift and tilt the pan to spread the batter to coat the pan's surface. This can be tricky, but you'll get better as you go along. You want a thin coat of batter in the pan.

5. Cook the batter until the edges and the surface start to get dry. The edges will begin to curl. When the underside of the crêpe is golden, hold the pan with the pot holder and use the metal or plastic spatula to gently get under the crêpe and flip it. Cook about 1 minute and then invert the pan over the serving platter and slide out the crêpe.

6. Repeat until all the batter is gone. Stack the crêpes on top of one another and cover with paper towels to keep them warm. Rub the pan with more oil if necessary.

7. Serve the crêpes with filling ingredients or store them in the refrigerator or freezer for later use.

Note: If you're filling the crêpes with savory foods like cheese or vegetables, eliminate the sugar and vanilla when making the batter. To store crêpes, separate them with individual sheets of waxed paper before stacking. Store them in a resealable plastic bag in the refrigerator for up to 2 days or in the freezer for up to 1 month.

Kid Comment

Inga Hazen, 11: "I love eating these crêpes with just sugar on them. I like the way they taste in the morning or anytime. The best thing about them is that me and my mom do them together."

Inga's mom, Helen, says: "I've been making these crêpes and eating them for 25 years, and I still love them!" Her favorite way to eat them is to sprinkle granulated sugar on the top while the crêpe is cooking. Do not flip the crêpe; instead, let the top dry out and the sugar caramelize.

Inga Hazen, 11

Kitchen Clue

The thickness of your fillings and the size of your crêpe will determine how you wrap or roll the crêpe.

Dessert crêpes, smeared with a thin layer of jam, cream cheese, or chocolate spread, can be rolled like a cigar and then dusted with confectioners' sugar. Eat them with a fork or your hands.

For thicker fillings, fold the crêpe over the filling about a third of the way up from the bottom and then fold in the two outer sides like a cone.

Fresh Vietnamese-Style Spring Rolls

If you've never had these fresh vegetable rolls, you're in for a treat. Fresh salad ingredients are wrapped in thin, transparent rice papers and then are drizzled or dipped with sauce for a refreshing combination of tastes and textures. The whole family can help prepare the ingredients and then fill and wrap their own rolls. My version of these rolls features some of our favorite fillings. But you can use any thinly sliced vegetables or cooked meats or shrimp to fill the wrappers.

The rice papers are fragile to work with at first, but once you get the hang of wrapping and rolling them, you'll be a pro. The key is to be organized and to work methodically with the ingredients set out, assembly-line style, in front of you.

How hard is this recipe? Intermediate

Adult help needed with the grater and cutting, at the stove, and organizing ingredients

Makes 16 salad rolls

Equipment

3-quart saucepan	cutting board	teaspoon
pot holder	sharp knife	clean kitchen towel
fork	grater or food processor with shredding disk	10-inch pie plate
timer	dry measuring cups	mixing spoon
strainer	4 large plates (for filling ingredients)	liquid measuring cup
large mixing bowl	serving platter	small bowl
kitchen scissors	2 tablespoons	plastic wrap
vegetable peeler		dinner plates

Ingredients

1 (3½-ounce) package cellophane noodles (see note)

7 red or green leaf lettuce leaves, washed and torn into bite-size pieces (tough center discarded)

2 large carrots, peeled and shredded (about 2 cups shredded)

32 fresh mint leaves, washed and patted dry

16 sprigs fresh cilantro, washed and patted dry (optional)

½ to ¾ cup dry roasted peanuts, chopped

¼ cup hoisin sauce

¼ cup plum sauce

16 8-inch round rice papers

1. Fill the saucepan three-quarters full with water and bring it to a boil. Have an adult drop the noodles into the water and use a pot holder to remove the pan from the heat. (The water should cover the noodles.) Poke the bunch of noodles in several places with a fork to loosen the pack. Soak for 5 minutes.

2. Drain the noodles in a strainer and rinse with cold water until cool. Shake to remove excess moisture and put drained noodles in the mixing bowl. Use kitchen scissors to cut them into small pieces.

continues

continued

3. Arrange an assembly line of plates with ingredients in this order: lettuce leaves, noodles, shredded carrots, mint and cilantro leaves, and peanuts. Set the serving platter at the end of the line. Put a tablespoon in the carrots and noodles and a teaspoon in the peanuts.

4. Place the clean towel, widthwise, next to the ingredients. Set the pie pan and the stack of rice papers next to the towel.

5. Mix the hoisin and plum sauce in a small bowl and set the mixture aside. (This is the dipping sauce.)

6. Fill the pie pan with very warm water and submerge one rice paper in the water. Soak it for 1 minute or until the wrapper becomes soft and pliable. (Soaking time may vary depending upon the freshness, thickness, and brand of the rice paper.) Handle the wrappers gently. (When dry, they are brittle and can crack easily. When wet, they can tear.)

7. With your fingers, grasp the edges of the wrapper and pull it out of the water. Let it drip over the pan and then lay it flat on the kitchen towel, toward the top. Fold the bottom of the towel over to cover the wrapper and gently pat to remove excess moisture. Wrapper will still be a little moist.

8. Fill the wrapper. Position a lettuce leaf toward the bottom half (closest to you) of the rice paper and then layer with 1 or 2 heaping tablespoons noodles, 1 heaping tablespoon carrots, a sprinkling (1 teaspoon) peanuts, 2 mint leaves, and a sprig of cilantro if you choose.

9. Wrap by gently folding the left and right edges of the rice paper over the filling. Fold the bottom edge toward the center and tightly tuck the rice paper in around the filling. (If the wrapper is too sticky to handle, wet your fingertips with water.) Continue to roll to the top end and press the wrapper so it sticks closed. Remove the salad roll to a serving plate.

10. Repeat with the remaining rice papers and ingredients, frequently changing the water used to soak. If the rolls look like they are drying out, cover them with plastic wrap.

11. Serve the rolls immediately with dipping sauce or refrigerate them to eat within several hours.

Note: Cellophane noodles are available in the Asian foods section of most supermarkets. The classic roll is made with rice stick noodles but I prefer using the cellophane noodles. They are compact, easy to handle, and readily available in supermarkets. Some large supermarkets carry rice papers (also marked spring rolls), or you can find them at a local Asian market. Look for transparent, wafer-like rounds about the size of tortillas.

Kid Comment

Andy Maletis, 11: "These are really fun to make. I'll help my mom make these for party appetizers."

His mom, Cyndy: "We've never attempted to make spring rolls before, and we were impressed with the outcome. We loved the dipping sauce! I liked to drizzle the sauce inside the roll. The kids liked to dip." The whole family had a great experience making this recipe. They all felt the rolls were "fresh and crunchy with a pretty presentation." The kids preferred to leave out the mint from the roll.

Andy Maletis, 11

Learn the Lingo

Wasabi is the Japanese version of horseradish. This green-colored seasoning comes in paste or dry powder form, which is mixed with water much like dry mustard. It has a sharp and fiery flavor. A small amount can be mixed with soy sauce for a dip used with the Japanese dishes sushi or sashimi.

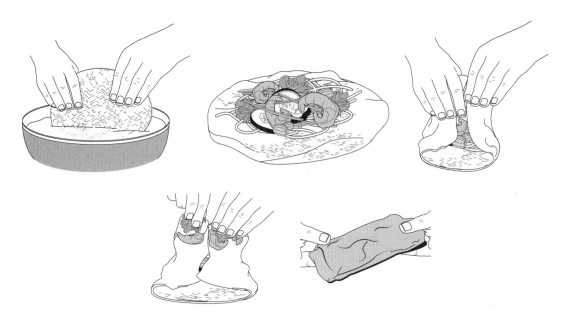

Filling and wrapping to create fresh Vietnamese-style Spring Rolls.

Chapter 24

Pasta and Pizza

Recipes

➤ Julia's Spaghetti with Fresh Basil and Garlic Tomato Sauce

➤ Easy Cheesy Zucchini Lasagna

➤ Homemade Macaroni and Cheese

➤ Mary's Sweet Noodle "Pie"

➤ Yakisoba Peanut Noodle Stir-Fry

➤ Julia's Tuna Noodle Express

➤ English Muffin Pizzas

➤ Portobello Mushroom Pizzas

When adults think of kid food, pasta and pizza usually are at the top of the list. If your family is anything like ours, you eat a lot of them. In fact, we've come to rely on pasta as the meal we turn to when we don't know what to make for dinner. It's so flexible and it always tastes great. It can be dressed with steamed or stir-fry vegetables or tossed with convenience foods, such as prepared roasted peppers and artichoke hearts in oil.

The recipes in this section introduce the whole family to classic pasta dishes. Enjoy my daughter's version of spaghetti with tomato sauce or make homemade macaroni and cheese. If you've never made lasagna without boiling the noodles, you and the kids will like my no-boil method. For speedy dinners, nothing beats the tortellini with pesto or the tuna noodle express. For something different, try Mary's Sweet Noodle "Pie" or Yakisoba Peanut Noodle Stir-Fry.

Kids will have fun making their own personal pizzas with toppings. Try them on an English muffin; or, for something different, on a meaty portobello mushroom.

Julia's Spaghetti with Fresh Basil and Garlic Tomato Sauce

My daughter Julia created this tomato sauce for a nutrition class assignment. Her friend Nikki Brams came to our house, and they cooked the sauce and took it with pasta to class the next day. Now every time Julia needs to bring a dish to school, she makes her pasta with tomato sauce. And, of course, we all look forward to when she makes it for a family dinner. Your house, like ours, will fill with the most wonderful aroma of simmering garlic and tomatoes when you cook this sauce.

How hard is this recipe? Intermediate

Adult help needed with cutting, at the stove, and draining the pasta

Serves 4 (makes 3½–4 cups sauce)

Equipment	Ingredients
cutting board	¼ cup extra-virgin olive oil
sharp knife	6 medium cloves garlic, peeled and very finely chopped
10- to 12-inch skillet or saucepan with lid	½ small onion, peeled and finely chopped
liquid measuring cup	6 to 8 large tomatoes, diced
timer	5 fresh basil leaves, torn into pieces
wooden spoon	2 bay leaves
measuring spoons	1 tablespoon plus ¼ teaspoon salt
6- to 8-quart pasta pot	1 pound imported spaghetti
colander	4 to 6 tablespoons freshly grated Parmesan cheese
pot holders	
ladle	
serving bowl or dish	
serving spoons or spaghetti tongs	
4 plates	

1. Heat the oil in the skillet over medium heat for 1 minute. Add the garlic and onion and sauté for 3 to 5 minutes or until the onion is translucent and golden and the garlic gives off a heady aroma.

2. Use the wooden spoon to mix in the tomatoes, basil, bay leaves, and ¼ teaspoon of salt. Cook this mixture, covered, for 20 to 25 minutes, stirring occasionally. Uncover and cook another 5 to 10 minutes. (If you prefer a thicker sauce, cook it, uncovered, to the desired consistency.)

3. Meanwhile, fill the pasta pot three-quarters full with water and turn the heat to medium-high. When the pasta water comes to a rolling boil, add 1 tablespoon of salt and have an adult drop in the pasta, stir, and cook according to the package directions. Put the colander in the sink. When the pasta is al dente—tender but firm to the bite—ask an adult to use pot holders to lift the pot and drain the pasta in the colander.

4. When the sauce is cooked, turn off the heat and let it stand 5 to 10 minutes. Remove the bay leaves.

5. Spread one or two ladles of sauce on the bottom of the serving dish, add the pasta, and ladle on the rest of the sauce.

6. Toss to cover the pasta with sauce and serve immediately with grated Parmesan cheese.

Note: We don't usually skin the tomatoes. If you prefer tomatoes without skins, refer to Chapter 13, "Let's Take a Cooking Lesson," for instructions on skinning tomatoes.

Julia Cooke, 15

Kid Comment

Julia Cooke, 15: "This sauce tastes great. It's light, but it has a lot of flavor because of the fresh tomatoes. It's fun to make and eat."

Easy Cheesy Zucchini Lasagna

I developed this recipe when I was the "In the Kitchen" columnist for *Barney Family Magazine*. I wanted to give families a vegetarian lasagna with some extra moisture and a slight crunch from shredded zucchini. Since then, I've started making it without boiling the noodles. Everyone can relax because kids don't have to worry about scalding their sensitive fingers. They just take any dry lasagna noodles (they don't have to be the special no-boil kind) and layer them with the other ingredients as if they were playing with toy building blocks. Adding water to the lasagna is what cooks the noodles during baking time.

continues

continued

How hard is this recipe? Intermediate

Adult help needed using the grater or food processor and the oven

Serves 10 to 12

Equipment

large mixing bowl	measuring spoons	pot holders
whisk	liquid measuring cup	cooling rack
dry measuring cups	13 × 9 × 2-inch baking dish	sharp knife
wooden spoon	aluminum foil	metal spatula
grater or food processor with shredding disk	timer	dinner plates

Ingredients

1 large egg

2 pounds part-skim ricotta cheese

1 pound part-skim mozzarella, shredded (about 4½ cups) and divided

¾ cup shredded Parmesan cheese, divided

2 tablespoons minced fresh parsley

1 (26-ounce) jar tomato-based pasta sauce

12 lasagna noodles, about ¾ pound

1 large zucchini, grated (about 2¼ cups)

1 cup water

1. Position the rack in the upper third of the oven and preheat the oven to 375 degrees F.

2. In the large bowl, lightly whisk the egg until blended and use the wooden spoon to mix it with the ricotta. Mix in 3 cups mozzarella, ½ cup Parmesan, and the parsley and combine well.

3. In the bottom of the baking dish, spread 1 cup tomato sauce. Place 4 uncooked lasagna noodles lengthwise and top with half the cheese mixture. Sprinkle on top half of the grated zucchini.

4. Place 4 uncooked noodles lengthwise over this and cover them with 1 cup sauce. Spread the remaining cheese mixture and zucchini over the sauce.

5. Top with 4 noodles lengthwise and cover with the remaining sauce. Sprinkle with the remaining mozzarella and Parmesan cheese. Pour the water around the inside edges of the baking dish.

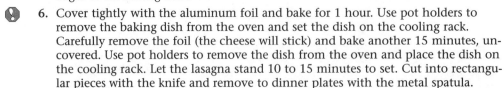

6. Cover tightly with the aluminum foil and bake for 1 hour. Use pot holders to remove the baking dish from the oven and set the dish on the cooling rack. Carefully remove the foil (the cheese will stick) and bake another 15 minutes, uncovered. Use pot holders to remove the dish from the oven and place the dish on the cooling rack. Let the lasagna stand 10 to 15 minutes to set. Cut into rectangular pieces with the knife and remove to dinner plates with the metal spatula.

William Bishop, 3½

Kid Comment

William Bishop, 3½, helped his mom make the lasagna from start to finish. He just kept saying, "Easiest recipe in the world." His mom, Suzanne, was thrilled. "I love this recipe! It's a very easy, quick, fun dinner. This is the first family meal we have ever had where everyone ate everything including dessert." Suzanne served the lasagna, stir-fry green beans, and the Harvest Crunch Fruit Bars (see Chapter 29, The Baker's Rack").

Homemade Macaroni and Cheese

If you've only tasted mac and cheese out of the box, you're in for a treat when you experience how flavorful this homemade version is. I've simplified the recipe by making the sauce from quick-mixing, superfine flour. This is great for kids because all they have to do is put the butter, milk, and flour in a pot and stir. My daughters like watching the sauce thicken and the cheese melt when they sprinkle it in. They enjoy seeing the dish come together when they mix the sauce with the pasta. We top the noodles with bread crumbs and make them crispy under the broiler for added flavor. The classic mac and cheese is made with elbow macaroni, but you can use any small pasta, such as shells or twists, with this recipe.

How hard is this recipe? Easy/Intermediate

Adult help needed using the grater or food processor, the oven and the stove, and draining the pasta

Serves 6 to 8

makes 7½ cups cooked pasta

continues

continued

Equipment

8-quart pasta pot

liquid measuring cup

dry measuring cups

small bowl

measuring spoons

fork

small strainer

cup

table spoon

grater or food processor
    with shredding disk

plate for cheese

3-quart sauce pan

table knife

liquid measuring cup

wooden spoon

timer

colander

pot holders

13 × 9 × 2-inch baking dish

rubber spatula

cooling rack

large serving spoon

serving bowls

Ingredients

½ cup seasoned Italian
    bread crumbs

1 tablespoon olive oil

¼ teaspoon dry mustard

¼ teaspoon salt

6 ounces sharp cheddar cheese,
    shredded (about 2 cups)

4 tablespoons butter, cut into small chunks

2 cups whole milk

2 tablespoons Wondra™ flour

12 ounces small elbow macaroni
    (or other small pasta such as shells or twists)

1. Fill the pasta pot with 5 quarts water and set it over medium-high heat to boil.

2. Position the rack on the highest rung in the oven and preheat the broiler. Keep the oven door slightly open.

3. Put the bread crumbs in a small bowl, add the oil, and use a fork to gently mix the oil with the crumbs until all the crumbs are moistened. Set them aside near the stove.

4. Sift the mustard through the strainer into a cup and then stir in ¼ teaspoon of the salt. Set this and the grated cheese beside the stove.

5. In the sauce pan, combine the butter with the milk and flour. Turn the heat to medium and bring it to a boil, stirring constantly with the wooden spoon. The sauce will thicken as you stir and might take up to 13 minutes to reach a boil. As soon as bubbles appear, cook 1 more minute and then immediately use pot holders to remove the saucepan from the heat.

6. Stir in the mustard mixture and the cheese until the cheese is melted. Set the sauce aside.

7. When the pasta water boils, add 1 tablespoon of salt and have an adult drop the pasta into the pot, stir, and cook it according to the package directions. The pasta is done when it is al dente, or tender but firm to the bite. Set the colander in the sink and have an adult use pot holders to lift the pot and drain the pasta into it. Spoon the pasta into the baking dish.

8. Use the rubber spatula to spoon the sauce on to the pasta. Mix well to coat the pasta.

9. Sprinkle the bread crumbs on top of the pasta to distribute them evenly over the surface. Use pot holders to place the baking dish in the oven and broil for 5 minutes or until the bread crumbs are evenly browned. Keep the oven door slightly open.

10. Use pot holders to remove the dish and place it on a cooling rack. Serve immediately.

Kid Comment

Madison Kaplan, 13: "This was a lot better than the boxed stuff that everybody's crazy about. I liked it a lot with the bread crumbs because it gave it a new flavor. It was really gourmet." Madison liked stirring the sauce and said she was surprised how easy it was to make mac and cheese from scratch.

Mary's Sweet Noodle "Pie"

 My friend Mary Chomenko Hinckley grew up eating this "pie" for breakfast. Her Ukranian mother would make it as a kind of shortcut skillet *kugel* or noodle pudding. Now that Mary has her own children, she makes it with them for a quick dinner. Kids can crack the eggs, stir in the ingredients, and mix the noodles. One favorite step is sprinkling the sugar on the finished dish.

How hard is this recipe? Easy/Intermediate

Adult help needed at the stove

Serves 2

Equipment

large mixing bowl
whisk
measuring spoons
dry measuring cups
2 large mixing spoons

10-inch nonstick skillet with
  flared edge and lid
table knife
timer
pot holders

plastic spatula
dinner plates
serving plate
sharp knife
table spoon

Ingredients

3 large eggs
2 tablespoons milk, any type
½ teaspoon salt

2 cups cooked angel hair pasta or spaghetti
3 tablespoons unsalted butter, divided
2 tablespoons sugar (or to taste)

1. In the mixing bowl, whisk the eggs together with the milk and salt.
2. Add the spaghetti and toss it well with the large spoons until all the spaghetti is coated with the egg mixture.
 3. In the skillet, melt 2 tablespoons of butter over medium-low heat. Pour the spaghetti mixture into the skillet, turn the heat to medium, and cook, covered, for about 10 minutes or until the underside of the pasta is golden in color and crispy.

continues

continued

 4. Use pot holders to remove the skillet from the burner. Use the spatula to loosen and slide the noodle pie onto a dinner plate. Set the skillet on the stove to melt the remaining tablespoon of butter. Cover the plate with another dinner plate. Invert the plates and, when the butter is melted, slide the noodle pie, uncooked side down, back into the skillet.

 5. Cook the pie, uncovered, for another 10 minutes or until the underside is golden in color and crispy.

 6. Use the spatula to slide the pie onto a serving plate; cut it into wedges. Sprinkle with sugar and serve while hot.

Note: The type of pan you use makes a big difference in the success of this pie. I once made it in an enamel pan, and the pie fell apart. Then I realized it was like a sweet noodle version of stir-fried rice. So I just cut up the noodles even more with the spatula, continued to cook it, and it still tasted great.

Kid Comment

Blake Hinckley, 11: "I've eaten this for so many years. It's simple yet it really tastes good. It's one of those simple things you can make at home, so it's an excuse not to go out when you don't want to cook." Blake likes to mix the eggs and noodles, but he says it's too hard for him to flip the pie.

His mother, Mary, calls this pie "the perfect solution to leftover spaghetti."

Blake Hinckley, 11

Learn the Lingo

A **kugel,** a classic Jewish dish, is a baked noodle pudding made in either sweet or savory versions. Kugels that are sweet contain raisins, nuts, spices, and sour cream. Meat, potatoes, or vegetables are baked in savory kugels. This dish can be served either warm or cold.

Yakisoba Peanut Noodle Stir-Fry

If you always order sesame peanut noodles at a Chinese restaurant, you're going to love learning how to make this dish. Kids can blend the peanut sauce and can help prepare the vegetables. The constant movement of the stir-fry might be tiresome for them, but they can chip in for a few stirs. With vegetables, tofu, and noodles, this dish is a complete meal in one pot. It's also very versatile. Use whatever vegetables are in your refrigerator or try substituting cooked shrimp or chicken for the tofu.

How hard is this recipe? Intermediate

Adult help needed with cutting and at the stove

Serves 4

Equipment

small sauce bowl	large mixing bowl	pot holders
dry measuring cups	serving plate	cooling rack
measuring spoons	large stir-fry pan or wok	large serving bowl
fork	timer	serving spoons
cutting board	wooden spoon or stir-fry paddle	dinner plates
sharp knife		

Ingredients

¼ cup peanut butter

2 tablespoons seasoned rice
    wine vinegar

1 tablespoon soy sauce

1 tablespoon honey

8 ounces firm tofu, cut into cubes

1 scallion, trimmed and sliced into rounds

10 small baby carrots, whole

½ green bell pepper, sliced into long,
    thin strips

2 pounds fresh yakisoba noodles

3 tablespoons vegetable oil, divided

continues

continued

1. Put the peanut butter in the small bowl and then slowly add the vinegar and soy sauce a little at a time. Press the mixture with a fork and stir to make a smooth paste. (Don't press too hard or the liquid will splash out of the bowl.) Mix in the honey. Set the sauce aside.

2. Assemble the tofu and vegetables in a bowl near the stove. Place the opened package of noodles and the serving plate nearby.

 3. Heat 2 tablespoons of oil in the stir-fry pan or wok over medium-high heat for 2 minutes. Add the tofu and vegetables and cook for 3 to 4 minutes, stirring constantly with the stir-fry paddle or wooden spoon. Lift the pan with a pot holder and return the cooked tofu and vegetables to the bowl.

4. Add the remaining 1 tablespoon oil and stir in the noodles, breaking up any large clumps with the stir-fry paddle or wooden spoon. Stir-fry, stirring constantly, until the noodles are heated through. This should take about 3 to 5 minutes. Use pot holders to remove the pan from the heat to the cooling rack.

5. Transfer the noodles to the serving bowl and toss them well with the peanut sauce. Toss in the vegetables.

6. Serve immediately.

Kid Comment

Madison Kaplan, 13: "It was exciting to make this because it took so little time to do something I get at a restaurant. The peanut sauce was absolutely delicious. It was just like the peanut sauce you get at a restaurant, and it goes good with everything." Madison said she was surprised she could make restaurant food so easily at home.

Madison Kaplan, 13

Kitchen Clue

You can find packaged fresh yakisoba noodles in the chilled foods aisle of the supermarket. Look in the Asian food section near the tofu.

Julia's Tuna Noodle Express

My daughter Julia came up with this recipe one night when she was baby-sitting for her sister. We had a box of mac and cheese on hand, but she wanted something more. So she looked through our pantry and decided to stir in some canned tuna fish and frozen peas for a protein and vegetable boost. It's become one of her favorite easy dinners, and she makes it for kids whenever she baby-sits. They always love it.

This is a good example of how you can create a dish based on what's in your refrigerator or cupboards.

How hard is this recipe? Easy

Adult help needed using the can opener, draining the pasta, and at the stove

Serves 2 to 4

Equipment

dry measuring cups	timer	liquid measuring cup
2 small bowls	colander	wooden spoon
can opener	pot holders	serving spoon
fork	table knife	serving bowls
3-quart sauce pan		

Ingredients

½ cup frozen peas

4–6 ounces canned solid white tuna, packed in water

1 (7¼-ounce) box macaroni and cheese

4 tablespoons butter

¼ cup milk

salt and pepper to taste

1. Put the peas in a small bowl of lukewarm water near the stove to thaw.
2. Flake the tuna in a small bowl and set it near the stove.

continues

continued

3. Fill the sauce pan three-quarters full with water and bring it to a boil on medium high heat. Have an adult add the pasta and cook according to the package directions. Set the colander in the sink and have an adult use pot holders to lift the sauce pan and drain the pasta in the colander.

   Using pot holders, return the pasta to the sauce pan and add the butter, milk, and packaged cheese sauce. Mix well with the wooden spoon.

4. Stir in the tuna and peas and mix well.

5. Serve immediately.

Kid Comment

Julia Cooke, 15: "This tastes like macaroni and cheese with a punch of flavor and nutrition. It's really easy to make."

Have-It-Your-Way Personal Pizzas

English Muffin Pizzas

I went into Oregon public schools and taught kids how to make this easy pizza as part of the Oregon Dairy Council's Cooking with Kids program. What I like about these pizzas is that they're quick, easy, and guaranteed to give your kids a successful cooking experience. Kids love having the power to choose their own toppings and create their own pizza. You can encourage them to experiment with new foods by setting out different topping choices. Take them to the store and walk through the produce section to see what fresh vegetables would be fun to put on their pizza.

How hard is this recipe? Easy

Adult help needed using the grater or food processor and at the oven or toaster oven

Makes 2 pizzas

Equipment

toaster or toaster oven

fork

cookie sheet, toaster oven tray,
   or microwave-safe plate

measuring spoons

grater or food processor with
   shredding disk

plate for cheese

dry measuring cups

timer

pot holders

metal spatula

serving plate

Ingredients

1 English muffin, split in half with a fork

4 tablespoons store-bought spaghetti sauce

½ cup (1½ ounces) shredded mozzarella cheese

sliced vegetables or other toppings

1. Position the rack in the center of the oven and preheat the oven to 400 degrees F.
2. Lightly toast the English muffins in the toaster.
3. Place the muffins on an ungreased cookie sheet or on the tray of the toaster oven. Spread 2 tablespoons sauce on each half. Sprinkle ¼ cup cheese on top of the sauce. Add any toppings you desire.
4. Bake for 10 minutes. The cheese will be melted, and the sauce will be heated.
5. Use pot holders to remove the cookie sheet from the oven or the tray from the toaster oven. Use the spatula to put the pizzas on serving plates. Allow the cheese to cool for several minutes before serving.

Microwave instructions: Follow steps 1 and 2. Place the pizzas on a microwave-safe plate. Microwave on high for 30 to 45 seconds or until the cheese is melted.

Kitchen Clue

When I was teaching an English Muffin Pizza class, we came up with an idea for zucchini pizza bites. We had a bowl of raw zucchini coins on the table along with lots of other left-over pizza toppings. We took a zucchini coin, topped it with sauce, and added some cheese. Then we just popped the whole thing in our mouths. We also tried adding sliced olives, bell peppers, and onions, all of which were interesting tastes. Try experimenting with your own zucchini bites. You can put these in the microwave or oven and heat them until warm.

Portobello Mushroom Pizzas

Jack Czarnecki, mushroom expert and author of several mushroom cookbooks, suggests using a portobello mushroom in place of pizza crust. I agree with him that it's a kid-friendly way to introduce kids to mushrooms. The beefy mushroom acts as a solid, almost meaty base for the sauce and melted cheese. Try experimenting with different flavored sauces or other soft cheeses to vary the taste. You'll find these mushrooms to be very thick, moist, and chewy, so you'll want to cut the pizza into wedges and eat it with a knife and fork.

How hard is this recipe? Easy

Adult help needed using the grater or food processor and the oven

Makes 2 mushroom pizzas

Equipment

paper towels	grater or food processor	pot holders
measuring spoons	with shredding disk	cooling rack
tablespoon	plate for cheese	spatula
nonstick cookie sheet	dry measuring cups	serving plates
or jelly roll pan	timer	
liquid measuring cup		

Ingredients

2 (4½- to 5-inch wide) portobello mushrooms

½ teaspoon olive oil

½ cup chunky, store-bought tomato sauce

1 cup (3 ounces) shredded mozzarella cheese

salt and pepper to taste

1. Position the rack in the center of the oven and preheat the oven to 375 degrees F.
2. Gently snap the stem from the gill side of the mushrooms. Take wet paper towels, wipe the mushrooms, and brush the gills to remove any excess dirt. Pat the mushrooms dry.
3. Coat the curved side of each mushroom cap with ¼ teaspoon oil, spreading it gently and evenly over the surface with a spoon or your clean finger.
4. On the cookie sheet or jelly roll pan, place the cap gill side up. Spread half the tomato sauce followed by half the cheese on each mushroom.

 5. Bake for 12 to 15 minutes. When the pizzas are done, the cheese should be melted and the mushroom and sauce warmed.

6. Use pot holders to remove the cookie sheet or jelly roll pan from the oven and place it on the cooling rack. Use the spatula to put the mushroom caps on serving plates. Allow the cheese to cool slightly before serving. Add salt and pepper to taste, if desired.

Note: Look for firm portobello mushrooms with a good rim or lip around the edge. This shape holds in moisture nicely, and it looks attractive when baked. Avoid mushroom caps that are flat around the edges. They'll lose their shape, and the juices will run during baking.

Kitchen Clue

When you're shopping for Portobello mushrooms, you may see them by other names. Sometimes they are labeled as portabella, portabello, or portobella. They are all the same great-tasting, meaty-style mushroom.

Chapter 25

Mealtime Magic

Recipes

➤ Tuna Melts

➤ One-Pot Italian Sausage Supper

➤ Shake-It-Up Chicken

➤ Chili with All the Fixins'

➤ Confetti Vegetarian Chili

➤ Tropical Pineapple Fish

➤ Turkey Hash with Red Peppers and Corn

➤ Super Stuffed Spuds

➤ Pork Chops with Caramelized Apples

The lunch and dinner hours have just gotten easier with the range of possibilities on the following pages. Look through this section to find delicious one-pot skillet meals, easy oven dishes, and mealtime solutions that satisfy the whole family such as Super Stuffed Spuds.

Got a night when everyone just passes through the kitchen on their way to different activities? Try making the recipes for a big pot of chili with meat or with vegetables. Keep it hot on the stove so everyone can dip in when they're ready for their dinner. On nights when you have more time, kids will enjoy preparing all the ingredients and setting up a chili bar with toppings.

Throughout this section, you'll see suggestions for how your kids can chip in to prepare the meal. If they're old enough to handle a knife, do what I do. Get them chopping vegetables and mixing ingredients by your side. You'll have a chance to catch up on the news of the day, and the meal will get on the table faster.

Tuna Melts

We like to make these melts for weekend lunches. Just make the tuna recipe in Chapter 22, "Super Soups and Salads," put it on a toasted English muffin, and then top it with a slice of cheese and broil. Vary the kind of cheese you use to add different flavors to the sandwich.

How hard is this recipe? Easy

Adult help needed using the can opener and at the oven

Makes 2 tuna melts

Equipment

fork	cutting board	pot holders
toaster	sharp knife	cooling rack
cookie sheet	measuring spoons	metal spatula
can opener	timer	serving plate
small mixing bowl		

Ingredients

1 English muffin

8 tablespoons Tuna Fish Salad (see Chapter 22)

2 slices cheese

1. Place the rack on the highest rung in the oven (about 4 inches below the heat source) and preheat the oven to broil. Keep the oven door slightly open.
2. Split the muffin with a fork and lightly toast it in the toaster. Place the muffin halves on the ungreased cookie sheet, rough side up.
3. Use the measuring spoon to spread 4 tablespoons tuna fish salad on each muffin. Cover each with 1 slice of cheese.
4. Broil just until the cheese is melted and starts to brown, about 2 to 3 minutes. Use pot holders to remove the sheet from the oven and place it on the cooling rack. Use a spatula to place the melts onto serving plates. Serve immediately.

One-Pot Italian Sausage Supper

This was an old supper standby in my Italian family when I was growing up, and it's one of the first meals I learned to make on my own. Kids can help cut up the potatoes and peppers and stir the ingredients at the stove. These days, I make it in a skillet for a quick meal, but if you have time and want the deep, rich flavors of slow cooking, you can put everything in a large casserole or baking dish and roast it in the oven. My kids make crusty garlic bread and a crisp green salad to round out the meal.

How hard is this recipe? Easy/Intermediate

Adult help needed for cutting and at the stove

Serves 4

Equipment

cutting board	wooden spoon or spatula
sharp knife	timer
measuring spoons	pot holder
large nonstick skillet with lid	serving plate

Ingredients

2 tablespoons olive oil

1½ pounds sweet Italian sausage, cut into 2-inch rounds

1 pound Yukon Gold, red, or white potatoes, unpeeled and cut into small chunks

1 medium onion, cut in half and sliced lengthwise

1 red or yellow bell pepper, sliced lengthwise

1 green bell pepper, sliced lengthwise

½ tablespoon dried Italian seasonings (optional)

1. Put the oil in the skillet and heat it for 1 minute over medium-high heat. Brown the sausage for 2 minutes and then add the potatoes and layer the onions and peppers on top. Add seasonings, if desired.

2. Cook, covered, for 20 minutes. Use the wooden spoon or spatula to stir frequently to continue browning the sausage and distributing the vegetables.

3. Reduce the heat to medium and cook, uncovered, for 5 minutes or until the meat is no longer pink and the potatoes and vegetables are tender. If the dish seems dry, add a little water.

4. Use the pot holder to hold the handle of the skillet while you remove ingredients to a serving platter. Serve immediately.

Oven directions: Roast, uncovered, in a 375-degree oven for 45 minutes to 1 hour, stirring occasionally.

Variation: Make this into an Italian hoagie sandwich by layering the ingredients between 2 large pieces of Italian bread or hoagie sandwich rolls.

Kid Comment

The Noto family was impressed by this dish because it was colorful, quick, easy, and a complete meal. "It's a great dish," said Peggy Noto. Her daughter, Emma, 5, and son, Torben, 8, helped cut up the vegetables and put them in the skillet. Their favorite ingredient was the sausage.

Shake-It-Up Chicken

Kids enjoy making this chicken because they get to squish it in yogurt in a plastic bag and then shake it with bread crumbs in another plastic bag. The yogurt coating keeps the skinless chicken moist during baking.

How hard is this recipe? Easy

Adult help needed handling raw chicken and using the oven

Serves 4

Equipment

tablespoon	fork	sharp knife
2 1-gallon self-sealing plastic bags	nonstick baking pan	cooling rack
timer	pot holders	dinner plates
dry measuring cups	tongs	

Ingredients

1 (8-ounce) cup plain yogurt

6 boneless, skinless chicken thighs (about 1½ pounds)

1 cup garlic-herb or other seasoned bread crumbs

1. Position the rack in the center of the oven and preheat the oven to 400 degrees F.
2. Use the spoon to scoop the yogurt into a plastic bag. Add the chicken thighs to the bag. Press out the air, seal the bag, and press lightly to spread yogurt all over the chicken. Refrigerate the chicken for 30 minutes.
3. Meanwhile, place the bread crumbs in the other plastic bag. Use the fork to take 3 pieces of chicken out of the bag with the yogurt and place them in the bag with bread crumbs. Shake the bag to coat all the chicken. Remove the chicken with the fork and place it in the baking pan.

4. Repeat with the remaining 3 pieces of chicken. Add more bread crumbs if you need the extra coating.

5. Bake for 40 to 45 minutes or until the chicken no longer is pink inside and the juices run clear when cut with the sharp knife. Use the tongs to turn the chicken after 20 minutes. Be careful not to rub off the bread crumb mixture. Wash the tongs in hot soapy water before using again.

6. Use pot holders to remove the pan to a cooling rack. Use the clean tongs to remove the chicken to dinner plates, again being careful not to scrape off the bread crumbs. Serve immediately.

Mary Bishop, 6

Kid Comment

Mary Bishop, 6: "This was fun to make. I liked finding the yogurt in the refrigerator to put on the chicken."

Chili with All the Fixins'

My kids definitely think that one of the best things about chili is all the fixins'. We like to set up a chili bar with bowls containing grated cheese, sour cream, scallions, chopped olives, green chili peppers, avocado, and tomato salsa. Everyone just piles what they want on top of the chili. Serve this with Mexican Spoon Bread (from Chapter 29, "The Baker's Rack") and a green salad and you've got a great meal.

How hard is this recipe? Intermediate

Adult help needed with cutting, using the can opener, and at the stove

Makes 6½ cups

continues

continued

Equipment

cutting board	measuring spoons	pot holders
sharp knife	timer	ladle
dry measuring cups	wooden spoon	serving bowls
Dutch oven or 5½-quart sauce pan with lid	can opener	

Ingredients

1 tablespoon olive oil	1 teaspoon cumin
1 medium onion, diced (about 1 cup)	2 tablespoons chili powder
	1 (28-ounce) can diced tomatoes in their juice
2 large cloves garlic, minced (about 1 tablespoon)	1 (15-ounce) can chili beans or pink beans
1 pound ground lean beef	

1. In the Dutch oven or saucepan, heat the oil for 1 minute over medium heat. Add the onion and garlic and sauté for 3 to 5 minutes, stirring frequently with the wooden spoon. The onion should be golden and transparent.

2. Add the beef, crumbling it with your clean hands as you add it to the pot. Use the wooden spoon to break up any large clumps of meat in the pot. Turn the heat to high and continue to cook the meat, stirring frequently, until it no longer is pink. This should take about 4 minutes.

3. Sprinkle the cumin and chili powder on the meat and stir in the tomatoes and beans. Reduce the heat to medium high.

4. When the chili begins to simmer, reduce the heat to medium and cook, covered, for 25 minutes.

5. Ladle into serving bowls and top with garnishes.

Kid Comment

Lizzie Cooke, 12: "It tastes yummy because it's so meaty. It tastes good with sour cream on it."

Confetti Vegetarian Chili

When you're in the mood for chili but don't want meat, try this colorful bean and corn version. It makes a hearty meal, especially when you top it with grated cheese, sour cream, salsa, and crumbled tortilla chips. Kids can help prepare the ingredients and put them in the pot. They also enjoy serving up bowls of toppings for the chili.

How hard is this recipe? Intermediate

Adult help needed using the can opener, cutting, and at the stove

Makes 12 cups

Equipment

liquid measuring cup	Dutch oven or 5½-quart sauce pan
timer	wooden spoon
kitchen scissors	can opener
measuring spoons	pot holders
cutting board	ladle
sharp knife	

Ingredients

3 sun-dried tomatoes

¼ cup warm water

3 tablespoons canola oil

1 medium onion, diced (1 cup)

3 cloves garlic, minced (1 tablespoon)

1 green bell pepper, diced (1½ cups)

1 tablespoon chili powder

1 teaspoon cumin

2 (28-ounce) cans diced, peeled tomatoes, in their juice

1 (15½-ounce) can chick peas, drained

1 (15-ounce) can black beans, drained

1 (15-ounce) can seasoned white beans with liquid

1 (15¼-ounce) can whole kernel corn, drained

1 (4-ounce) can chopped green chilies

1. Soak the sun-dried tomatoes in ¼ cup warm water for 15 minutes or until softened. When ready, cut them into small pieces with kitchen scissors. Set aside, reserving the liquid.

2. Meanwhile, put the oil, onion, and garlic in the sauce pan over medium-high heat and sauté for 5 minutes. The onions should be golden and shiny and should give off an aroma with the garlic.

3. Stir in the green pepper, chili powder, cumin, and sun-dried tomatoes with their liquid. Cook for 10 minutes, stirring frequently.

4. Add the tomatoes, beans, corn, and green chilies. Stir to combine all the ingredients. Bring the chili back to a boil and then turn down the heat to medium-low.

5. Simmer, uncovered, for 40 to 45 minutes, stirring once or twice.

6. Serve immediately, with or without toppings, or refrigerate for later use.

Note: This chili keeps well either refrigerated or frozen. When defrosting, just pour off any extra water that collects when the chili thaws.

Kid Comment

Jeremy Wearn, 10: "I thought cooking this dish was fun. The flavor was good. I liked the liquid soupy part. I thought it had enough tang; it was perfect." He added that, if he made it again, he would make it even thicker by adding more corn.

Jeremy's dad, Fred: "The whole family loved this vegetarian chili. This is hard to beat." The Wearns suggested using puréed tomatoes instead of diced tomatoes, although we like the chunkiness that the diced tomatoes give the sauce. You can try it both ways and see which one you like better.

Kitchen Clue

Make big batches of vegetarian or meat chili for those hectic nights when everyone seems to be on different schedules. Keep the chili hot on the stove so everyone can just dig in as they come into the kitchen. If the chili gets too thick and needs more sauce, just add some more tomatoes or a little water. These dishes also are good the next day or two after cooking because the spices and seasonings have a chance to meld.

Tropical Pineapple Fish

 If you're looking for a really quick but delicious dinner, this is it. The fish is moist, and the fruit topping gives it an elegant look and a tasty finish. The pineapple chunks and peach preserves appeal to kids who might be otherwise skittish about eating broiled fish.

How hard is this recipe? Easy

Adult help needed using the can opener and the oven

Serves 4

Equipment

broiler pan with rack   dry measuring cups   cooling rack
aluminum foil   can opener   fork
measuring spoons   pot holders   kitchen towel
paper towels   timer   serving plate
small bowl   metal spatula   dinner plates
spoon

Ingredients

1 teaspoon vegetable oil
    for greasing the pan

⅓ cup peach preserves

2 tablespoons apple cider vinegar

½ cup pineapple tidbits

1¼ pounds halibut steaks or
    other lean fish steaks

1. Position the rack in the upper part of the oven and preheat the oven to medium broil. Keep the oven door slightly open. Line the rack of the broiler pan with aluminum foil and spread the oil on the pan with paper towels.

2. In a small bowl, mix the preserves with the vinegar and gently stir in the pineapple with the spoon. Set the mixture aside with the spoon near the oven.

3. Place the fish on the broiler pan and use pot holders to slide the pan on the rack. (The fish should be about 4 inches beneath the heat source.) Broil for 3 to 4 minutes.

4. Use pot holders to remove the fish from the oven. Set the pan on the cooling rack and use the spatula to turn over the fish in one piece. Return the pan to the oven, using pot holders, and broil for about 3 more minutes or until the fish flakes easily when pierced with a fork. Do not overcook. Wash and dry the spatula for later use.

5. Use pot holders to remove the fish from the oven. Set the pan on the cooling rack and spoon the fruit mixture on top of the fish. Broil for 1 more minute.

6. Use pot holders to remove the broiler pan from the oven and place it on the cooling rack. Use the clean spatula to put the fish onto the serving plate. Spoon the sauce from the pan onto the fish. Serve immediately.

Kid Comment

Jake Sadle, 10: "Yum. This has a nice taste to it. It has a sweetness and tartness in every bite. I'd like to try making it with other kinds of fish. (We used halibut.) It's an easy recipe to follow."

Kid Quiz

Guess how you can get perfectly cooked fish every time?

Follow the 10-minute rule. Measure the thickness of your fish (at the thickest part if it's not a fish steak). For every inch, allow 10 minutes of cooking time. How long would you cook a fish that is 1¼ inches thick? Ten minutes for the inch plus one-quarter of 10 (or 2½ minutes) for a total of 12½ minutes.

Turkey Hash With Red Peppers and Corn

If you like hash brown potatoes, you'll go for this dish. For a hash, you pan-fry shredded potatoes with cooked meat or fish and any vegetables you like. We like to make chicken or turkey hash and add corn and red peppers for color and crunch. Try this festive-looking version and then come up with some of your own creative combinations.

How hard is this recipe? Intermediate

Adult help needed cutting and at the stove

Serves 6 to 8

Equipment

10- to 12-inch nonstick skillet

wooden spoon

timer

pot holder

plate for meat

measuring spoons

cutting board

sharp knife

dry measuring cups

plastic spatula

serving bowl

Ingredients

1¼ pounds commercially packaged turkey breast strips

4 tablespoons canola oil, divided

1 small onion, finely diced

1 red bell pepper, diced

1 (20-ounce) bag refrigerated, shredded hash brown potatoes

1 cup fresh or frozen whole kernel corn

1 teaspoon chili powder

¼ teaspoon salt

1. In the skillet, cook the turkey strips over high heat for 4 minutes. Set them aside in a clean dish along with any cooked meat juices.

2. Add half the oil, the onion, and the red pepper to the skillet and stir fry with the wooden spoon on medium-high heat for 3 minutes. Add the potatoes, corn, chili powder, and salt. Stir to combine with other ingredients.

3. Pat down with a spatula to flatten the mixture. Pan-fry, without stirring, for 8 to 10 minutes. The potatoes should be golden and the edges should turn brown.

4. Drizzle the remaining oil over the top and stir in the cooked meat. Turn the mixture over and cook, without stirring, for another 5 to 8 minutes or until the potatoes are cooked and golden.

5. Transfer to the serving bowl and serve hot.

Kid Comment

Lucy McVicker, 14: "This was really pretty to look at. I could make this on my own."

Super Stuffed Spuds

My kids started eating stuffed potatoes for lunch at a lodge during winter ski trips a few years ago, and before we knew it, they wanted to make them for dinner. They've become a standby for a simple, nutritious dinner. They satisfy everyone's appetite because you customize them with your own favorite toppings. My kids line up ingredients buffet-style, and then we all just pile our choices onto the cooked potato. The kids' favorites are grated cheddar cheese, sour cream, and snipped fresh chives. We always put out bowls of raw or steamed vegetables as toppers or nibbles.

How hard is this recipe? Easy

Adult help needed cutting and using the vegetable peeler and the oven

Serves 4

Equipment

vegetable brush or plastic mesh sponge	tongs
vegetable peeler	small knife
fork	serving plate or dinner plates
pot holders	bowls and tablespoons for toppings
timer	

continues

continued

Ingredients

4 large russet potatoes, about 8 to 10 ounces each

salt and pepper to taste

toppings

low-fat sour cream	guacamole
low-fat yogurt	sliced black olives
shredded hard cheese	shredded zucchini
tomato or fruit salsa	diced peppers
raw or cooked broccoli	peas

1. Position the rack in the center of the oven and preheat the oven to 425 degrees F.

2. Under cool running water, scrub the potatoes with the vegetable brush or plastic mesh sponge to remove dirt. Pick out any "eyes" with the tip of a vegetable peeler.

3. Pierce the potatoes on all sides with a fork. (This lets the steam escape while cooking.) Use pot holders to pull out the oven rack and position potatoes directly on the rack at least 2 inches apart.

4. Bake for 45 minutes to 1 hour or until the center can easily be pierced by a small knife.

5. Use pot holders to pull out the oven rack and remove the potatoes with tongs. Place them on a serving plate or dinner plates. Cut the top of the potato lengthwise and make two crosswise cuts on either side halfway between the center and end of the potato. When cool enough to touch, lightly push on either end to open the potato.

6. Fill and top potatoes with your favorite ingredients.

Note: Try melting the cheese on top of the potato the way my kids do. My daughter Julia sprinkles the potato with salt, pepper, and cheese and microwaves it for 30 seconds to 1 minute or until all the cheese is melted. She then adds a dollop of sour cream and a sprinkling of fresh chives.

Kid Comment

Julia Cooke, 15: "It tastes heavenly. The potato gets all cheesy and a little creamy, and it's got a lot of flavor."

Heads Up!

When baking potatoes, don't wrap them in foil. The skin will get soggy, and the potatoes get gummy because the foil traps the steam and moisture. Potatoes wrapped in foil also can pose a health hazard. The oxygen-free environment gives toxins, like botulism, the perfect climate in which to grow.

Remember that cooked potatoes are a perishable food that should not be kept between 40 and 140 degrees F for longer than 2 hours. After 2 hours at room temperature, the bacteria multiply and pose a risk for food-borne illness.

Pork Chops with Caramelized Apples

This simple skillet meal combines two great tastes; it's the classic combination of pork and apples. The addition of the dried herb thyme adds a subtle and interesting flavor. Kids can help chop the apples, turn the meat, and add the ingredients to the pot.

How hard is this recipe? Easy

Adult help needed with cutting and at the stove

Serves 4

Equipment
cutting board
sharp knife
vegetable peeler
10- to 12-inch nonstick
    skillet with lid
measuring spoons
timer

wooden spoon or plastic spatula
pot holders
instant-read thermometer
tongs
large serving plate

Ingredients
2 tablespoons olive oil
4 loin pork chops with bone, ¾-inch thick (about 1½ pounds)
2 large apples, cored, peeled, and coarsely chopped
¼ teaspoon dried thyme
1 tablespoon brown sugar

continues

continued

1. In the skillet, heat the oil over medium-high heat for 90 seconds. Add the meat and cook for 1 to 2 minutes on each side or until the sides are browned.

2. Add the apples, sprinkle in the thyme, and cook for 8 to 10 minutes, covered. The meat is cooked when the internal temperature registers 160 degrees F on an instant-read thermometer or when only the slightest blush of pink remains.

3. Use tongs to remove the chops to a large serving plate.

4. Sprinkle the brown sugar over the apples and toss them to coat. Cook for 2 more minutes or until the sugar has melted.

5. Remove the apples and put them on top of the chops with any remaining juice. Serve immediately.

Variation: I like to add store-bought bottled sauerkraut or sweet-and-sour red cabbage after step 2 and heat it just long enough to warm the cabbage. If you make these additions, omit steps 3 through 5 and serve everything all at once.

Kid Comment

Kevin McVicker, 5: "I never had apples with pork chops, but I like the flavor. I'd like to make this again for my dad."

His mom, Yolanda, said Kevin and his two siblings ate the whole meal, even though the combination of caramelized apples and pork was new to them.

Kevin McVicker, 5

Chapter 26

Very Veggies and Sides

Recipes

➤ Dippin' Hearty Artichokes

➤ Helen Mandel's Artichoke Dipping Sauce

➤ Incredible Shrinking Spinach

➤ Honey-Glazed Carrot Coins

➤ Brown Sugar Butternut Squash

➤ Cheesy Zucchini Boats

➤ Stir-Fry Veggies with Sesame Seeds

➤ Mashed Potato Mountains

➤ Polenta Stars and Shapes

➤ Oven-Roasted Baby Potatoes with Herbs

➤ Pink Rice

➤ Fluffy Couscous with Golden Raisins

When it comes to veggies and side dishes, get kids involved in making them and they'll usually eat them. I've created recipes in this section that offer kids a new take on some old standbys. How can they refuse mashed potatoes when they make them into mini-mountains? How can they resist eating rice when they turn it red with chili powder and tomato juice?

They might be more willing to try new dishes, such as polenta, when they can cut them into stars and top them with melted cheese. They might try couscous when it's paired with a favorite everyday food like raisins.

I hope your whole family discovers recipes in this section that make the extras dishes on the dinner plate a little more interesting.

Dippin' Hearty Artichokes

When I was growing up, we always looked forward to nights when we would have artichokes. We got to eat them with our hands—you just pull off the cooked leaves, dip them in your favorite sauce, and run the leaf through your teeth to scrape off the fleshy inside. And at the center (past the "choke," which you discard) was a sweet, tender "heart." Preparing artichokes and eating them can be an adventure for your kids. My kids always ask for them come spring and fall when they're in season. We all know that artichokes take time to eat, but that's part of their attraction. We have some of our best conversations when we're sitting around the table, pulling off and eating our artichoke leaves.

How hard is this recipe? Easy

Adult help needed with cutting and at the stove

Serves 4

Equipment

cutting board	steaming basket (optional)
sharp knife	fork
kitchen scissors	pot holders
8-quart nonreactive pasta pot with lid or Dutch oven	tongs
	large serving plate
lemon reamer or juicer	
timer	

Ingredients

4 artichokes

½ lemon

Favorite Dippers

    melted butter and lemon juice

    mayonnaise, either plain or with some seasonings

    plain yogurt blended with mayonnaise

1. Ask an adult to help you prepare the artichoke. Use the sharp knife and cutting board to cut about an inch off the top and the stems at the base. Pull off the small bottom leaves. Snip off the thorny tips of the leaves with scissors if necessary. (Some varieties of artichokes don't have these pricklies.)

2. Wash the artichokes under running water. Push out the leaves slightly so the water flows over the insides. If the artichokes are really sandy, dunk them under water in a large pot.

3. Fill the pot with about 2 inches of water and use the lemon reamer or juicer to juice the lemon right into the water. Don't worry about pits. If you're using a steamer, put it in the pot. Stand the artichokes by their stems in the steamer basket or the pot.

4. Cover the pot, turn on the heat to medium-high, and let the artichokes steam for 25 to 45 minutes. The cooking time will vary depending on the artichokes' size. They're cooked when a knife or fork can easily be inserted into the base, just like a potato, or when the outside leaves and those near the center pull out easily. Test them to be sure you're not overcooking them.

5. When the artichokes are done, turn off the stove, use the tongs to remove them, and put them on the serving plate. Serve at room temperature with dipping sauces.

Helen Mandel's Artichoke Dipping Sauce

This easy-to-make sauce tastes great with artichokes, as a dipper for vegetables, or on fish. I've even used it cold for tuna fish salad in place of mayonnaise. I like the scallions, but if they're too strong for you, reduce the amount to your taste before serving.

How hard is this recipe? Easy

Adult help needed with cutting and at the stove

Makes 1½ cups

Equipment	Ingredients
cutting board	4 tablespoons unsalted butter
sharp knife	½ cup low-fat mayonnaise
dry measuring cups	½ cup plain yogurt (regular or low-fat)
lemon reamer or juicer	1 teaspoon lemon juice
measuring spoons	1 tablespoon Dijon-style mustard
small saucepan	⅛ teaspoon sugar (optional)
whisk	2 scallions, finely chopped (optional)
large spoon	
serving board	

1. Melt the butter over low heat in a small saucepan or in the microwave.
2. Whisk in the ingredients in the order listed.
3. Serve the sauce warm or at room temperature.

Kid Comment

Jake Sadle, 10: "I like to shape the leaves in a circle around the plate as decoration after each leaf is devoured. I like artichokes because they're fun to eat and taste yummy. My grandmother's recipe [Helen Mandel's Artichoke Dipping Sauce] for artichoke sauce is the best. Even if kids don't like Dijon mustard, mayonnaise, or green onions, when they're blended together it won't taste the same way the ingredients taste by themselves. If you have a sauce, artichokes take the flavor of the sauce. Artichokes have a kind of warm and meaty texture."

Jake Sadle, 10

Kid Quiz

Can you guess what artichokes have in common with bananas and with oranges?

Artichokes have the same amount of potassium as a banana, and like oranges, they also are a source of vitamin C.

Kitchen Clue

How do I eat an artichoke?

Artichokes come in small, medium, and large sizes. Remove the leaves of the cooked artichoke one by one. Dip the wide leaf end into the sauce. Bite down on the fleshy inside of the leaf and pull it through your teeth. Do not eat the leaf. When you get to the center, the leaves will get softer. They cover a fuzzy "choke." Don't eat the choke. Scoop it out with a knife or a spoon, being careful to get out all the fuzzy center. (My daughter Lizzie cuts the artichoke bottom in half so she can see where the choke ends to make it easier to scoop.) Underneath, you'll find the prize—a tender, flavorful heart. The bigger the artichoke, the bigger the heart. Eat the heart plain or dip it in your sauce. Don't worry if you can't eat the whole artichoke. It's fun to snack on the leaves the next day, either cold or reheated.

Incredible Shrinking Spinach

 You'll be amazed when you see fresh spinach leaves shrink before your eyes as they cook. Just put them in the pot and watch what happens. You'll like the full-bodied flavor of freshly cooked spinach, especially when you put a pat of butter or a drizzle of oil on top. We also like to give it a squirt of lemon. This is the way they serve spinach in some Mediterranean countries.

How hard is this recipe? Easy

Adult help needed at the stove

Makes 3½ cups cooked spinach

Equipment

colander   wooden spoon

waxed paper   pot holders

measuring spoons   serving bowl

8-quart saucepan

timer

liquid measuring cup

Ingredients

1 (24-ounce) bag prewashed
    fresh spinach leaves

3 garlic cloves

3 tablespoons extra-virgin olive oil

salt and pepper to taste

1 to 2 large lemons, cut into quarters

1. Check the spinach to see if it needs further washing. If it does, put it in a colander and wash it under cool running water. Shake off the excess water.

continues

continued

2. Put the garlic between two sheets of waxed paper. Take the pot and smash the garlic cloves to crush them. Remove the papery garlic peel and discard, along with the waxed paper.

3. Heat the oil in the saucepan over medium-high heat for 2 minutes. Add the garlic and cook for 1½ minutes.

4. Have an adult drop in the spinach leaves. Be careful not to get burned by the splatters. Pour ½ cup water over the leaves. Cook for 8 to 10 minutes, stirring frequently to distribute the spinach. The spinach is ready when all the leaves have shrunk and are tender.

5. Use pot holders to lift the pan and, with the wooden spoon, remove the spinach to a serving bowl and serve it warm. Season it with salt and pepper to taste and squirt it with a quarter of a lemon.

Kid Quiz

Why does Popeye eat so much spinach?

Popeye eats spinach because it's full of vitamins A and C. Vitamin A helps you see properly in the dark, protects you from infections, promotes the healthy growth of cells, and might help prevent cancer. Vitamin C protects you from bruising, heals cuts and wounds, and keeps your gums and your immune system healthy. Spinach also contains iron, but an acid in spinach prevents the iron from being absorbed by the body. Too bad. That acid also is what gives spinach its slightly bitter taste.

Honey-Glazed Carrot Coins

Crisp, tender carrots, sweetened with honey and brown sugar, hit the spot at dinnertime. Peter Rabbit would have been pleased to munch on some of these. Kids can help prepare this dish by peeling the carrots, cutting them into coins, and stirring in the sweeteners. For a lighter variation of this rich dish, cut the butter in half.

How hard is this recipe? Easy

Adult help needed with cutting and at the stove

Serves 4

Equipment

10-inch skillet	pot holders
cutting board	colander
vegetable peeler	table knife
sharp knife	measuring spoons
dry measuring cups	wooden spoon
timer	serving bowl

Ingredients

4 medium carrots, peeled and sliced into ¼-inch coins (about 2 cups)

2 tablespoons butter

2 tablespoons honey

1 teaspoon brown sugar

1. Fill the skillet halfway with water and bring it to a boil over medium heat. Drop in the carrots and cook, uncovered, for 10 minutes. The carrots should be slightly crunchy.

2. Have an adult use pot holders to drain the water and carrots in the colander. Rinse with cold water.

3. Put the butter, honey, and sugar in the skillet and cook over medium heat until the butter is melted, stirring constantly with the wooden spoon. Stir in the carrots to coat well with the sauce and cook, uncovered, for 10 minutes, stirring occasionally.

4. Remove the carrots and the sauce to the serving bowl. Serve immediately.

John Maletis, 12

Kid Comment

John Maletis, 12: "My favorite part was stirring the carrots in the pan. They were sweet and crunchy to eat. Good with chicken or meat."

Brown Sugar Butternut Squash

In the winter, we enjoy baking all the different colorful squash we find at farm stands and supermarkets. One of our favorites is butternut squash with its pale-tan hard skin, bright orange flesh, and a long neck and bulb-like bottom. The shape always reminds us of a stringed musical instrument called the mandolin. Cutting through the squash is definitely adult work, but kids can help scoop out the flesh and seeds, prepare the squash for baking, and drop in the butter and brown sugar at the end.

How hard is this recipe? Easy/Intermediate

Adult help needed with cutting and using the oven

Serves 4

Equipment

cutting board	aluminum foil	table knife
large chef's knife	timer	fork
tablespoon	pot holders	tongs
4-quart baking pan	cooling rack	serving plate
liquid measuring cup	measuring spoons	

Ingredients

2 large butternut squash   4 teaspoons butter (or to taste), divided

1 cup water   4 tablespoons brown sugar, divided

1. Position the rack in the center of the oven and preheat the oven to 400 degrees F.
2. Have an adult cut the squash in half. Kids can scrape out the flesh and seeds with a tablespoon.
3. Place the squash, flesh side up, in the baking pan. Fill the bottom of the pan with the water. Cover the pan tightly with aluminum foil.
4. Bake the squash for about 40 minutes. (This might vary depending on size of the squash.) Have an adult use pot holders and remove the pan from oven, uncover and discard the foil (taking care not to get burned from the steam), and then drain the water. Place on the cooling rack. Kids can help put 1 tablespoon brown sugar and 1 teaspoon butter into the hollow of the squash.
5. Use pot holders to return the squash to the oven and bake, uncovered, for about 5 minutes. The squash is ready when the butter-sugar mixture is melted and the orange squash flesh can be easily pierced with a fork.
6. Have an adult use pot holders to remove the pan to a cooling rack. Let it cool for several minutes. Use tongs to place the squash on a serving plate.
7. Serve immediately. (Scoop out the flesh in the neck of the squash first, dipping it into the butter-sugar mixture.)

Variation: In place of brown sugar and butter, put maple syrup or honey in the hollow when you're ready to serve the squash.

Kid Quiz

Is butternut squash a summer or winter squash?

Butternut is one of the many varieties of hard-skinned winter squash. These squash have hard seeds and a deep yellow to bright orange flesh. Other varieties of winter squash are acorn, Hubbard, spaghetti, buttercup, and turban.

The other type of squash is known as summer squash. These squash have thin skins and soft seeds that you can eat. Zucchini, yellow crookneck, and pattypan are typical varieties of summer squash. Look for squash at farmers' markets, farm stands, and your supermarket.

Cheesy Zucchini Boats

The bubbly cheese topping adds flavor to these summer squash boats. My mom taught me how to make this recipe, and now my kids help make them for our family. They like the flavor and enjoy sprinkling the cheese on top of the boats.

How hard is this recipe? Easy/Intermediate

Adult help needed with cutting and using the oven

Serves 4 (makes 8 small zucchini boats)

Equipment

cutting board	pot holders
sharp knife	table knife
fork	measuring spoons
jelly roll or baking pan	cooling rack
liquid measuring cup	spatula
timer	serving plate

Ingredients

2 large zucchini, washed	2 to 3 tablespoons butter
½ cup water	8 tablespoons grated Parmesan cheese

1. Position the rack in the upper third of oven and preheat the oven to 425 degrees F.

continued

continued

2. Slice the ends off the zucchini and discard. Cut each zucchini in half crosswise and then cut each half lengthwise down the middle to make 8 boats. Run a fork lightly down the center of the flat side of each zucchini. (This helps the butter and cheese sink into the zucchini.)

3. Put the zucchini, cut side up, in the pan and add ½ cup of water to the bottom of the pan. (The water will steam the zucchini during baking.) If you like really crunchy zucchini or if the skin of the zucchini is very thin and tender, you can reduce the amount of water or omit it altogether.

4. Cook the zucchini for 10 to 15 minutes or until they are tender. Cooking time varies with size of the zucchini. When cooked, a fork should pierce them easily. When done, transfer the pan to a cooling rack.

5. Turn the oven off and reset it to high broil. Keep the oven door slightly open.

6. Cut the butter into thin slivers and distribute them evenly over the surface of each zucchini. (The butter will begin to melt.) Sprinkle 1 tablespoon cheese all along the surface of each boat.

7. Keeping the oven door slightly open, broil the zucchini for 3 to 5 minutes or until the cheese topping turns golden and starts to bubble.

8. When done, use pot holders and transfer the pan to the cooling rack. Use the spatula to lift up the zucchini and put them on a serving plate. Serve immediately.

Stir-Fry Veggies with Sesame Seeds

This colorful stir-fry is a quick and easy way to cook veggies and give them lots of flavor. When you're in a hurry, use packaged precut vegetables or whatever vegetables you have on hand. You can put the veggies on rice or pasta, or you can even toss in some tofu toward the end of cooking for more substance—and protein. Kids can help prepare the vegetables, try stir-frying, drizzle the sauce, and sprinkle the seeds on the cooked vegetables.

How hard is this recipe? Easy

Adult help needed with cutting and at the stove

Serves 4

Equipment

small bowl	timer
measuring spoons	wooden spoon or stir-fry tool
cutting board	liquid measuring cuo
sharp knife	pot holder
large bowl	spoon
wok or 10- to 12-inch skillet with lid	serving bowl

Ingredients

1 tablespoon soy sauce

½ teaspoon sesame oil

1 tablespoon vegetable oil

8 ounces carrots, sliced lengthwise (about 2 cups)

8 ounces broccoli florets (about 2 cups)

½ red bell pepper, sliced lengthwise into slivers

½ yellow or orange bell pepper, sliced lengthwise into slivers

¼ cup water or chicken broth

1 tablespoon toasted sesame seeds

1. In the small bowl, combine the soy sauce and sesame oil; set it aside.
2. Heat the vegetable oil over medium-high heat for 1 minute. Add the carrots and cook, constantly tossing, for 1 minute.
3. Add the remaining vegetables and stir-fry for 3 minutes.
4. Pour in ¼ cup water or chicken broth, cover, and cook for 2 minutes or until all the liquid is gone. Vegetables should be slightly crisp but tender.
5. Use the pot holders to lift the wok or skillet and, with the wooden spoon, put the vegetables in the serving bowl. Use the spoon to stir the soy sauce and sesame oil and then drizzle it over the vegetables. Toss to distribute sauce. Sprinkle sesame seeds over the vegetables. Serve immediately.

Mashed Potato Mountains

Fluffy mashed potatoes go with just about any American meal. They are the ultimate comfort food. Once you learn how to make them, you'll find yourself wanting to fix them again and again. Mash them right in the saucepan and watch how they turn into a creamy mass as you whip them. Just mound them into little mountains right on everyone's plate.

How hard is this recipe? Easy/Intermediate

Adult help needed with cutting and at the stove

Serves 4 (makes 4 cups potatoes)

Equipment

cutting board

vegetable peeler

paring knife

medium saucepan with lid

measuring spoons

timer

colander

fork

pot holders

kitchen towel or hot pad

potato masher

liquid measuring cup

whisk

wooden spoon

dinner plates

Ingredients

5 to 6 medium russet or Idaho potatoes, about 2 pounds

½ teaspoon kosher salt

3 tablespoons butter

½ cup nonfat milk

salt and pepper to taste

continued

continued

1. On the cutting board, use the vegetable peeler to remove the potato skins. Rinse the board and the potatoes under cold running water. Place the potatoes on the board and cut each potato into quarters.

2. Put the potato chunks into the saucepan and cover them with water to about ½ inch above the potatoes. Sprinkle the ½ teaspoon of salt into the water.

3. Put the pot on the stove and turn the heat to high. Bring the potatoes to a boil (it will take about 10 minutes) and then immediately turn the heat to low. Cover the saucepan and simmer for about 15 minutes.

4. While you're waiting, set up the colander in the sink and clean the cutting board and potato peels.

5. Check the potatoes. They're done if they are soft and tender when you pierce them with the fork. If not ready, cook for another 2 minutes and test again.

6. When the potatoes are done, ask an adult to use a pot holder to remove the pot from the stove and drain the contents of the pot into the colander. Grasp the handles of the colander with pot holders and return the drained potatoes to the saucepan.

7. Put the saucepan back on the burner over low heat and shake the pan to let the potatoes dry out. When they appear dry, turn off the burner.

8. Use pot holders to remove the pot from the stove and place it on the counter on a kitchen towel or hot pad. Hold the handle of the saucepan while you mash the potatoes with a masher until they are in small chunks and start to look smooth.

9. Whisk in the butter and then slowly add the milk. The potatoes will become creamy and fluffy. Season with salt and pepper to taste.

10. Use the wooden spoon to mound the potatoes onto dinner plates and serve immediately.

Polenta Stars and Shapes

Make polenta into stars by pressing a cookie cutter into cooked polenta rounds. If you top the stars with cheese, you've got a dish that will brighten any dinner plate. You get two recipes in one with these stars. Use the leftover shapes from the rounds by sprinkling them with oil and Italian seasonings and baking them alongside the stars.

How hard is this recipe? Easy/Intermediate

Adult help needed with cutting and using the oven

Makes 15 stars

Equipment

cutting board

sharp knife

kitchen scissors (optional)

table knife

kitchen ruler

2-inch star cookie cutter

2 nonstick baking or jelly roll pans

measuring spoons

pot holders

timer

cooling racks

plastic spatula

serving plate

serving bowl

Ingredients

1 (24-ounce) package precooked polenta in a log (about 7½ inches long)

2 teaspoons extra-virgin olive oil

¼ teaspoon Italian seasoning

2½ ounces mozzarella cheese, cut into 2 half-inch slices

1. Position the racks in the top and middle of the oven and preheat the oven to 375 degrees F.

2. Use the sharp knife or kitchen scissors to cut and remove the plastic packaging from the polenta. (Water will squirt out.) Cut the roll crosswise into ½-inch rounds. (Kids can do this with a table knife.) Put a kitchen ruler at the top of the log to help guide you.

3. Place all the rounds, flat side down, on the cutting board. Center the star cookie cutter on each round and press down to cut out the star. Lift the star up, push the polenta out, and put the excess pieces from the round on a baking pan.

4. When you've finished cutting out the stars, drizzle the oil over the polenta tidbits. Sprinkle the herbs evenly over the pieces and toss with your clean hands. Set this aside.

5. Use your clean hands to put the stars, flat side down, onto the second baking pan.

6. Cut the mozzarella slices like a pie into 8 wedges and put a wedge on top of each star. (You'll have one left over.)

7. Use pot holders to place the pan holding the polenta tidbits on the upper rack in the oven and put the stars on the middle rack. Bake for 15 minutes.

8. When done, use pot holders to move the pans to the cooling racks. Use the spatula to transfer the stars to a serving plate and the tidbits to a serving bowl. Allow cheese to cool slightly, and then serve at once.

Variation: Try different cheeses on top of the stars. We like to brush the stars with olive oil and sprinkle each star with ½ teaspoon grated Parmesan or pecorino romano cheese.

Oven-Roasted Baby Potatoes with Herbs

These potatoes are a dinner standby in our house because they cook up so quickly, taste so good, and go with so many main dishes. The oil and herbs give them a rich and crispy texture as the potatoes roast. Try experimenting with different dried herbs to see how the flavor changes.

How hard is this recipe? Easy

Adult help needed with cutting and using the oven

Serves 4

continued

continued

Equipment

cutting board	measuring spoons	fork
sharp knife	wooden spoon	cooling rack
nonstick jelly roll pan, roasting pan, or 10-inch pie pan	pot holders	serving plate
	timer	

Ingredients

1¼ pounds red new potatoes, scrubbed and eyes removed

2 tablespoons virgin or extra-virgin olive oil

1 tablespoon dried fine herbs, or Italian seasonings

¼ teaspoon salt

1. Position the rack in the upper third of the oven and preheat the oven to 425 degrees F.

2. Cut the potatoes in half and place them in the baking pan. Drizzle oil over the potatoes and toss them with the wooden spoon to coat them evenly with the oil. Sprinkle the herbs on the potatoes and toss them again.

3. Bake, uncovered, for 30 to 40 minutes, stirring occasionally to allow even browning. When cooked, the potatoes will be browned and can be pierced easily with a fork.

4. Use pot holders to remove the pan from the oven and place it on the cooling rack. Sprinkle with salt. Serve immediately.

Pink Rice

My friend Helen Cunningham made up this shortcut version of Mexican or Spanish rice. The rice typically contains tomatoes, but in this recipe, you use tomato juice and chili powder to give it color and flavor. Wait until you see the bright color it turns the rice. Kids can sprinkle in the chili powder and pour in the juice.

How hard is this recipe? Easy

Adult help needed at the stove

Serves 4

Equipment	**Ingredients**
measuring spoons	2 tablespoons olive oil
3-quart saucepan with lid	1½ cups parboiled, enriched white rice
timer	2 cups fat-free chicken broth
dry measuring cups	1 cup tomato or tomato-vegetable juice
wooden spoon	½ teaspoon salt
liquid measuring cup	1 tablespoon chili powder
fork	
pot holder	
serving board	

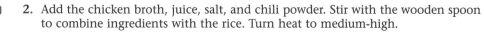

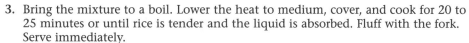 1. Heat the oil in the saucepan for 1 minute over medium heat. Add the rice, stir to coat, and cook for 2 minutes.

2. Add the chicken broth, juice, salt, and chili powder. Stir with the wooden spoon to combine ingredients with the rice. Turn heat to medium-high.

3. Bring the mixture to a boil. Lower the heat to medium, cover, and cook for 20 to 25 minutes or until rice is tender and the liquid is absorbed. Fluff with the fork. Serve immediately.

Jeremy Wearn, 10

Kid Comment

Jeremy Wearn, 10: "This is fun and easy to make. This is good as a side dish. It reminds me of Spanish rice."

Kitchen Clue

With so many different types of rice so readily available today, it's fun to experiment with various types. Take a tour of the rice aisle at your supermarket or the bulk bins at a local health food store. We like the nutty flavor and chewy texture of short-grain brown rice. The kids also like the stickier consistency of sushi rice.

Fluffy Couscous with Golden Raisins

If you were to visit North Africa, you would see many people eating pale yellow granules called couscous. When I was a student traveling in Morocco, I learned to eat it by using my cupped hand as a scooper to put the couscous in my mouth. Eating couscous is a communal event, and our hosts would bring out steaming mounds of it with chicken and chick peas on a large bronze tray. We'd sit around the tray and talk as we ate our meal with our hands. It was very exotic and fun to experience the customs of another culture. These days at my home we don't eat couscous with our hands, but we do make it often as a side dish in place of rice or pasta. Instant couscous is quick and easy to cook and can be served plain with butter or oil or mixed with nuts, raisins, and your favorite dried fruits.

How hard is this recipe? Easy

Adult help needed at the stove

Makes 4 cups

Equipment		Ingredients
liquid measuring cup	table knife	2 cups chicken broth
3-quart saucepan with lid	wooden spoon	1½ cups instant couscous
dry measuring cup	serving bowl	½ cup golden raisins
pot holder		2 tablespoons butter
timer		pinch of salt

1. Bring the chicken broth to a boil in the saucepan over medium-high heat.
2. Sprinkle in the couscous and raisins. Use the pot holder to remove the saucepan from the heat and let it stand, covered, for 5 minutes. The grains should taste tender.
3. Use the wooden spoon to stir in the butter and salt. As the butter is melting, use the spoon to toss the grains so they appear fluffy. Serve immediately.

Kitchen Clue

Cooking times will vary depending on the type of couscous you use. If you buy noninstant couscous from the bulk bin of your market, follow step 1. Add the couscous and raisins, cover, and reduce the heat to let the couscous simmer for 15 minutes. Be sure to check the cooking directions for the type of couscous you purchase.

Chapter 27

Snacktime

> ## Recipes
>
> ➤ Veggies and Dip
>
> ➤ Crunchy Celery Logs with Homemade Peanut Butter
>
> ➤ Guacamole
>
> ➤ Hard-to-Resist Homemade Tortilla Chips
>
> ➤ Fresh Tomato Salsa
>
> ➤ Out-of-This World Hummus
>
> ➤ Crispy Crunchy Pita Chips
>
> ➤ Quesadillas
>
> ➤ Finger Lickin' Dippin' Fruit
>
> ➤ Fruit Face
>
> ➤ Melon Boat with People
>
> ➤ Lizzie's Super Smushes

Snacks give kids a chance to refuel and keep their energy up during the day. I've always viewed snacks as a way to get in some vitamins, minerals, and other nutrients, no matter what your age. That's not to say that snacks have to be boring. In fact, kids will eat their fruits and veggies willingly when they're enticed by a good dip or a chance to be creative. You'll find opportunities for both of these on the following pages. Kids will enjoy dipping fresh fruits into yogurt and learning how to make their own chips, salsas, and dips. The whole family can become food artists by making fruit faces and melon boats.

Because many kids will be fixing snacks on their own, I've included several no-cook, no-cut, and do-ahead snacks. Flip through the following pages to find nutritious, fun-to-make, and fun-to-eat nibbles.

Veggies and Dip

 I always try to keep a few bags of tender baby carrots and sliced veggies in the refrigerator for after-school snacking. My kids like to fill up a plate with these handy vegetables and dunk them in hummus, dressings, or dips. In the morning or the night before, slice some zucchini, bell peppers, celery, broccoli, and cucumbers and refrigerate them in covered containers or plastic bags so they're ready when hunger strikes as you step in the door. What an easy way to get in your 5-a-Day! If you are serving more than one person, multiply the ingredients by the number of people.

How hard is this recipe? Easy

Adult help needed with cutting

Serves 1

Equipment		Ingredients
cutting board	dry measuring cup	2 cups chopped vegetables
sharp knife	small bowl	1 cup hummus, prepared dip, or yogurt
serving plate		

1. Set the vegetables out on a plate.
2. Put dip in a small bowl.
3. Dunk vegetables into dip.

Kitchen Clue

To save time when preparing veggie snacks, pick up prewashed, precut vegetables at the supermarket. Warehouse clubs also sell large bags of these veggies at good prices. Make sure the vegetables look freshly cut with no brown edges.

Crunchy Celery Logs with Homemade Peanut Butter

Celery slathered with peanut butter was one of the first snacks my kids learned to make, and it's still a favorite. The grainier texture and full-bodied taste of homemade peanut butter goes well with the celery. Kids can make a batch of peanut butter and can cut up celery sticks with adults at night. This way, as soon as they get home the next day, they'll be able to fix a no-cook, no-cut snack. It's also interesting for kids to see how to make something from the original food source instead of eating it out of a jar. In this case, they're making peanut butter from the nuts.

How hard is this recipe? Easy

Adult help needed with cutting and using the food processor

Serves 2 (makes ¼ cup peanut butter)

Equipment

dry measuring cup	sharp knife
food processor	container with lid
rubber spatula	resealable plastic bag
small bowl	table knife
paper towels	serving plate
cutting board	

Ingredients

1 cup shelled, dry-roasted or cocktail peanuts

vegetable oil, if necessary

2 stalks celery

1. Make the peanut butter by placing the nuts in the bowl of the food processor. Process for about 2 minutes. The peanuts first will break up into fine bits, then they'll become moist with their own oil, and then they'll start to clump together. When a ball forms, continue to process for another 30 seconds to smooth out the texture. If the peanut butter seems too dry, drizzle in a little oil. Rub some peanut butter between your fingers. If it seems too grainy, process a few seconds more. Use the rubber spatula to remove the peanut butter to the bowl.

2. Wash the celery under cool running water and pat it dry. Cut off and discard the tough, white bottom part of the stalk along with the leaves, just below where they join the stalk. Cut the stalk into 2- to 3-inch pieces. Repeat for the second stalk.

3. If you're not using it immediately, refrigerate and store the peanut butter in a closed container. Store the celery in a resealable plastic bag.

4. When you're ready to assemble, use the table knife to spread the peanut butter into the hollow of the celery. Put it on a plate and serve.

Guacamole

 My kids grew up eating guacamole because our first baby sitter was from Guatemala, and she happily shared her family's recipe with us. This creamy dip, made with mashed avocados, is eaten in Mexico and other Latin American countries, such as Guatemala. You'll find different versions, some of which use lemon juice instead of lime juice or use different seasonings. Scoop up your guacamole with homemade tortilla chips (see the next recipe) or use it as a spread on sandwiches or tortilla wraps.

How hard is this recipe? Easy

Adult help needed with cutting

Makes 1½ cups

Equipment

cutting board	potato masher or fork
sharp knife	measuring spoons
tablespoon	plastic wrap
large bowl	

Ingredients

2 medium ripe avocados (about 6 ounces each)

1 medium ripe tomato, finely diced (about ¾ cup)

½ small onion, finely diced (about ¼ cup)

1 tablespoon plus 1 teaspoon fresh lime juice

2 tablespoons finely minced fresh cilantro leaves

¼ teaspoon salt, preferably kosher

 1. Cut the avocado in half by piercing the skin with a sharp knife until it hits the pit. Move the knife lengthwise all the way around the pit. Do not try to cut through the pit.

 2. Twist the avocado halves and pull to separate the halves. To remove the pit, hit it with the long edge of the knife. Turn the knife, still stuck in the pit, clockwise until the pit loosens. Use the spoon to scoop out the flesh and place the avocado in the large bowl. Discard the avocado shell and the pit.

3. Mash the avocado with a potato masher or a fork until it's smooth. If you prefer, you can mash it less for a chunkier texture.

4. Add the tomato, onion, lime juice, cilantro, and salt. Stir with the tablespoon to combine.

5. Serve immediately or refrigerate, covered with plastic wrap, for up to 3 hours.

Kid Comment

Lizzie Cooke, 12: "Make sure you wear an apron; otherwise, the avocado will get all over you. It's a lot easier to mash the avocado with a potato masher instead of a fork."

Heads Up!

If left out in the open, the avocado in the guacamole turns brown from the oxygen in the air. If you're not going to eat the guacamole right away, cover it with plastic wrap and press the wrap onto the surface of the dip. This prevents the air from discoloring the avocado.

Kitchen Clue

Avocados are a fruit with a rich, buttery texture. You'll find two types: The Haas is purply-black with a pebbly skin, and the Fuerte is green with a thin, smooth skin. For guacamole, we prefer the darker Haas variety with its smaller pit and creamier texture.

Choose avocados without blemishes or dark, sunken spots. Ripe avocados will be firm, but when you press them, they should feel a little soft under the skin. Store ripe avocados in the refrigerator for up to a week and store unripe ones at room temperature until they ripen.

Most avocados in the market are hard and are not ripe. To speed up ripening, put them in a paper bag with an apple. (The apple emits a gas that ripens other fruits and vegetables.) Close the top but pierce the bag in several places and keep it at room temperature for up to 3 days.

Hard-to-Resist
Homemade Tortilla Chips

Did you know that you can make your own tortilla chips in the oven? They're fast and easy to bake, and they're much more healthy than the packaged ones because they're not deep-fried in oil. Enjoy these chips with your guacamole, other dips, or just as a crunchy munchy. We like to use a pizza wheel to cut up the tortillas.

How hard is this recipe? Easy

Adult help needed with cutting and using the oven

Makes 32 chips

Equipment

cutting board	timer
pizza wheel or sharp knife	metal spatula
measuring spoons	wire cooling rack
jelly roll or baking pan	serving bowl
pot holders	covered container or resealable plastic bag

Ingredients

4 corn tortillas

1 (5-ounce) can vegetable oil spray

$\frac{1}{8}$ to $\frac{1}{4}$ teaspoon salt

1. Position the rack in the upper part of the oven and preheat the oven to 400 degrees F.

2. Place the tortillas on the cutting board and lightly spray each side with the vegetable spray. Sprinkle the salt on the tortillas.

3. Stack 2 tortillas on top of each other. Use the pizza wheel or a sharp knife to cut the tortillas like a pie into 8 triangular pieces. (Cut the whole in half, then cut the half in half to make fourths, and then cut the fourths in half to make eighths.) Repeat with the other two tortillas and set them aside. Place the 16 pieces in one layer on the ungreased pan.

4. Use pot holders to place the pan in the oven and bake for 8 minutes or until the tortillas are lightly browned and crisp. Look through the oven window to see how the tortillas change and curl up and start to look like chips.

5. Remove the tortillas from the oven, place them on a wire rack, and let them cool in the pan for about 5 minutes. Use the spatula to push the tortillas from the pan into a bowl. Bake the remaining tortilla pieces, let them cool, and add them to the bowl.

6. Serve the chips immediately or store them in a resealable bag or container.

Variation: Instead of using salt, try sprinkling some chili powder or Mexican seasoning on the tortillas before baking.

Fresh Tomato Salsa

 Making homemade salsa is simple, and it's so much better than the store-bought variety because you know it's really fresh and preservative-free. When tomatoes are in season, the salsa bursts with their succulent flavor. Add finely diced jalapen[td]o pepper if you want some heat. Use this salsa as a dip for tortilla or pita chips or as a topping for chili, meat, or fish.

How hard is this recipe? Easy

Adult help needed with cutting

Makes 2½ cups

Equipment

cutting board	lemon reamer or juicer	spoon
sharp knife	small strainer	plastic wrap
dry measuring cups	small bowl	timer
measuring spoons	large bowl	

Ingredients

4 medium tomatoes, diced (about 2½ cups)

½ small onion, finely diced (about ⅓ to ½ cup)

2 tablespoons fresh cilantro, finely minced (leaves from about 6 sprigs)

2 tablespoons lime juice (about ½ lime juiced)

¼ teaspoon salt

1. Put all the ingredients in a large bowl and mix them thoroughly to blend.
2. Refrigerate the mixture, covered with plastic wrap, for 30 to 60 minutes to allow flavors to meld. Serve cold.

Out-of-This-World Hummus

 Hummus is a smooth and creamy Middle Eastern dip made from chick peas and traditionally served with pita bread. The bread is torn into bite-size pieces and then dipped into the hummus. (You'll also see this word spelled "hoomus.") This recipe was given to me by my friends Carol and Edward Dayoob, and it was handed down in Edward's Lebanese family. Their kids, now grown, used to help make the dip by squeezing the lemons and putting the ingredients into the blender.

How hard is this recipe? Easy

Adult help needed with cutting and using the food processor or blender and can opener

Makes 3 cups

continues

continued

Equipment

cutting board	measuring spoons	liquid measuring cup
sharp knife	lemon juicer or reamer	rubber spatula
food processor or blender	strainer	serving bowl or plate
can opener	small bowl	

Ingredients

2 large cloves garlic, peeled and trimmed	½ teaspoon salt
2 (15½-ounce) cans chick peas, drained	½ cup cool water
6 tablespoons roasted sesame tahini	1 tablespoon olive oil
2 lemons, juiced (about ½ cup)	1 tablespoon chopped parsley
¼ teaspoon cumin	

1. Drop the garlic cloves into the blender or food processor, secure the lid, and blend or process for several seconds to chop the garlic.
2. Add the chick peas, tahini, lemon juice, cumin, and salt to the container and refit the lid on tightly.
3. Blend on medium speed or process for several minutes until the ingredients are well-mixed and smooth, scraping down the sides of the container as needed with the rubber spatula. The dip will be somewhat dense. Slowly drizzle the water through the hole in the lid or feed tube and continue to blend or process until the dip becomes light and fluffy.
4. Use the spatula to put the hummus in the bowl. Drizzle the oil on top and sprinkle with the parsley.
5. Serve immediately with pita bread or cover with plastic wrap and refrigerate for later use.

Note: If the oil has risen to the top of the tahini in the jar, mix it in before you measure the tahini for the hummus.

You can use a blender to make the dip but it works much better in a food processor.

For a colorful and attractive presentation, put the hummus on the serving plate and surround the dip with wedges of tomatoes and pita, sliced into triangular-shaped wedges.

Learn the Lingo

Tahini is a paste made from ground sesame seeds. It traditionally is used to flavor hummus and another dip made from eggplant called **baba ghanoush.** Originally only available in Middle Eastern markets and natural foods stores, tahini is now widely distributed in supermarkets. The oil tends to separate and rise to the top of the tahini, and it should be thoroughly blended before using.

Kitchen Clue

Save yourself a step when a recipe calls for adding chopped garlic to ingredients in a blender or a food processor. Just drop the garlic in the container first and blend or process for a few seconds. The garlic will be chopped, and you can just add the rest of the ingredients.

Crispy Crunchy Pita Chips

When we're in the mood for something crunchy, we like to make these pita chips. They're more healthful than processed snack chips, and they make great dippers for spreads. Sprinkle the pita bread with seasonings or grated cheese before you bake them to create different flavor combinations.

How hard is this recipe? Easy

Adult help needed with cutting and using the oven

Makes 32 pita chips

continues

continued

Equipment

cutting board	pastry brush	timer
pizza wheel or	jelly roll pan	serving bowl
sharp knife	pot holders	covered container or
liquid measuring cup		resealable plastic bag

Ingredients

2 (6-inch) pita breads

¼ cup olive or canola oil

grated cheese or seasonings to taste

1. Position the rack in the center of the oven and preheat the oven to 400 degrees F.
2. Put the pita bread on a cutting board and use the pizza wheel or a sharp knife to cut the pita bread into 8 wedges, like a pie.
3. Take each wedge and pull it apart at the seam of the joined end to create two triangles.
4. Brush the rough side of the triangle with oil and sprinkle it with the seasonings.
5. Place the bread in a single layer, oiled side up, on the jelly roll pan and bake for 8 to 10 minutes or until crispy and golden brown.
6. Use the pot holders to remove the chips from the oven and put them in a serving bowl. The chips can be stored in a covered container for several days.

Kitchen Clue

There's almost no limit to the seasonings you can use to flavor the pita bread. Try chili powder, cumin or coriander (together or separate), garlic powder, onion powder, fine herbs, grated Parmesan or romano cheese, curry powder, or cracked pepper. For a sweet chip, kids can try cinnamon sugar.

Kid Quiz

What part of the world does pita (pronounced PEE-tah) bread come from?

This round bread comes from the Middle East. It's a flat bread made from either white or whole wheat flour. The bread splits to make a pocket, which is why it also is called pocket bread. Stuff the pocket with ingredients to make a sandwich. If you visited the Middle East, you'd be served whole pita breads with meals, or you could tear off bite-size pieces to dip into hummus or other spreads.

Quesadillas

Tortillas with melted cheese are a quick and easy afternoon snack. Kids love to make them and watch the cheese melt. They're like a grilled cheese sandwich made with tortillas. Make them in the microwave or flip them at the stove. Eat the quesadillas plain or add your favorite seasonings or even green chilies.

How hard is this recipe? Easy

Adult help needed with cutting, using the grater or food processor, and at the stove

Makes 1 quesadilla

Equipment

cutting board	measuring spoons	pot holder
sharp knife	10-inch nonstick skillet or	plastic spatula
grater or food processor with a grating disk	microwave-safe plate	dinner plate
	paper towel	
large plate for grated cheese	timer	

Ingredients

¼ teaspoon vegetable oil

2 (6- to 8-inch) flour or corn tortillas

3 to 4 tablespoons grated, low-fat hard cheese, such as cheddar or Monterey Jack

4 teaspoons each salsa, beans, and sour cream (optional)

1. Put the oil in the skillet and spread it with a folded paper towel to create a thin film of oil.

continues

continued

2. Place 1 tortilla on the skillet and sprinkle the cheese on top. Try to keep the cheese away from the edges so it doesn't seep out of the tortilla when it melts. Put the second tortilla on top of the cheese.

3. Put the skillet on the stove and turn the heat to medium. Cook, uncovered, for about 4 minutes.

4. Grasp the skillet handle with the pot holder and use the spatula to flip the tortilla and cook it for another 2 to 3 minutes on the other side.

5. With the spatula, remove the quesadilla from the skillet and place it on the dinner plate. Let it cool for 2 minutes and then cut it into four wedges. Serve immediately.

6. Put 1 teaspoon salsa, sour cream, or beans on each wedge, fold it over, and eat immediately.

Microwave directions: Prepare the tortilla with the cheese as previously directed. Put the tortilla on a microwave-safe plate and cook it for 30 seconds. Use pot holders to remove it from the microwave and let it cool for 2 minutes. Cut it into four wedges and serve.

Heads Up!

The cheese in the quesadilla is very hot just after being cooked. Be sure to wait 2 minutes and slice the quesadilla into wedges before eating so you don't burn your tongue. Use a pizza wheel for easy slicing.

Kid Quiz

What fruits are good for super-simple frozen snacks?

Answer: Bananas and grapes, although grapes should not be eaten by young children who are at risk for choking on them. For a banana treat, peel it, cut it up into rounds, and freeze the rounds in a plastic bag. Spread the coins out flat. To eat them, take the rounds out of the freezer, put them in a bowl, let them soften for a few minutes, and then mash them together. The flavor is sweet, and the consistency is like a frozen dessert. For a grape snack, put the grapes in the freezer for a few hours. To eat them, remove them from the freezer, let them thaw for a few minutes, and then pop them in your mouth.

Finger Lickin' Dippin' Fruit

 When you get home from school, cut up some fruit, put it on a big plate, and then use a skewer to dip it into your favorite flavored yogurt. Try this combination of fruits or see what you've got in the refrigerator to make your own platter. If an adult isn't home to help you cut, put together no-cut fruits, such as grapes, berries, and bananas. You also can make this for your family for a nice dessert after dinner.

How hard is this recipe? Easy

Adult help needed with cutting

Serves 4

Equipment

cutting board	large plate	spoon
sharp knife	small bowl	4 (8-inch) bamboo skewers
table knife		

Ingredients

8 large red or green grapes, washed and patted dry

8 medium strawberries, washed and patted dry

1 large ripe banana, peeled and cut into rounds

2 kiwi, skinned and cut into chunks

1 small apple, peeled, cored, and cut into chunks

1 (8-ounce) container low-fat vanilla yogurt

continues

continued

1. Arrange the washed and cut-up fruit on a large plate.
2. Spoon the yogurt into a small bowl.
3. Use skewers to pierce the fruit and dip it into the yogurt.

Kid Comment

Lizzie Cooke, 12: "It's fun to dip the fruit in the yogurt and eat off the skewer. This is a great after-school snack."

Fruit Face

 Create this green-haired funny face on your plate with fruit. What a way to eat your 5-a-Day fruits! Can you think of another face to make with some of your other favorite fruits?

How hard is this? Very Easy

Adult help needed with cutting and using the can opener

Makes 1 fruit face

Equipment

paper towels	table knife
can opener	dinner plate
cutting board	

Ingredients

2 red grapes	2 pineapple rings
22 green grapes	8 mandarin orange slices
1 large strawberry, green stem removed	½ medium banana, cut into rounds

1. Wash the grapes and the strawberry. Pat them dry with paper towels.
2. On the plate, make eyes by arranging the pineapple rings next to each other toward the top. Place the red grapes in the holes. For eyebrows, place 3 mandarin slices above each eye.
3. To make hair, scatter the green grapes above and around the pineapple eyes.

4. For the nose, place the strawberry, stem side down, between and slightly below the pineapple rings.

5. For the smile, arrange the banana rounds into a semicircle at the bottom edge of the plate.

6. Finally, for the ears, place a mandarin slice beside the pineapple rings on the left and right rim of the plate. Serve immediately.

Kid Comment

Lizzie Cooke, 12: "These are really fun to make because you get to create a face, and it really looks neat with all the colors. Once you actually make it, you might as well eat it."

Melon Boat with People

 Turn a slice of melon into an edible boat with a grape sail and strawberry people. This looks pretty and tastes fresh and juicy.

How hard is this recipe? Easy

Adult help needed with cutting

Makes 1 melon boat

Equipment

paper towels	4 toothpicks	sharp knife
bamboo skewers, 9" or longer	cutting board	dinner plate

Ingredients

8 green grapes	3- to 4-inch wedge cantaloupe,
4 small strawberries	honeydew, or crenshaw melon with skin

1. Wash the grapes and strawberries and pat them dry with paper towels. Remove the stems from the strawberries.

2. Push the skewer through the middle of each grape, from one point to the other point, to make a string of grapes on the skewer.

3. Push a toothpick through the center of each strawberry from stem to tip.

4. Cut a small slice off the bottom of the melon wedge to allow it to lay flat and steady. Set the melon slice, skin side down, on the plate to make a boat. Attach the sail by poking the skewer with grapes into one end of the boat. Put the "people" on the boat by sticking the strawberries on toothpicks into the curve of the melon.

Kid Comment

Lizzie Cooke, 12: "Once you get done making this, you get to eat it. The grapes look like little green pearls on a string."

Lizzie's Super Smushes

 If you like the flavors of chocolate, marshmallow, and peanut butter, you're going to love this treat. All you do is spread a little bit of each on a graham cracker, smush the crackers together, and snack away. Yum! My daughter Lizzie came up with this snack using a favorite European chocolate-hazelnut spread, Nutella™, and I love eating it with her. It's like an easy-to-make s'more with peanut butter, and it tastes great with a big glass of cold milk.

How hard is this recipe? Easy

No adult help needed—except to eat!

Makes 7 smushes

Equipment

dry measuring cups   3 table knives   1 large plate

Ingredients

1 package (11 pieces) graham crackers

¼ cup chocolate-hazelnut spread (such as Nutella™)

¼ cup marshmallow cream

¼ cup smooth peanut butter

1. Break all the graham crackers in half and arrange them into seven piles of three each. (You'll have one extra half. Dunk it in milk and eat it!)

2. Working with 3 crackers at a time, smear the first cracker with chocolate, the second with marshmallow, and the third with peanut butter. Use separate knives to dip into the chocolate spread, the marshmallow, and the peanut butter.

3. Put 2 crackers together with the filling facing up and top it with a third cracker with the filling facing down.

4. Gently smush the cracker sandwich together. Repeat for the remaining sets of crackers.

5. Eat immediately, licking the filling off the sides of the crackers the way you do with an ice cream sandwich.

Variation: Make a traditional s'more by using only the chocolate and marshmallow cream.

Chapter 28

Delectable Desserts

Recipes

➤ Mom's Sweet "Egg on Toast" Wannabe

➤ Moon on a Melon

➤ Sunshine Sundae

➤ Caramel–Chocolate Chip Ice Cream Pie

➤ Danish Rice Pudding

➤ Creamy Coconut Custard

➤ Crispy Chocolate Treats

Italians have a great idea about desserts. No matter what sweets go on the table, they always set out a bowl of fresh fruit. I grew up with this ever-present fruit bowl, often accompanied by cheese, at the end of a meal. It was a great way to learn to appreciate and taste new fruits; whenever I can, I try to keep up the custom.

But what about those sweets? Why not go one step further and combine the sweet treat with the fruit? Nearly half the recipes in this chapter do just that to team up the great taste of fruit with traditional dessert components such as cake and ice cream.

Kids will enjoy preparing these and other end-of-the-meal treats. They can help make some ahead of time, such as the Danish Rice Pudding, Creamy Coconut Custard, or ice cream pie. With others, they'll have fun assembling dessert just before it's "ready to serve." Of course, desserts take many forms, so don't forget to look through Chapter 29, "The Baker's Rack," for pies, cookies, and cakes. They always taste great with that last glass of milk for the day.

Mom's Sweet
"Egg On Toast" Wannabe

 My mom made this as a teenager in the 1920s, I made it and ate it as a kid in the 1950s, and then my kids started making it again in the 1990s. Take a piece of pound cake—the "toast"—and make a pretend "egg" on top using an inverted peach half for the yolk and whipped cream all around the edges for the white. You'll end up with a yummy dessert that looks like an egg on toast. My kids' favorite part—besides the eating—is squirting the whipped cream around the peach.

How hard is this recipe? Easy

Adult help needed using the can opener and with cutting

Serves 4

Equipment

cutting board   sharp knife   can opener   fork   4 serving plates

Ingredients

4 slices store-bought pound cake (in loaf shape)

4 canned or fresh skinned peach halves

1 (7-ounce) can whipped cream

1. Put a slice of pound cake on each plate.
2. Center a peach half, flat side down, on each slice of cake.
3. Squirt whipped cream all around the outside edge of the peach to make a rim of white.
4. Serve immediately.

Kid Comment

Lizzie Cooke, 12: "This is a good mix of flavors. It's very easy, and it's really fun to make."

Moon on a Melon

 Put a scoop of ice cream or frozen yogurt in the curve of a melon slice and you have an instant dessert. The sweet, juicy melon and the cold ice cream make a great color, texture, and flavor combination. Let kids scoop the ice cream onto the melon and watch how they gobble down one of their fruits for the day.

How hard is this recipe? Easy

Adult help needed with cutting

Serves 4

Equipment

cutting board	tablespoon	4 plates
sharp knife	ice cream scoop	

Ingredients

1 cantaloupe

4 scoops vanilla or chocolate ice cream

1. Cut the melon in half. With the spoon, scrape out the seeds and discard them. Cut the halves in half, making four wedges. Slice a sliver off the bottom skin of each wedge so the melon rests flat.
2. Place each melon wedge on a plate and scoop ice cream on top of each wedge. Serve immediately.

Sunshine Sundae

 When you're in the mood for fruit and frozen yogurt, put together this colorful dessert. You'll enjoy using your hands to build the "sun" and its rays and to layer all the ingredients. You can make this into a different dessert by substituting other sun- and sunset-colored fruits and by topping them with different sauces and fruits.

How hard is this recipe? Easy

Adult help needed using the can opener

Serves 4

Equipment

can opener	4 plates	measuring spoons
fork	ice cream scoop	

Ingredients

4 slices canned pineapple rings

1 (11-ounce) can mandarin orange slices

4 scoops vanilla frozen yogurt

4 tablespoons pineapple topping, divided

4 tablespoons strawberry or raspberry sauce, divided

1 (7-ounce) can whipped light cream

4 strawberries or raspberries

continues

continued

1. Put a pineapple ring—the sun—on a plate.

2. Gently fan 10 mandarin oranges out from the edge of the pineapple. Position them so that one end touches the pineapple and they all face the same direction. They should look like rays coming out of the sun.

3. Put a scoop of frozen yogurt, round side up, in the center of the pineapple ring.

4. Drizzle 1 tablespoon pineapple topping onto the center of the frozen yogurt mound so the sauce runs down the sides. Follow with 1 tablespoon strawberry or raspberry sauce, again drizzled in the center.

5. Squirt a dollop of whipped cream in the center of the frozen yogurt. Top with a strawberry or raspberry.

6. Repeat the steps with the remaining ingredients. Serve immediately.

Variation: For a simple dessert, just use the pineapple, orange slices, and frozen yogurt without the toppings.

Caramel–Chocolate Chip Ice Cream Pie

 Making a homemade ice cream pie is easier than you think. Start with a prepared cookie crust and fill it with ice cream, chocolate chips, and caramel sauce for a pie that's even better than a store-bought one. You'll surprise the whole family with this treat.

How hard is this recipe? Easy

Adult help needed with cutting to serve pie

Makes 1 nine-inch pie

Equipment
dry measuring cups	large mixing bowl	measuring spoons	sharp knife
large serving spoon	rubber spatula	aluminum foil	serving plates

Ingredients

3 cups (1½ pints) low-fat vanilla ice cream or frozen yogurt

1 cup miniature chocolate chips

5 tablespoons store-bought caramel sauce (about 4 ounces)

1 (9-inch) cookie pie crust

1. Scoop the ice cream into the mixing bowl and allow it to soften. Using your thoroughly cleaned hands or the spatula, mix in the chocolate chips.

2. Drizzle in the caramel sauce and blend. The sauce will appear streaky in the ice cream.

3. Scoop the ice cream into the cookie pie crust and flatten the top with the back of the spatula. Cover the pie with aluminum foil. Freeze until firm.

 4. Slice into pieces with the sharp knife and serve immediately after removing from freezer. If pie is too hard to cut, let stand for several minutes or until soft enough to slice easily with the knife.

Heads Up!

Kids naturally use their hands as tools when cooking. If they want to use their hands to mix the ice cream with the chips, make sure their hands are very clean. They shouldn't lick their fingers while making the pie!

Kid Comment

Lizzie Cooke, 12: "I like the way the sauce gets marbleized in the ice cream. This was lots of fun to make, especially when I squished the ice cream through my hands to mix in the chips."

Danish Rice Pudding

This creamy rice pudding is customarily served on Christmas Eve, but I think it's too good to eat only on a holiday. The Noto family shared this recipe with me along with the Danish traditions surrounding the dessert. They hide an almond in the pudding, and when the pudding is served, the lucky person who gets the almond wins a small prize, usually a marzipan treat or a box of chocolates. Everyone looks forward to discovering who the lucky person will be. In Denmark, the pudding is made and then left in the barns at Christmas for the *nisser* or elf-like Christmas spirits. Tradition says that, if you leave them pudding, they'll do nice things for you all year; if you don't, they'll play little tricks on you. When the Noto children help make this pudding, they whip the cream, blend in the ingredients, and stir the pudding at the stove.

How hard is this recipe? Easy/Intermediate

Adult help needed with cutting, at the stove, and using the mixer

Serves 8

continues

continued

Equipment

small mixing bowl	wooden spoon	rubber spatula
hand-held electric mixer or large whisk	timer	2-quart shallow bowl
	knife	aluminum foil
liquid measuring cup	cutting board	serving spoon
2-quart saucepan	pot holder	serving bowls
dry measuring cup		
measuring spoons		

Ingredients

1 quart whole milk	½ cup blanched slivered almonds	2 teaspoons vanilla
¾ cup long-grain white rice		1 blanched whole almond
	1 cup chilled whipping cream	candy or treat for the winner (optional)
3½ tablespoons sugar	2 teaspoons almond extract	

1. Put the small mixing bowl and the whisk or mixer beaters in the refrigerator to chill them. (This makes it easier to whip the cream.)

2. Pour the milk into the saucepan and bring it to a boil over medium heat. Stir in the rice and sugar with the wooden spoon.

3. Lower the heat to medium low and simmer, uncovered, for about 25 minutes. When ready, the rice should be soft, and most of the liquid should be absorbed. Test the rice by rubbing a grain between your forefinger and thumb. The rice is ready if you don't feel a hard kernel at the center.

4. While the rice is cooking, prepare the almonds and whipped cream. An adult should chop the almonds into small pieces with the knife on the cutting board. Use the hand-held mixer or wire whisk to whip the cream in the chilled small bowl.

5. When the rice is cooked, grasp the handle of the pot with the pot holder and use the rubber spatula to scoop the rice mixture into the shallow bowl so it cools quickly to room temperature. Stir in the chopped almonds and the almond and vanilla extracts. If necessary, cover loosely with aluminum foil and refrigerate to cool.

6. When the rice has cooled, use the rubber spatula to gently fold in the whipped cream. (The rice has to be cool enough so the whipped cream doesn't turn into liquid upon contact with the rice.) Bury the whole almond in the bowl of pudding and refrigerate, covered, until ready to serve.

7. To serve, spoon into bowls, making sure the almond is hidden in one of the bowls.

Note: This dessert often is served with a fruit sauce or syrup.

Torben Noto, 8

Kid Comment

Torben Noto, 8: "Rice pudding is awesome, even if you don't win the prize."

Emma Noto, 5: "This is SOOOO easy to make. I won the prize when I was four." The Notos' mom, Peggy, says that this dessert is always a hit, and the kids look forward to making and eating it.

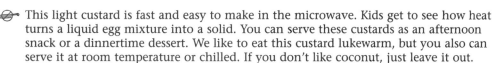

Creamy Coconut Custard

This light custard is fast and easy to make in the microwave. Kids get to see how heat turns a liquid egg mixture into a solid. You can serve these custards as an afternoon snack or a dinnertime dessert. We like to eat this custard lukewarm, but you also can serve it at room temperature or chilled. If you don't like coconut, just leave it out.

How hard is this recipe? Intermediate

Adult help needed handling hot cups out of the microwave

Makes 6 (6-ounce) servings

Equipment

4-cup microwave-safe liquid measuring cup

timer

2- to 3-quart mixing bowl

whisk

dry measuring cups

measuring spoons

pot holder

ladle

6 (6-ounce) microwave-safe custard cups

wooden spoon

Ingredients

2 cups whole milk

3 large eggs

½ cup sugar

½ teaspoon vanilla

⅛ teaspoon salt

¼ cup sweetened flaked coconut

nutmeg to sprinkle if desired

continues

continued

1. Pour the milk into the liquid measuring cup and microwave it on high for 2 to 4 minutes or until small bubbles appear around the rim of the milk. Do not let the milk boil.

2. Meanwhile, lightly whisk the eggs in the bowl and whisk in the sugar, vanilla, salt, and coconut to combine.

3. Use the pot holder to remove the milk from the microwave. Slowly add the hot milk to the mixture, whisking lightly to combine with other ingredients. Ladle equal amounts of the mixture into the custard cups.

4. Place the cups in a ring on the outer edge of the microwave platter. Microwave on medium (50 percent power) for about 4 to 8 minutes. Check every 2 minutes to see if the custard is cooked. The custards are done when they are slightly firm and are set within about an inch from the edge of the cup. The center will look like soft-set gelatin. Remove any custards that are done and continue to cook the others, checking every 30 seconds. Do not let the custards boil. (If the microwave platter doesn't move, use a wooden spoon to push the cups half a turn to the left every 2 minutes.)

5. When done, remove the custards from the microwave with the pot holders. (The cups will be very hot.) Sprinkle with nutmeg if you like and let the custards cool, uncovered, on the counter for up to 2 hours. They will continue to cook, and the center will set as it cools. If you are not eating them within 2 hours, refrigerate.

6. Serve when the custards are set.

Heads Up!

The wattage or power of your microwave oven will affect how fast the custards cook. This is why there's a range in the cooking time. You don't want the custards to boil; this is why you cook at medium power. At this power, the heat spreads slowly throughout the custard.

Crispy Chocolate Treats

Bite into these crunchy, gooey treats for mouthfuls of peanut and chocolate wrapped around your favorite light, crackling cereal. This family favorite tastes even better the second day.

How hard is this? Intermediate

Adult supervision needed at the stove and for mixing and cutting

Makes 24 two-inch squares

Equipment

dry measuring cups	14-inch sheet waxed paper	small rubber spatula
large mixing bowl	table knife	pot holders
wooden spoon	3-quart nonstick saucepan or	metal spatula
sharp knife	3-quart microwave-safe bowl	serving plate
13 × 9 × 2-inch baking pan	timer	

Ingredients

5 cups rice cereal	3 tablespoons butter
½ cup dry roasted peanuts	12 ounces large marshmallows (about 50)
½ cup miniature chocolate morsels	¼ cup reduced-fat peanut butter
nonstick spray or butter for greasing	

1. Combine the cereal, peanuts, and chocolate morsels in the large bowl. Generously grease the wooden spoon, sharp knife, baking pan, and one side of the waxed paper. Place the bowl, paper, and pan near the stove.

2. Melt the butter in the saucepan over moderately low heat. Add the marshmallows and stir with the greased spoon until melted. This should take about 8 minutes. Use the rubber spatula to scoop out the peanut butter and add it to the marshmallows. Stir with the wooden spoon just until combined. This should take about 1 minute.

3. Pour the cereal mixture into the saucepan and stir to combine it with the sauce. Kids will need help here because the mixture will be very sticky and hard to stir.

4. Use pot holders to lift the saucepan and immediately spoon and spread the mixture into the baking pan. Cover it with the waxed paper, greased side down, and use your hands on the waxed paper to press and shape the mixture into the pan.

5. Cut with the greased knife into 2-inch squares. Let them cool, then use the metal spatula or knife to lift the squares onto a serving plate.

Microwave version: Place butter and marshmallows in a 3-quart or larger microwave-safe bowl. Microwave on high for 2 minutes. (Watch how the marshmallows puff up!) Using pot holders, remove the bowl, add the peanut butter, and stir. (The mixture will be very sticky, and the bowl will be hot.) Microwave on high for 1 minute. Remove the bowl from the oven, stir with the wooden spoon and blend in the cereal mixture. Follow steps 4 and 5 above.

Kid Comment

Samuel Carlisle-Sullivan and Emma Noto, both age 5: "We like how the stove made the chocolate melt and look like marbles." The kids liked pouring the cereal and chips into the saucepan. Sam added: "It was too hard to stir on the stove, but I like the feeling of cooking over a hot stove, and I like the peanuts in it." When the kids made the microwave version, they were able to stir it themselves.

Samuel Carlisle-Sullivan, 5

Chapter 29

The Baker's Rack

Recipes

➤ Nightcap Cookies

➤ Peanut Butter Crisps

➤ Betty's Brownies

➤ Harvest Crunch Fruit Bars

➤ Chocolate Nut Triangles

➤ Mom's 1–2–3–4 Cake

➤ Judy's Apple Cake

➤ Easy as Apple Pie

➤ Southern Baking Powder Biscuits with Honey Butter

➤ Ellen's Mexican Spoon Bread

➤ Quick and Easy Tomato Bread

➤ Best-Ever Garlic Bread

➤ Banana Chocolate Chip Surprise

➤ Irish Grandma's Bread

➤ Wecke Bread (Swiss Sweet Bread)

➤ Lemon Poppy Seed Mini-Muffins

Kids love to bake. The mixing, measuring, pouring, and kneading captivates them, and they revel in getting elbow-deep in flour. It's magical to see raw ingredients turn into something delicious to eat, and the wonderful aroma of baked goods fills everyone with anticipation for the result.

In this chapter, I give young bakers a good cross-section of recipes and experiences using the oven. Beginners will have great success with the four-ingredient Nightcap Cookies or the one-pan Harvest Crunch Fruit Bars. For cakes and pies, kids will enjoy making no-fail treats such as Judy's Apple Cake or Easy As Apple Pie. My mom's 1-2-3-4 cake has lots of steps, but testers say it was a simple recipe, and it looks and tastes wonderful.

Finally, you and your kids will find lots of choices in the breads, biscuits, and muffins section. I was fortunate to have been given two very special family recipes: the Irish Grandma's Bread and the Wecke Bread (Swiss Sweet Bread). The former is just about the easiest introduction to bread-making there is, and the latter is one of the more challenging recipes in the book. I hope you enjoy making all these Baker's Rack specials as much as my family and our young recipe testers have.

Nightcap Cookies

 The Hillis family from central Oregon has been making these flourless peanut butter cookies for generations. They call them nightcap cookies because they're so quick and easy to make that they hit the spot when you get the night munchies. This is a good first cookie recipe for kids because it's foolproof and is guaranteed to give them a feeling of success. With only four ingredients, it's simple to mix, it's fast to make and bake, and the result is both sweet and satisfying with the rich taste of peanut butter.

How hard is this recipe? Easy

Adult help needed using the oven

Makes about 3 dozen cookies

Equipment

large mixing bowl	table knife to level ingredients	pot holders
wooden spoon	cookie sheets	timer
dry measuring cups	ruler	cooling racks
tablespoon	fork	metal spatula

Ingredients

1 large egg	1 teaspoon vanilla
1 cup sugar	1 cup regular or reduced-fat peanut butter

1. Position the rack in the middle of the oven and preheat the oven to 350 degrees F.
2. Crack the egg into the mixing bowl and use the wooden spoon to beat the egg. Mix in the sugar and beat until well combined.
3. Mix in the vanilla, followed by the peanut butter.

4. Shape the dough into 1" balls. Place about 2 inches apart on ungreased cookie sheets. Press each cookie with a fork and then turn the fork and press again to make a crisscross pattern.

5. Bake, one cookie sheet at a time, for 10 to 12 minutes or until the cookies turn golden brown.

6. Use pot holders to remove the cookie sheet from the oven and place it on a cooling rack to cool for 5 minutes, or until the cookies can be easily lifted with the spatula. Use the spatula to transfer the cookies to the cooling racks.

Note: These cookies are moist and chewy. If you prefer a crisper cookie, increase the baking time to 15 minutes.

Variation: Place a peanut in the center of each cookie before baking.

Campbell Clarey, 6

Kid Comment

Campbell Clarey, 6: "I liked crisscrossing the cookies with a fork." Her mother, Molly, who was impressed with how easy the recipe was, said Campbell loved the taste of the peanut butter. "They tasted like peanut butter cups."

Kitchen Clue

When measuring sticky ingredients (such as peanut butter) in dry measuring cups, grease the cup with a little oil or vegetable spray before measuring. The ingredients will then slip out easily.

Peanut Butter Crisps

My kids really like the crispness of this peanut butter cookie. It's light, and it tastes like a peanut-sugar cookie. Kids will have fun pressing the fork into the dough to make the crisscrosses on top.

How difficult is this recipe? Easy

Adult help needed using the mixer and the oven

Makes about 5 dozen cookies

Equipment

large mixing bowl	sifter or strainer	pot holders
dry measuring cups	tablespoons	timer
small rubber spatula	cookie sheets	cooling racks
hand-held electric mixer	table fork	metal spatula
measuring spoons		
medium mixing bowl		

Ingredients

1 cup (2 sticks) unsalted butter, softened	¾ cup sugar	2 cups all-purpose flour
	2 large eggs	½ teaspoon baking soda
1 cup regular or reduced-fat peanut butter	1 teaspoon vanilla	½ teaspoon salt
¾ cup brown sugar		

1. Position the rack in the center of the oven and preheat the oven to 325 degrees F.
2. In the large bowl, cream the butter, peanut butter, and sugars with the electric mixer on medium speed. Add the eggs and vanilla and continue to mix just until blended.
3. In the medium bowl, sift together the flour, baking soda, and salt. Add this to the butter mixture and blend just until combined with the mixer on low speed.
4. Drop the dough by tablespoonfuls onto the ungreased cookie sheets, leaving 3 inches between cookies. (Once cooked, the cookies will spread to about double the size.) Press each cookie with a fork and then turn the fork to press again and make a crisscross pattern.
5. Bake one sheet at a time (for even cooking) for 15 to 18 minutes. The cookies are done when the edges begin to brown and the center is a golden color.
6. Use pot holders to remove the cookie sheet, place it on the cooling rack, and let it cool for 5 minutes. Use the spatula to transfer the cookies to the cooling racks.

Note: Because these cookies are like thin sugar cookies, they spread and the crisscross imprint is very faint on the baked cookie. Kids like to make the crisscross, but the cookie taste doesn't suffer without it!

Kid Comment

Robert Bishop, 9: "It's really fun to make these. They are really good, but they're even better with a glass of milk."

Betty's Brownies

My friend Betty Shenberger created these yummy brownies. They have a nice crust on the outside, but the inside is moist and chewy and reminds my family of toffee. What do you think?

Kids can help cream the butter, mix the ingredients, and spread the batter in the pan.

How hard is this recipe? Easy

Adult help needed with cutting, using the mixer and the oven

Makes 16 brownies

Equipment

8 × 8 × 2-inch baking pan	measuring spoons	rubber spatula
large mixing bowl	medium mixing bowl	pot holders
hand-held electric mixer	wooden spoon	timer
dry measuring cups	waxed paper	cooling rack
		sharp knife

Ingredients

butter for greasing pan	2 teaspoons vanilla	¼ teaspoon salt
1 stick (½ cup) unsalted butter, softened	¾ cup all-purpose flour	½ teaspoon baking powder
1½ cups sugar	⅓ cup unsweetened cocoa powder	1 cup chopped pecans
2 large eggs		

1. Position the rack in the center of the oven and preheat the oven to 350 degrees F. Grease the pan.
2. In the large mixing bowl, cream the butter with the mixer on low speed. Add the sugar, eggs, and vanilla and blend on low speed until combined.
3. In the medium mixing bowl, mix the flour, cocoa powder, salt, and baking powder using the wooden spoon. Sift the mixture onto a sheet of waxed paper.
4. Blend the dry mixture into the butter mixture with the beater on low speed or with the wooden spoon. Fold in the nuts. (The batter will be thick.)

continues

continued

 5. Spread the batter into the baking pan with the rubber spatula and then bake for 30 minutes. When done, the brownies will pull slightly away from the sides of the pan, but they will still be soft within.

 6. Use pot holders to remove the pan, place it on the cooling rack, and cool the brownies in the pan. Cut into 16 squares.

Kitchen Clue

Did you know that bar cookies, like the brownies and fruit bars in this book, actually get better with age? If these sweets don't get devoured on the first day, try eating them the next day to see for yourself. If you have to bring bar cookies to a school event, you can make them a day or two ahead. Cookies usually last, unrefrigerated, for about five days. You also can freeze them. They're often just as good right out of the freezer.

Harvest Crunch Fruit Bars

I added toasted wheat germ and sesame seeds to graham crackers to make a crunchy cookie crust that's full of flavor and nutrition. I top these bars with dried fruit for a healthful boost. Like frozen candy bars, these cookies taste great if you eat them right out of the freezer. When preparing the bars, kids like crushing the crackers in a plastic bag and then layering everything in the baking pan. This is a good beginner's recipe with virtually no mixing and no mess because almost everything is done right in the pan.

How hard is this recipe? Easy

Adult help needed with cutting, the can opener, at the oven, and pouring

Makes 24 squares

Equipment

1 one-gallon resealable plastic bag
measuring spoons
table knife
13 × 9 × 2-inch baking pan
pot holders

timer
cooling rack
rubber spatula
can opener

dry measuring cups
wooden spoon
sharp knife
aluminum foil

Ingredients

1 (11-cracker) packet graham crackers

3 tablespoons toasted wheat germ flakes

3 tablespoons sesame seeds

1 stick (½ cup) unsalted butter, cut into seven chunks

1 (14-ounce) can fat-free sweetened condensed milk

½ cup sweetened flaked coconut

½ cup semisweet or milk chocolate morsels

½ cup sweetened dried cranberries

1. Position the rack in the center of the oven and preheat the oven to 350 degrees F.

2. Fill the plastic bag with the graham crackers, squeeze out the excess air, and seal well. Now comes the fun part. Place the bag on a flat surface, make a fist, and pound the bag with the side of your hands to make course crumbs. (You also can scrunch the contents together—through the bag—between your hands.) Open the bag and add the wheat germ and sesame seeds. Reseal and shake to mix ingredients well.

3. Put the butter in the pan. Use pot holders to put the pan in the oven for about 3 minutes to melt the butter. Watch to make sure the butter doesn't burn.

4. Use pot holders to remove the pan from the oven and set it on the cooling rack on the counter. (The pan will be hot for a few minutes, so don't touch it or allow the plastic bag to touch it.) When the pan is cool enough to touch, open the plastic bag and pour the ingredients evenly into the pan. Start at one end and work your way to the other end, letting the crumbs slowly flow in a stream out of the bag. Use your clean fingers or the spatula to moisten all the crumbs with butter and to distribute the mixture well throughout the pan.

5. Pour the condensed milk over the crumbs to cover them. The milk will be heavy and sticky, so start at one end and drizzle it in wide ribbons across the crumbs. Use the spatula to scrape the extra milk from the can. If necessary, use the spatula to spread the milk evenly.

6. Sprinkle the remaining ingredients on top of the milk. Start with the coconut, add the chocolate morsels, and then add the cranberries. Use the wooden spoon to distribute the ingredients evenly across the top if necessary.

7. Bake for about 20 minutes or until the edges begin to brown. Check after 15 minutes to be sure the bars don't burn. Use pot holders to remove the pan to the cooling rack and let the bar cookies cool for 15 minutes in the pan. Cut them into 24 squares and allow the bars to cool completely before serving. You also can wrap them securely in foil to freeze.

Variation: Sprinkle ½ cup chopped, dried apricots in place of the dried cranberries or experiment with other favorite dried fruits. If desired, add ½ cup chopped nuts.

Kid Comment

Emma Noto, 5: "It was really fun to sprinkle all of the treats on top."

Torben Noto, 8: "These are healthy treats, and they actually taste good."

Their mom, Peggy, said everyone in her family loved the taste of these cookies. "These are great. And there's no clean-up!"

Kitchen Clue

Cookies baked in pans with dark or dull surfaces will brown and bake more quickly than cookies cooked in pans with shiny surfaces. Because your oven and the type of equipment you use will make a difference in timing, always check your cookies at least 5 minutes before the recipe says they're done. Otherwise, they could burn and you'd be disappointed.

Chocolate Nut Triangles

These whole wheat shortbread-style cookies, topped with chocolate and crunchy nuts, never last long in our house. They're especially good when dunked in a glass of cold milk. Kids love to see how the hard chocolate bits, when warmed in the oven, can be smoothed into a spreadable topping. If your kids don't like nuts just omit them or do as our creative testers did—make half the pan with nuts and half without.

How hard is this recipe? Easy/Intermediate

Adult help needed with cutting and using the oven

Makes 24 triangles

Equipment

9 × 13 × 2-inch baking pan

medium mixing bowl

dry measuring cups

hand-held electric mixer

large mixing bowl

measuring spoons

rubber spatula

pot holders

timer

cooling rack

table knife or frosting spatula

sharp knife

metal or plastic spatula

serving plate

Ingredients

butter for greasing the pan

1 cup all-purpose flour

1 cup whole wheat flour

2 sticks (1 cup) unsalted butter, softened

1 cup dark brown sugar

1 large egg

1 teaspoon vanilla

1½ cups (9 ounces) bittersweet chocolate morsels

¾ cup chopped pecans, walnuts, or hazelnuts

1. Position the rack in the center of the oven and preheat the oven to 350 degrees F. Grease the baking pan.

2. In the medium bowl, combine the flours and then set them aside.

3. Put the butter and sugar in the large bowl and blend with the electric mixer until light and fluffy. This should take about 2 to 3 minutes.

4. Add the egg and vanilla and blend. Gradually beat in the flours and blend just until combined.

5. Use the rubber spatula to scoop and spread the mixture into the baking pan and smooth it so it covers the surface evenly.

6. Bake 25 to 30 minutes. The cookies will be light brown and soft to the touch.

7. Use pot holders to remove the pan from the oven to a cooling rack and sprinkle chocolate morsels evenly on top of the cookies. Use pot holders to return the pan to the oven for 2 more minutes.

8. Use pot holders to remove the pan from the oven and use the table knife or spatula to lightly spread the chips to make a coating. Sprinkle evenly with nuts.

9. Let the cookies cool in the pan for 15 minutes. Use the sharp knife to cut into 12 squares by making two lengthwise cuts and three widthwise cuts in the pan. Cut each square in half on the diagonal to make triangles.

10. When the chocolate begins to harden, remove the triangles with the spatula and place them on the serving plate.

Kid Comment

Torben Noto, 8: "I really like this a lot 'cuz it sort of tastes like cake and cookies mixed together. It was neat when it came out of the oven. The chocolate chips looked normal, but when you touched it with the spatula, it became a chocolate sauce."

Emma Noto, 5: "I liked it because of the chocolate." Both kids liked the soft and crumbly texture of the cookie.

Kitchen Clue

When making bar cookies, avoid scratching the pan and make cutting easier by using this aluminum foil trick. Before starting, invert the pan and mold and cut foil over the outside of the pan. Then turn the pan right side up and line the inside of the pan with the foil. Grease the foil as you would the pan and, when you're ready to cut, lift the foil up and out of the pan. This trick works especially well for the Chocolate Nut Triangles.

Kid Quiz

What can you do if your butter is cold and hard and the recipe calls for soft butter?

Grate it or microwave it. To grate it, unwrap the end of the stick of butter and grate it against the largest holes on your hand-held grater. To microwave, heat the butter on a microwave-safe plate, uncovered, on medium-low. For 1 stick of butter, allow 15 to 25 seconds; for half a stick, allow 10 seconds.

Special Cakes and Apple Pie

Mom's 1-2-3-4 Cake

This citrus-flavored cake is so light and moist that you won't be able to stop eating it. My mom made this as a young girl, and I rediscovered her recipe when I began to write this book. We made it in a Bundt (fluted) pan and found it gave the cake a lovely crust and an elegant look. We also had a cooking mishap that had a happy ending—we doubled the amount of milk and orange juice in the original recipe by mistake, but it gave the cake extra moisture. In olden days, this cake was named 1-2-3-4 so bakers could remember the ingredients easily. Can you tell from the ingredient list what the numbers mean?

How hard is this recipe? Intermediate

Adult help needed for beating, grating, greasing the pan, and using the oven

Makes 1 large Bundt cake

Equipment

table knife	hand-held electric mixer	pot holders
12-cup Bundt pan	grater or zester	timer
measuring spoons	waxed paper for zest and icing	clean kitchen towel
dry measuring cups	2-cup liquid measuring cup	cooling rack
sifter or large strainer	small whisk	plastic wrap or
2 large mixing bowls	rubber spatula	aluminum foil

Ingredients

For the cake:

1 cup (2 sticks) plus 1 tablespoon
    unsalted butter, softened

3 cups plus 1 tablespoon
    all-purpose flour

4 teaspoons baking powder

¼ teaspoon salt

2 cups sugar

1½ tablespoons orange zest

4 large eggs, lightly beaten

1 cup milk

1 cup orange juice

For the glaze:

¾ cup confectioners' sugar

4 teaspoons orange juice

1. Position the rack in the center of the oven and preheat the oven to 375 degrees F.

2. Use 1 tablespoon butter to grease the Bundt pan. Be sure to get into all the creases. Lightly sprinkle the pan with 1 tablespoon flour and tap to coat the entire surface. Shake out excess flour.

3. Sift the flour, baking powder, and salt into a large bowl.

4. In another large bowl, use the electric mixer on medium speed to cream the butter, sugar, and orange zest for about 3 minutes or until batter is smooth and light in color. Add the eggs and mix for about 2 minutes or until blended.

continues

continued

5. Combine the milk and orange juice with the whisk in the liquid measuring cup. Add half the milk-juice blend and half the flour mixture to the butter mixture. Beat on low speed for 20 to 30 seconds. Repeat with the remaining ingredients and beat just until combined. This should take about 20 to 30 seconds. Do not overbeat.

6. Use the rubber spatula to scrape the batter into the Bundt pan. Bake for 45 minutes. When done, the cake will start to pull away from the sides of the pan.

7. Meanwhile, wash and dry the whisk and the liquid measuring cup and prepare the glaze. Put the confectioners' sugar in the liquid measuring cup. Add the orange juice and whisk until combined and smooth. Set aside.

8. Use pot holders to remove the cake from the oven and let it cool for 10 minutes. Tap the sides of the pan with the handle of a table knife. Ask an adult to put a cooling rack on the open end of the pan, hold the bottom of the pan with pot holders, and quickly invert the pan and rack together to turn the cake onto the rack. The cake should slip out. Tap the pan again if it doesn't.

9. Place the rack on top of a piece of waxed paper. Drizzle the glaze onto the cake while the cake is still warm. Follow the curves of the cake from the inside to the outside, working your way around the cake. Spoon any icing from the waxed paper onto the cake. You can serve the cake immediately or store it at room temperature for up to 2 days. For longer storage, wrap the cake in plastic and refrigerate it for up to 2 more days or freeze in aluminum foil.

Kitchen Clue

A hand-held grater has different size holes to use for making fine and coarse shreds. To grate the peel of citrus fruits, put waxed or parchment paper over the smallest holes and grate through the paper. The peel will cling to the paper. Just scrape it off the paper with the measuring spoon to collect the desired about of zest. In recipes, the terms zest and peel mean the same thing.

Kid Comment

Torben Noto, 8: "It is amazing that these things turn into a cake. It's like science or magic."

Emma Noto, 5: "This cake is perfect for tea parties."

Their mom, Peggy, enjoyed making the cake with them. "There are lots of steps but each step was easy. Great cake. It lasted a week and it was still fresh!"

Emma Noto, 5

Judy's Apple Cake

In the fall, when apples are in season, our neighbor Judy Matarazzo goes with her family to pick apples and then comes home to bake them into this cake with her 6-year-old son, Harrison. She made the same cake as a child with her mother, and she says it's perfect for kids because all you do is mix everything together and put it in the oven. Kids get to measure, stir, chop apples, and pour the batter.

How hard is this recipe? Easy/Intermediate

Adult help needed with cutting and using the oven

Makes 1 cake

Equipment

10 × 13-inch glass cake dish	liquid measuring cup	pot holders
large mixing bowl	measuring spoons	timer
cutting board	wooden spoon	cooling rack
sharp knife	small bowl	cake knife or metal spatula
dry measuring cup	rubber spatula	

continues

continued

Ingredients

butter for greasing dish

4 to 5 Granny Smith apples
(4 to 4½ cups chopped)

1 cup light or dark brown sugar

1 cup sugar

1 cup vegetable oil

1 tablespoon vanilla

1 cup coarsely chopped nuts
such as pecans, walnuts, or hazelnuts

2 cups all-purpose flour

2 large eggs

1 teaspoon baking soda

2 teaspoons cinnamon

1 teaspoon salt

1. Position the rack in the center of the oven and preheat the oven to 350 degrees F. Grease the baking dish with butter.

2. In the large mixing bowl, combine the apples, sugars, oil, vanilla, nuts, and flour using the wooden spoon.

3. Crack the eggs into the small bowl and add them, along with the baking soda, cinnamon, and salt, to the apple mixture.

4. Mix all the ingredients until combined into a batter.

5. Pour the batter into the greased baking dish and use the rubber spatula to scrape the sides of the bowl.

6. Bake the cake for 60 minutes or until it pulls away from the sides of the pan.

7. Transfer the baking dish to the cooling rack. Serve this cake warm, right from the baking dish.

Note: The apples don't need to be exactly the same size, but they should be chopped small; otherwise, they will be too chunky in the cake. You also can use Rome or Red or Golden Delicious apples for this cake.

Variation: Try serving this cake with ice cream and caramel sauce.

Kid Comment

Harrison Matarazzo, 6: "I like cutting the apples by myself. The cake tastes like cinnamon." His mom, Judy, says this cake is very forgiving, especially for young cooks who don't chop apples exactly the same size. "You cannot wreck it," says Judy.

Harrison Mattarazzo, 6

Easy as Apple Pie

When I ran the Apple Pie for Kids workshop at the Woodlawn Elementary School in Portland, Oregon, 65 fourth and fifth graders baked this apple pie for the very first time. I know the recipe is fun and not too difficult because, before the workshop, I had my daughter Lizzie, who was 11 at the time, bake it by herself several times to test it! The fourth and fifth graders were aided by food professionals in this workshop sponsored by the International Association of Culinary Professionals. If you've never baked an apple pie, try this one. Do what we do at home: Put a scoop of vanilla ice cream on top for pie à la mode!

How hard is this recipe? Easy/Intermediate

Adult help needed with cutting, rolling dough, and using the oven

Makes 1 double-crust 9-inch pie

Equipment

2 large mixing bowls	cutting board	baking sheet
dry measuring cups	waxed paper	aluminum foil
measuring spoons	rolling pin	pot holders
2 wooden spoons	9-inch pie pan	timer
paring knife	metal spatula	fork
liquid measuring cup	ruler	cooling rack
plastic wrap		

Ingredients

For the crust:

2 cups all-purpose flour

½ teaspoon salt

11 tablespoons cold, unsalted butter (about 1⅓ sticks), cut into ½-inch chunks

¼ cup cold water

For the apple filling:

4 tablespoons sugar

2 tablespoons all-purpose flour

1 tablespoon ground cinnamon

5 to 6 large Granny Smith or other firm apples, peeled and coarsely chopped (about 6 cups)

2 tablespoons unsalted butter, cut into small chunks

To make the crust:

1. In a large bowl, mix the flour and salt together using a wooden spoon.
2. Add the butter to the flour mixture. Using clean fingertips, pinch the butter into the flour until it looks like big crumbs, almost like uncooked oatmeal.
3. Sprinkle in the water a little at a time and press the dough together until it makes a ball. Add a few more drops of water if the dough seems too dry.
4. Gather any extra bits of dough into the ball and then divide the dough into two balls, one a little larger than the other. Wrap the dough in plastic wrap and refrigerate it while you make the filling.

continues

continued

To make the filling:

1. In a large bowl, combine the sugar, flour, and cinnamon using a wooden spoon.

2. Add the apples and toss them with the sugar mixture until they are well-coated. Set them aside.

To prepare the pie:

1. Position the rack in the middle of the oven and preheat the oven to 425 degrees F.

2. Remove the dough from the refrigerator to a clean work surface and unwrap. Put the larger dough ball on a big piece of waxed paper or plastic wrap and press it down gently once or twice with the heel of your hand or a rolling pin. Cover it with another piece of waxed paper or plastic wrap. Roll out the dough into a circle. Work from the center using short quick motions and roll only in one direction out toward the edges. Rotate the dough in quarter turns, after you roll it in each direction, to flatten the dough evenly. The circle should be about 1½ inches bigger than the pie pan. Put your pie pan upside down over the circle to help measure it.

3. Remove the top piece of waxed paper or plastic wrap and fit the circle of dough into the pan. Put the pie pan upside down on top of the dough and quickly flip the pan and the dough so the dough falls inside the pan. Carefully peel the dough away from the waxed paper or plastic wrap. (Use the metal spatula to get under the dough, if necessary.) If the dough breaks, gently pinch it back together. Lightly press and shape the dough into the inside of the pan, up the side, and along the edge.

4. Fill the pie pan with the apples. Dot the remaining 2 tablespoons butter on top of the apples. Set the pan aside.

5. Put the second ball of dough on a piece of waxed paper or plastic wrap, press it down, and cover it with another piece of waxed paper or plastic wrap. Roll it as you did before into a circle only slightly larger than the top edge of the pan. (Measure with a ruler.) Remove the top sheet of waxed paper or plastic wrap. Fit the crust over the top of the pie by picking up the waxed paper or wrap and flipping it over to cover the apples. Gently peel the dough off the paper or wrap. (Use the metal spatula to get under the dough, if necessary.)

6. Seal the pie by pinching together all the dough around the edges of the pan with your fingers. Cut away any extra dough from the edges and use it to make decorations, such as your initials. Press these into the top pie crust.

7. Use a knife to make slits on the top crust so steam can escape during baking.

To bake the pie:

1. Place the pie on a baking sheet covered with aluminum foil and put it on the middle rack of your oven. Bake for 15 minutes at 425 degrees F. Then lower the oven temperature to 350 degrees F and bake for another 30 to 40 minutes or until the pie is done. The crust will be golden, and some apple juices will be bubbling on the edges. Pierce the middle of the pie with a fork. If the fork goes through the crust easily and the apples are soft, the pie is ready.

2. Use pot holders to remove the pie to a cooling rack and let the pie stand for 15 minutes before cutting.

Proud young bakers show off their pies at an IACP Apple Pie for Kids workshop.

Photo credit: IACP

Kid Comment

Shanae Mejia, 11: "It was fun to put all the ingredients together to see what it would make."

Jordon Winkel, 10: "I liked learning how to make the pie because, in the future, I may need that skill for a job in case there isn't any other. I liked doing the dough part because it was fun to flatten it out and put it over the pan."

Mau Nomani, 10: "The cinnamon apples inside the crust tasted great. I liked making the edges. That was fun to put your finger in (the edge of the crust) and go around and make designs on it."

Biscuits, Breads, and Muffins

Southern Baking Powder Biscuits with Honey Butter

The Hudson family from Tennessee has been making these biscuits for generations. Down South, they like to serve them with honey butter and thick slices of country ham or a paste made from brewed coffee and honey. Judy Hudson Matarazzo shared this family recipe, which she made growing up and now makes regularly with her 6-year-old son, Harrison. He likes kneading the dough and cutting out the biscuits.

How hard is this recipe? Easy

Adult help needed using the oven

Makes 20 biscuits

Equipment

large mixing bowl	waxed paper	biscuit cutter or 3- to 4-inch-wide glass
dry measuring cups	table knife	
measuring spoons	liquid measuring cup	cookie sheet
wooden spoon	cutting board or clean surface for rolling	pot holders
sifter or strainer to sift		timer
	rolling pin	cooling rack

Ingredients

2 cups all-purpose flour

4 teaspoons baking powder

1 teaspoon salt

2 to 4 tablespoons cold unsalted butter, cut into small chunks

¾ cup milk or water

flour for dusting biscuit cutter or glass

1. Position the rack in the middle of the oven and preheat the oven to 450 degrees F.

2. In the large bowl, mix the flour, baking powder, and salt together and sift the mixture twice onto the waxed paper. Return the mixture to the bowl.

3. Add the butter to the flour mixture. Using clean fingertips, pinch the butter into the flour mixture until it looks like big crumbs. With the wooden spoon, stir in the milk or water very gradually just until it forms a soft dough.

4. Turn out the dough onto a floured board or clean, flat surface. Pat the dough out into a circle and use a floured rolling pin to gently roll to a ½-inch thickness.

5. Dip the biscuit cutter or glass in flour and cut the dough into circles. Place the biscuits on the ungreased cookie sheet and bake for 12 minutes or until the tops of the biscuits are golden brown.

 6. Use pot holders to remove the cookie sheet from the oven and set it on the cooling rack. Serve the biscuits warm, with or without honey butter (the honey butter recipe follows).

Kid Comment

Harrison Matarazzo, 6: "My favorite part is eating the biscuits and making jam sandwiches with the biscuits."

Honey Butter

This sweet butter is delicious and can be spread on warm biscuits, toast, or sandwiches such as the spiral sandwiches. (See Chapter 23, "Let's Wrap and Roll," for the recipe.)

How hard is this recipe? Easy

Adult help needed using the food processor

Makes 1 cup

Equipment

food processor   rubber spatula

liquid measuring cup   small container with lid

timer

Ingredients

½ cup (1 stick) unsalted butter, cut into small chunks

½ cup honey

 1. Place the butter in the bowl of the food processor. Process the butter for 10 seconds. While continuing to process, pour the honey through the feed tube. Process for about 45 to 60 seconds or until the honey and butter are mixed and form a soft paste.

2. Remove the lid and use the rubber spatula to scrape the butter into the small container. Refrigerate, covered, until ready to use. Be sure to use by expiration date on the butter container.

Ellen's Mexican Spoon Bread

My friend Ellen Bogart taught me how to make this bread 10 years ago. She learned it from an aunt in Missouri and used to make it often when she was growing up. Spoon bread got its name because it's soft enough to eat with a spoon. Over the years, I've changed the recipe to include more corn and some chili powder, either of which you can leave out. Kids will like making this recipe because they get to pour the batter and then layer ingredients in the baking pan. We eat this bread anytime, but we find it's particularly good when paired with the chili, fajitas, and potato corn chowder recipes in this book.

How difficult is this recipe? Easy/Intermediate

Adult help needed cutting and using the grater, the can opener, and the oven

Serves 8 to 10

Equipment

1½-quart casserole or 9 × 9-inch baking dish

microwave-safe bowl or saucepan to melt butter

cutting board

sharp knife

grater

waxed paper (for under grater)

large mixing bowl

dry measuring cups

measuring spoons

can opener

tablespoon

liquid measuring cup

wooden spoon

rubber spatula

pot holders

timer

cooling rack

Ingredients

butter for greasing pan

1 cup cornmeal

½ teaspoon baking soda

1 (16-ounce) can creamed corn

4 ounces whole corn (optional)

¾ cup milk

⅓ cup melted unsalted butter (about 5 tablespoons solid butter)

2 large eggs, lightly beaten

¼ teaspoon chili powder (optional)

1 (4-ounce) can chopped green chilies

1½ cups shredded cheddar cheese (about 5 ounces), divided

1 green onion coarsely chopped

1. Position the rack in the middle of the oven and preheat the oven to 400 degrees F. Grease the pan with butter.

2. In the large mixing bowl, combine the cornmeal and baking soda. Add the creamed corn, whole corn (if using), milk, melted butter, eggs, and chili powder (if using). Mix well with the wooden spoon.

3. Pour half the batter into the casserole dish. Spread the green chilies, onions, and ¾ cup cheese on top of the batter.

4. With the rubber spatula, scrape out the remaining batter from the mixing bowl into the pan. Smooth to cover the other ingredients. Top the batter with the rest of the cheese.

5. Bake for 40 to 45 minutes. When done, the outside edges will be browned, but the bread will still be very moist. Remove the casserole dish from the oven and set it on a cooling rack. Serve the bread warm as a side dish or at room temperature.

Quick and Easy Tomato Bread

Squishing the tomatoes is the fun part of making this delicious bread. I learned how to prepare this in Barcelona, Spain, where it's favored as part of a complete meal or as a snack. Like garlic bread, this recipe is one that kids can make easily, allowing them to be involved in the dinnertime routine. Parents can cut and toast the bread; the kids will have fun rubbing it with the garlic and squeezing the tomato on the bread.

How hard is this recipe? Easy

Adult help needed with cutting and using the oven

Makes 1 loaf

Equipment

paper towels	cookie sheet or baking pan	measuring spoons
sharp knife	pot holders	tongs
cutting board	timer	serving plate
serrated bread knife	cooling rack	

Ingredients

2-4 large ripe tomatoes

2 large garlic cloves

1 large loaf Italian or other dense bread

1 teaspoon extra-virgin olive oil

salt and pepper to taste

1. Position the rack on the highest rung in the oven and preheat to medium high broil. Keep the oven door slightly open.

2. Wash the tomatoes under cool running water and dry with paper towels. Have an adult slice the tomatoes in half crosswise, peel the papery skin off the garlic cloves, and cut each clove in half crosswise.

3. Cut the bread in half crosswise and then cut each half lengthwise. Place the bread, cut side up, on the ungreased cookie sheet.

4. Use pot holders to slide the cookie sheet into the oven and toast the bread for about 1 minute or until lightly toasted. Keep the oven door slightly open. Use pot holders to remove the sheet from the oven and place it on a cooling rack.

5. Take a piece of the bread, being careful not to touch the hot cookie sheet, and rub a piece of garlic up and down the bread. The rough edges of the toast will catch some pieces of the garlic and its juice.

6. Squeeze 1 to 2 tomato halves over the bread and then rub the tomatoes up and down the length of the bread. Throw away the remnants of the tomatoes and the garlic. Finish by drizzling ¼ teaspoon of extra virgin olive oil along the bread and sprinkling with a pinch of salt and pepper.

7. Do the same with the remaining 3 slices of bread, garlic, and tomatoes. Use the tongs to put the bread on the serving plate. Serve immediately as an appetizer or a side dish.

Variation: Sprinkle 1 teaspoon grated Parmesan cheese on each slice of bread.

Kid Comment

Lizzie Cooke, 12: "This is easy and simple. It's fun to squirt the tomatoes. It's like squishing grapes. I would make this as an after-school snack. The different flavors together are delicious."

Kitchen Clue

To remove the smell of garlic (or onion as well), rub salt on your hands as if you were washing them. Follow by washing and rinsing your hands with water. Another method is to rub your hands under cool running water with a stainless steel spoon or another stainless steel object.

Best-Ever Garlic Bread

After you taste this homemade version, you'll never want to eat store-bought garlic bread again. Kids have fun squeezing the garlic press and watching the garlic come out the other end. They also like to spread the garlic oil on the bread. My three sisters and I, as children, would always take turns making the garlic bread in our house. It was an easy way for us to be involved in the hubbub of the kitchen with a safe, doable task. Now my kids do the same. We hope you enjoy our family's version of garlic bread.

How hard is this recipe? Easy

Adult help needed with cutting and using the oven

Makes 1 loaf of bread

Equipment

cutting board	garlic press	cooling rack
serrated bread knife	table knife	cloth or large paper napkins
cookie sheet or baking pan	tablespoon	tongs
small bowl	pot holders	serving plate
measuring spoons	timer	

Ingredients

1 loaf French or Italian bread (about 13 inches long)

6 tablespoons extra-virgin olive oil

3 large cloves garlic, papery skin removed

1. Position the rack on the highest rung in the oven and preheat to medium broil. Keep the oven door open slightly.

2. Cut the loaf of bread in half crosswise and cut each half in half lengthwise. Put the four pieces of bread, cut side up, on the ungreased cookie sheet.

3. Pour the olive oil into the bowl. Put a garlic clove in the press and squeeze it over the bowl. Use the table knife to scrape the bottom of the press and put the garlic into the bowl. Scrape out the garlic from the inside of the press and put it in the bowl. Repeat with the remaining garlic cloves.

4. Mix the garlic and oil well with the tablespoon and then spoon it onto the cut side of the bread slices. Distribute the garlic pieces evenly.

5. Use pot holders to slide the cookie sheet into the oven and toast the bread for about 2 to 3 minutes or until the tops are golden brown and crusty. Keep the oven door slightly open.

6. Use pot holders to remove the sheet from the oven and place it on the cooling rack. Spread the napkins on the serving plate. Use the tongs to put the bread on the napkins and then wrap it to keep it warm. Serve immediately.

Variations: Make an herbed garlic bread or a cheese garlic bread by sprinkling the bread slices with dried Italian seasonings or grated Parmesan cheese (to taste) before toasting.

Banana Chocolate Chip Surprise

I love the taste of old-fashioned banana bread, but I began wondering what would happen if I added miniature chocolate chips and a surprise in the center—a whole banana or maybe even peanut butter spread on the banana. The result is a moist, chocolaty bread with a treat in the middle. Top this with a scoop of ice cream and you've got an instant dessert. This bread was a big hit with our recipe testers.

How hard is this recipe? Easy/Intermediate

Adult help needed with mixing and using the oven

Makes 1 loaf

continues

continued

Equipment

9 × 5 × 3-inch loaf pan	fork	cutting board
large mixing bowl	whisk	table knife
dry measuring cups	wooden spoon	pot holders
measuring spoons	oven-safe bowl or sauce	timer
sifter	pan to melt butter	sharp knife
2 small mixing bowls	large rubber spatula	cooling rack

Ingredients

butter for greasing pan	2 large very ripe bananas, mashed (about 1 cup)
2 cups all-purpose flour	1 cup sugar
½ teaspoon baking soda	3 tablespoons unsalted butter, melted and cooled
½ teaspoon baking powder	½ cup semisweet chocolate miniature morsels
1 teaspoon salt	1 large firm banana
2 large eggs, lightly beaten	

1. Position the rack in the center of the oven and preheat the oven to 350 degrees F. Grease the loaf pan with butter.

2. In the large bowl, sift together the flour, baking soda, baking powder, and salt.

3. In the small bowl, add the eggs to the mashed banana with the wooden spoon. Stir in the sugar and melted butter to combine.

4. Add the banana mixture to the flour mixture and stir with the wooden spoon just to combine. Do not overbeat. Add the chocolate morsels and lightly stir to mix evenly.

5. Use the spatula to pour half the batter into the loaf pan. Peel the firm banana, trim the ends, and slice it in half crosswise. Cut it in half lengthwise, following the curve of the banana.

6. Lay the banana pieces, cut side down, along the length of the pan down the center. Cover them with the remaining batter.

7. Bake for about 1 hour or until the edges of the cake pull away from the sides of the pan.

8. Use pot holders to remove the pan to a cooling rack. Run the sharp knife along the inside edges of the pan to loosen the bread, and let it stand for 15 minutes. Turn the bread out onto the cooling rack to cool completely.

Variation: Spread peanut butter on the bananas before you lay them down in the batter.

Kid Comment

Robert Bishop, 9: "This is really good. Can we try this with peanut butter next time?" His mom, Suzanne, said: "Everyone liked this a lot. I loved the banana in the center."

Irish Grandma's Bread

My friend Siobhan Loughran learned how to make this Irish soda bread at her mother's knee. Born in Limerick, Ireland, she moved with her family to Chicago when she was a youngster. Now that she has her own two young boys, she makes it with them almost weekly as a way to keep up the family traditions. Her kids love to mix and measure the ingredients, knead the bread, and shape it into loaves. This simple, straightforward recipe results in delicious fresh bread. Making it is a wonderful way to introduce kids to baking bread and the customs of another country.

How hard is this recipe? Easy/Intermediate

Adult help needed using the oven

Makes 1 large or 2 small loaves

Equipment

cookie sheet or
    2 nine-inch pie pans
large mixing bowl
dry measuring cups
measuring spoons

sifter or large strainer
table knife
liquid measuring cup
fork

sharp knife
pot holders
timer
cooling rack

Ingredients

butter for greasing
4 cups plus 2 tablespoons all-purpose flour
1⅔ cups whole wheat flour
1 tablespoon baking soda

1 tablespoon plus 2 teaspoons sugar
1 teaspoon salt
3 tablespoons unsalted butter
2½ cups buttermilk

1. Position the rack in the center of the oven and preheat the oven to 350 degrees F. If you are baking one large loaf, grease the cookie sheet and sprinkle it with a tablespoon of flour. Shake off any excess flour into the sink. If you are baking two loaves, grease and flour each pie pan.

2. In the large bowl, sift together the flours, baking soda, sugar, and salt.

continues

continued

3. Add the butter to the flour mixture. Using clean fingertips, pinch the butter into the flour mixture until it looks like coarse crumbs.

4. Make a hole in the center of the flour mixture and pour the buttermilk into it. Use a fork to mix the milk into the flour to form dough. Pat it lightly with your fingers into a ball.

5. Lightly sprinkle a clean, flat surface with a tablespoon of flour. Turn the dough ball onto the surface and gently knead it to form a soft, smooth dough. Work it with your hands a few times, but do not overknead.

6. Shape the dough into a large round loaf and put it on the cookie sheet or divide the dough into the two pie pans. Cut a cross into the top of each loaf with the sharp knife. (This makes it easy to divide into quarters, called farls.)

7. Use pot holders to put the bread in the oven. Bake it for 1 hour if you are baking one large loaf or for 45 minutes if you are baking two smaller loaves. The bread becomes golden brown and pulls slightly away from the pan edges.

8. Use pot holders to remove the bread to a cooling rack.

9. When the bread has cooled, cut it into quarters and serve.

Variation: To give the bread a nutty texture, add ¼ cup bran or ¼ cup pinhead or steel-cut oats to the dry ingredients in step 2.

Kid Comment

Joseph Taylor, 5: "I like to make Irish Grandma's Bread. It's fun to squeeze it in my fingers. And we get to listen to stories about my mom and grandma when we make it. My dad really likes to eat it."

James Taylor, 8: "Irish Grandma's Bread is special. It's part of our tradition. It reminds me about my family and where we came from."

Joseph Taylor, 5

James Taylor, 8

Wecke Bread (Swiss Sweet Bread)

I first had this delicious Sweet Bread when one of the Kuenzi clan from Silverton, Oregon made it for our family years ago. When I was looking for a good bread recipe with which to show kids how to use yeast, I immediately thought of this. Connie Kuenzie says this recipe has been in her family for generations, and it's a traditional Swiss Sweet Bread. You can make it into a regular loaf or braid it before rising, which is fun for kids. We also shape the dough into rolls for what we like to call sweet dinner nuggets. Try eating them warm and spread with honey butter.

Don't be intimidated by this recipe. It looks long and complicated, but all the details will actually help you succeed every step of the way. Be sure to read it through and understand it before you get started. If this is your first time making yeast bread, check out the tips and photos for breadmaking on Web sites listed in Appendix B, "The Resource Guide." Take advantage of the baking hot lines listed in the guide.

How hard is this recipe? Advanced

Adult help needed throughout the entire recipe, mixing, kneading, using the knife, and using the oven

Makes 1 loaf or 12 dinner rolls

Equipment

small saucepan or microwave-safe liquid measuring cup

table knife

instant-read thermometer or candy thermometer

liquid measuring cup

teaspoon

small bowl

whisk

measuring spoons

small cup

plastic wrap

large mixing bowl

dry measuring cups

wooden spoon

pastry scraper

2 clean kitchen towels

timer

rolling pin

ruler

9 × 5 × 3-inch loaf pan

kitchen scissors or sharp knife (for braiding or rolls)

cookie sheet (for braided bread or rolls)

pastry brush

pot holders

cooling rack

Ingredients

1 cup half-and-half

3 tablespoons unsalted butter

¼ cup warm water

1 package active dry yeast

2 large eggs

1 tablespoon cool water

4 cups all-purpose flour, ½ cup reserved

⅓ cup sugar

1 teaspoon salt

butter for greasing

continues

continued

1. In a saucepan or in the microwave, heat the half-and-half until it begins to simmer. (Bubbles begin to form around the edges.) Do not boil it. Add the butter to melt it. Set this aside and allow it to cool to 115 degrees F. (Use the thermometer to check the temperature.)

2. Fill the liquid measuring cup with hot tap water to warm it. Let it stand for 1 minute. Pour it out and refill with ¼ cup warm water. Use the thermometer to be sure the water is between 105 and 115 degrees F. (The water should feel like warm bath water.) Gently sprinkle in the yeast and stir with the teaspoon to dissolve. The yeast should begin to foam on the surface of the water.

3. In a small bowl, lightly beat the eggs using the whisk. Remove 1 tablespoon of the egg and mix it with 1 tablespoon water in a small cup. Cover this with plastic wrap and refrigerate it for later use. Add the cooled half-and-half and the yeast mixture to the eggs and whisk to combine.

4. In a large bowl, combine the 3½ cups of the flour, sugar, and salt with the wooden spoon. Make a hole in the center of the ingredients.

5. Pour the liquids into the hole in the flour and gently stir in a circular motion with the wooden spoon until all the flour is mixed in.

6. Take the remaining ½ cup of flour and sprinkle 2 tablespoons of it on a clean, flat surface. Set the rest nearby for use during kneading. Scrape out the dough onto the surface and form it into a loose ball.

7. Flour your clean hands and knead the dough for 10 minutes with a push, fold, and turn motion. First push the dough away from you in a rolling motion with the heels of your hands. Then fold it over toward you and turn the dough a quarter turn. Add small amounts of flour if necessary to make the dough and kneading surface less sticky. The dough will be ready when it is smooth, satiny, and elastic. If you push your finger lightly into it, the dough should spring back.

8. Wash and dry the large bowl and grease it with butter. Put the dough ball into the bowl, and turn it over so all the surfaces are coated with butter.

9. Grease a length of plastic wrap to fit over the bowl and use it to cover the bowl with the greased side facing the dough. Remove the bowl to a draft-free, warm place to rise until it is double in size (about 1 hour to 1½ hours, depending on the temperature). To test whether the dough has doubled, quickly and lightly push two fingertips about ½ inch into the edge of the dough. If they leave a dent, the dough is ready.

10. When risen sufficiently, punch down the dough by making a fist and pushing it into the center of the dough. The dough will lose its air. Fold the edges of the dough toward the center and shape it into a smooth ball. Turn the dough out onto a clean, lightly floured surface.

11. To shape the dough for the loaf pan, lightly pat and roll the doll with the rolling pin into a 14 × 17 inch rectangle. Start at the shorter end and roll tightly, pressing the dough into a smooth roll. Pinch the edges and the ends to seal the dough. Put the dough into a greased loaf pan, cover it with a clean kitchen towel, and allow it to rise until double its size or until your fingertips leave a dent when the dough is pressed. (The rising should take about 45 minutes to 1½ hours.)

12. If you are braiding the dough, after you turn the dough onto the floured surface, use the knife or dough scraper to divide the ball into three equal pieces. Roll each piece into a 12-inch rope and braid the ropes. Place the dough on a greased cookie

sheet or baking pan, cover it with a clean kitchen towel, and allow it to rise until double in size or until your fingertips leave a dent when the dough is pressed. (This should take about 45 minutes to 1½ hours.)

13. Meanwhile, position the rack in the center of the oven and preheat the oven to 350 degrees F. When the dough has risen, use the pastry brush to "paint" the surface of the dough with the egg mixture (the one you reserved in the refrigerator). Bake for 30 to 40 minutes or until the loaf is golden brown and pulling away from the sides of the pan.

14. Use pot holders to remove the pan to a cooling rack and let the bread cool for 10 minutes in the pan. Turn out the loaf onto the rack to finish cooling completely. You can also check if the bread is ready by inserting an instant-read thermometer into the center of the loaf. When it registers 190 degrees F, the bread is finished baking.

Variation: This dough makes excellent sweet rolls. Follow the recipe to step 10 and then cut the dough in half with kitchen scissors. Snip six equal pieces of dough from each half and form them into balls. Set the 12 balls on greased cookie sheets, cover them with greased plastic wrap, and let them rise for about 45 minutes or until they double in size. Snip an X on the tops of each ball with kitchen scissors and paint them with the egg wash. Bake for 20 to 25 minutes or until the internal temperature registers 190 degrees F on an instant-read thermometer. Use pot holders to remove the cookie sheet to a cooling rack and let the rolls cool for 10 minutes in the pan. Turn out the rolls onto the rack to finish cooling completely.

Lemon Poppy Seed Mini-Muffins

These muffins are the perfect size for snacking. They're lemony and smooth, and the poppy seeds give a little crunch in your mouth. If you don't like poppy seeds just leave them out; the muffins still taste great. We also like the sweet glaze on top.

How hard is this recipe? Easy/Intermediate

Adult help needed at the stove, grating, filling muffins, and using the oven

Equipment

3 mini-muffin tins	waxed paper	timer
foil or paper mini-muffin cups	measuring spoons	liquid measuring cup
saucepan or microwave-safe bowl for melting butter	wooden spoon	cutting board
	medium mixing bowl	sharp knife
table knife	large whisk	lemon reamer or juicer
large mixing bowl	rubber spatula	small strainer
dry measuring cups	2 tablespoons	small whisk
grater or zester	pot holders	cooling racks

continues

continued

Ingredients

For the muffins:

6 tablespoons unsalted butter

1¾ cups all-purpose flour

¾ cup sugar

zest of 1 lemon
    (about 1 tablespoon)

¼ teaspoon salt

2 tablespoons poppy seeds

¾ teaspoon baking soda

1 teaspoon baking powder

1 large egg

1 (8-ounce) container
    fat-free vanilla yogurt

For the glaze:

¾ cup confectioners' sugar

3 teaspoons lemon juice

⅛ teaspoon vanilla

1. Position the racks on the middle and top rungs of the oven and preheat the oven to 400 degrees F. Line the muffin tins with baking cups.

2. Melt the butter in the saucepan over medium low heat or in the microwave. Set aside to cool.

3. In the large mixing bowl, mix the flour, sugar, lemon zest, salt, poppy seeds, baking soda, and baking powder with the wooden spoon. Make a hole in the center of the mixture.

4. In the medium bowl, lightly whisk the egg and whisk in the yogurt and the butter.

5. Use the rubber spatula to add the yogurt mixture to the flour mixture and stir with the wooden spoon just until blended. The batter will be lumpy and thick.

6. Use a tablespoon to scoop the batter and then, with another tablespoon, scrape it into each muffin cup. The batter should come to the top of the cup.

7. Bake for about 12 minutes or until golden brown. Check the muffins after 8 minutes and, if necessary, rearrange the tins in the oven to allow even baking.

8. While the muffins are baking, prepare the glaze. Measure the sugar into the liquid measuring cup. Add the lemon juice and vanilla and whisk to combine.

9. When done, use pot holders to remove the muffins from the oven and place them on cooling racks. (The tops should spring back lightly to the touch.) Let them cool in the pan for 5 minutes.

10. Turn out the muffins and set them on cooling racks over pieces of waxed paper. Drizzle some glaze on top of each muffin. (Have fun licking the glaze drippings off the waxed paper!)

Kid Comment

Robert Bishop, 9: "This is delicious. I really like these. It's fun to feel the poppy seeds popping in your mouth."

Robert Bishop, 9

Chapter 30

Holiday Happenings

Recipes

➤ Chocolate Truffles

➤ Crunchy Caramel Apples

➤ Libby's Famous Pumpkin Pie

➤ Mom's Snowball Cookies

Holidays are the perfect time to bring kids into the kitchen. The whole family gets swept up in the excitement of the preparations, and kids can easily participate in the festivities.

It's also a good time to start food traditions with your kids. When you make the same thing every year, they have something to look forward to and can mark each year with this special kitchen time.

The recipes in this section are geared toward specific seasons, but you needn't only make them at that time of year. Valentine truffles, for instance, make a festive Christmas gift. Kids can enjoy making caramel apples any time of the year, and if your family is anything like ours, pumpkin pie is always a welcome dessert. When you're looking to bake cookies, Mom's Snowball Cookies make an easy and delicious treat.

So turn to these recipes at holiday times or any time of the year for fun kitchen adventures with your kids.

Chocolate Truffles

Next Valentine's Day you can impress your loved ones with a box of handmade chocolate truffles. These rich morsels of chocolate look elegant, but they are easier to make than you think. All you do is melt butter with chocolate, heavy cream, and vanilla. Let the mixture harden and then shape it into little balls. You can serve them as is or roll them in toppings. Then just place them in foil or paper candy cups, which can be found in kitchen stores.

We started making truffles for teachers' gifts several years ago when my daughters were 7 and 10 years old. It wasn't until I took a chocolate class at the Disney Institute in Orlando, Florida, however, that I learned some tricks for easy truffle-making. I've adapted the Institute's recipe, and I find it works well for kids because it's simple, it heats in one pot, and it incorporates three easy-to-follow techniques. First, you pour and spread the melted chocolate into a jelly roll pan and refrigerate or freeze it. This hardens the chocolate quickly, which is especially important when working with impatient kids. Second, you scrape a small scoop (or melon baller or teaspoon measure) along the pan of hardened chocolate to form the ball. This eliminates the mess of melting chocolate in your hands as you form the balls. Finally, you pierce the truffles with a fork to hold them if you're dipping them in toppings. (I find that a bamboo skewer also works well.) This avoids making another chocolate mess in your hands.

Measure and set up all your ingredients next to the stove. Kids can have the special job of watching for the bubbles on the cream. Then let them add the chocolate chunks, butter, and vanilla and let them stir until the ingredients are melted.

When it comes to scooping the hardened chocolate, your child may or may not have difficulty squeezing the handle. Practice pressing the scooper handle ahead of time. If it's too hard, your child can still scrape the chocolate into the scoop and then let you squeeze it out.

How hard is this recipe? Easy/Intermediate

Adult help needed with cutting, at the stove, and forming truffles

Makes about 30 truffles

Equipment

2-quart saucepan	pot holder	large serving plate
liquid measuring cup	cooling rack	bowls or waxed paper for toppings
timer	cookie sheet or	truffle, cocktail, table, or
cutting board	jelly roll pan	fondue fork
sharp knife	parchment paper	serving plate
wooden spoon	rubber spatula	container with cover for
table knife	small disher (scoop)	storing truffles
measuring spoons	or melon baller	paper or foil candy cups (optional)

Ingredients

½ cup heavy or whipping cream

11 ounces good-quality dark chocolate, coarsely chopped

3 tablespoons unsalted butter, softened

¼ teaspoon vanilla

Truffle Toppings

> unsweetened cocoa powder (the classic covering)
>
> powdered spices—cinnamon, ginger, nutmeg
>
> chocolate sprinkles
>
> coconut chips or shavings
>
> finely chopped nuts—walnuts, pecans, hazelnuts, peanuts, pistachios
>
> finely chopped dried fruits
>
> melted white or dark chocolate

1. In the 2-quart saucepan, heat the heavy cream over moderate heat just until it comes to a slow boil. Be sure to watch it carefully so it doesn't burn or overboil.

2. When the bubbles start to break, add the chocolate and gently stir with the wooden spoon until the chocolate is melted. This should take about 1½ minutes. Mix in the butter and vanilla and continue to stir until the mixture becomes a thick sauce and all the butter is melted. This should take about 2 minutes. Use the pot holder to remove the pot from the heat to a cooling rack.

3. Line the cookie sheet or pan with parchment paper. Pour and spread the chocolate with the rubber spatula into a thin layer (about ¼ inch) in the pan and refrigerate until firm. This could take up to an hour depending on how cold your refrigerator is. Alternatively, place the chocolate on the sheet or pan in the freezer for about 20 minutes.

4. When the chocolate is set, drag the disher (scoop), melon baller or measuring spoon along the length of the sheet to collect the chocolate into a ball. (If the chocolate seems too glossy or wet, chill it more.) Release the chocolate ball onto a plate by squeezing the handle of the disher or pushing out of the ball or spoon.

5. Use the tip of your finger to gently roll the ball against the flat surface of the plate to make it evenly round. You can eat the truffles plain or sprinkle or coat them with toppings (step 6). Store the truffles in a closed container in the refrigerator.

6. Place the toppings in individual bowls or on separate pieces of waxed paper. Use a fork or a bamboo skewer to pick up a truffle and dip and roll it in the topping. Set the truffles in individual paper or foil candy cups before serving.

Kitchen Clue

Spray your disher (scoop), baller, or measuring spoon lightly with nonstick vegetable spray occasionally before scooping up the truffle mixture. The spray helps the truffle slip out easily. If you want to know what a disher looks like, just picture the servers on the deli or lunch line with their scoops. The disher used in truffles is the same kind of scoop but smaller.

Heads Up!

Burning the chocolate and cream will ruin the flavor of your truffle mixture. To prevent burning, watch carefully as the ingredients heat and stir them nearly continually. When the cream begins to form bubbles on the surface, it's time to start adding the chocolate. When the chocolate is just melted, add the butter and vanilla. Again, remove the pot from the heat just as all the ingredients are blended into a thick sauce.

Caramel Apples for Halloween

Crunchy Caramel Apples

 What's Halloween without caramel apples? They're deliciously juicy and sweet. They can be a little tricky to make, though, between the hot caramel syrup and all the dipping so adults should supervise this activity. Just set up an assembly line and work quickly, and you should have no trouble. Try the toppings we've suggested or come up with some of your own, such as chopped peanuts or small chocolate morsels. For a different flavor, try using chocolate caramels in place of the vanilla ones.

How hard is this recipe? Intermediate

Adult help needed throughout the recipe, especially at the stove and dipping the apples

Makes 5 apples

Equipment

1½-quart saucepan or microwave-safe bowl	pot holders	wooden spoon
paper towels	small bowl	measuring spoons
waxed paper	dry measuring cups	timer
5 wooden popsicle sticks	tablespoon	large plate

Ingredients

1 (14-ounce) package vanilla caramels (about 48 candies)

5 medium apples

½ cup granola, crushed to break up large chunks

¼ cup coconut

butter for greasing

2 tablespoons water

1. Unwrap the caramels and put them in the saucepan.

2. Wash and dry the apples thoroughly with the paper towels and set them on a piece of waxed paper on the counter. Press a wooden stick into the stem end of each apple. Set a pot holder on the counter next to the apples.

3. In the small bowl, combine the granola and coconut, mix with the tablespoon, and set the mixture next to the pot holder.

4. Tear off another sheet of waxed paper large enough to hold the apples and grease it with butter. Set it aside, greased side up, next to bowl. Generously grease the wooden spoon and set it on top of the waxed paper.

5. Add 2 tablespoons water to the caramels and place the saucepan over low heat. Cook the caramels for about 15 minutes or until they melt and become smooth. (Stir the caramels with the greased spoon as they cook.)

6. Use pot holders to remove the saucepan from the heat and place it on top of the pot holder on the counter. Watch not to burn yourself with the hot pot or the caramel.

7. Hold the apple by the stick and dip it as far as you can into the caramel mixture. Quickly flip the apple right side up to spread the caramel sauce, and then turn it upside down again. Alternatively, instead of flipping the apple, use the wooden spoon to pour caramel on the surface of the apple. (If the caramel sauce hardens, reheat it on the stove.)

8. Place the apple on the piece of waxed paper with the stick pointing upward. Repeat the same process with each apple.

9. When you've finished the apples, slide the plate underneath the waxed paper so the apples are on the plate. Refrigerate for about an hour or until the coating is firm.

Microwave version: Follow steps 1 to 4. Put the caramels and 2 tablespoons water in a deep, microwave-safe bowl. Microwave on high for 2½ to 3½ minutes, stirring every minute. Proceed with steps 6 to 9.

Kid Comment

Colleen Wearn, 14: "This is kind of messy. Be sure to hold the apple by the stick and don't touch the caramel. It burns you." Colleen found she had to work quickly before the caramel hardened. It was tricky to get the granola to stay on the apple if the caramel started cooling down. "The caramel was very hard and chewy. My brother lost his [loose] tooth while trying to eat it!" she said. Their mom, Maureen, said: "This is a good after-school snack."

Colleen Wearn, 14

Kitchen Clue

For easy clean-up, soak the pots, bowls, and utensils used to melt the caramels in very hot, soapy water immediately after use.

Libby's Famous Pumpkin Pie

Every few years, my birthday falls on Thanksgiving day. Even though my kids always present me with a birthday cake, the pumpkin pie is never far behind. Thanksgiving wouldn't be the same without a pumpkin pie, and one recipe that stands out is the Libby's Famous Pumpkin Pie. My daughter Julia baked our pumpkin pie this year, and was surprised by how easy it was to make. Here's our kid-friendly version of the Libby recipe.

How hard is this recipe? Easy

Adult help needed using the can opener, knife, and oven

Makes 1 deep-dish 9-inch pie or 2 shallow 9-inch pies, 8 servings each

Equipment

small bowl	large bowl	pot holders
dry measuring cups	whisk	timer
measuring spoons	can opener	small knife
wooden spoon	rubber spatula	wire cooling rack

Ingredients

¾ cup sugar

½ teaspoon salt

1 teaspoon ground cinnamon

½ teaspoon ground ginger

¼ teaspoon ground cloves

2 large eggs

1¾ cups (15- or 16-ounce can) solid pack pumpkin

1½ cups (12-ounce can) evaporated milk

1 deep-dish unbaked 9-inch (4-cup volume) pie shell or 2 shallow unbaked 9-inch (2-cup volume) pie shells

whipped cream or nuts for garnish if desired

1. Position the rack in the center of the oven and preheat the oven to 425 degrees F.

2. Combine the sugar, salt, cinnamon, ginger, and cloves in the small bowl and mix with the wooden spoon.

3. In the large bowl, beat the eggs lightly with the whisk. Stir in the pumpkin and sugar-spice mixture with the wooden spoon. Gradually stir in the evaporated milk. Use the rubber spatula to pour the batter into the pie shell (or shells).

4. Bake for 15 minutes. Reduce the temperature to 350 degrees F. Bake 40 to 50 minutes more for a 4-cup-volume pie or 15 to 20 minutes more for 2 shallow pies. Pies are done when a knife inserted about 1 to 1½ inches from the center comes out clean.

5. Use the pot holders to remove the pan (or pans) from the oven to the wire cooling rack. Leave to set for 2 hours. Serve immediately when set or chill for later use. (Do not freeze pumpkin pie because freezing causes the crust to separate from the filling.) Garnish with whipped cream and nuts if desired.

Note: For a lower-fat and lower-calorie pie, substitute nonfat or low-fat evaporated milk.

Heads Up!

Be sure to place the rack in the center of the oven; even heating prevents a crust from forming on the top of your pumpkin pie. Also be sure to watch baking time carefully: Overbaking can cause the pie filling to crack or pull away from the crust.

Mom's Snowball Cookies

Every family seems to have its own special holiday cookie. Ours is my mom's nut butter balls. The powdery white mounds remind us of snowballs because we roll the little balls in confectioners' sugar.

How hard is this recipe? Easy/Intermediate

Adult help needed using the food processor, electric mixer, and oven

Makes about 4 dozen cookies

Equipment

large mixing bowl
hand-held electric mixer
dry measuring cups
rubber spatula
measuring spoons
food processor or nut grinder

plastic wrap
timer
cookie sheets
parchment paper
tablespoon

pot holders
cooling racks
small bowl
serving plate
cookie tin

Ingredients

1 cup (2 sticks) unsalted
    butter, softened
½ cup sugar
½ teaspoon salt
2 teaspoons vanilla

2 cups sifted all-purpose flour, divided
1 cup finely ground walnuts,
    pecans, almonds, or hazelnuts
½ cup confectioners' sugar

1. In the large bowl with the mixer on medium speed, combine the butter and sugar until light and fluffy. Scrape down the sides of the bowl with the rubber spatula as needed.

2. Mix in the salt, vanilla, and half the flour. The dough will be crumbly at first, but when it starts to come together, slowly add the remaining flour to combine.

3. Add the nuts and mix just until the dough forms a mass.

4. Use the rubber spatula to scrape the dough onto the plastic wrap, wrap it tightly, and refrigerate it until it's easy to handle. This should take about 1 hour.

5. When you're ready to bake, position the rack in the center of the oven and pre-heat the oven to 350 degrees F. Line cookie sheets with parchment paper.

6. Use the tablespoon to scoop dough into the palm of your hand. Roll it lightly into a 1-inch ball. Place the balls about 2 inches apart on the cookie sheet.

7. Bake for 10 to 12 minutes or until cookies start to turn light brown.

8. Use pot holders to remove the sheets from the oven and place them on a cooling rack. Let the cookies set for about 5 minutes.

9. Meanwhile, fill the small bowl with confectioners' sugar. Roll the tops of the still-warm cookies in the sugar and set them on the serving plate. The sugar will melt slightly and coat the cookies. These cookies keep well in a covered tin.

Variation: Shape the dough into an S or a crescent moon shape or make a thumbprint cookie by pressing the cookie mound with your thumb. Bake the cookies and then, when cool, fill the thumbprints with red jelly or spreadable fruit.

Heads Up!

Be aware that the type of cookie sheet you use will make a difference in your cookies. Because air-bake sheets are insulated, they don't get as hot as regular sheets, and you'll have to bake cookies longer. Try to use shiny sheets rather than black steel ones. Because the black steel speeds browning on the bottom surface, you run the risk of overbrowning the bottom of your cookies. Always check your cookies 5 minutes before the minimum baking time because no two ovens are alike and the cookies could be ready. Try to make your cookies the same size so they bake at the same rate.

Kitchen Lingo Glossary

al dente   This Italian term means "to the tooth" and refers to cooking pasta so it is tender yet firm when bitten.

bake   To cook food by surrounding it with dry heat, usually in an oven. Foods can be baked covered or uncovered. Recipes will tell you at what temperature (degrees) the oven must be set and whether the food should be covered.

batter   An uncooked mixture of flour, liquid, and other ingredients that is able to be poured or spooned.

beat   To stir ingredients together quickly and vigorously in a circular motion so they become light and smooth by adding air. You can beat with a wire whisk, a wooden spoon, a rotary egg beater, or an electric mixer. Some recipes, in particular those requiring egg whites, will include detailed information about how to beat the ingredients.

blend   To mix food in an electric blender or to mix ingredients together with a hand tool. When you blend, you mix foods until they are smooth and well-combined and until you no longer see the separate ingredients.

blender   An electric appliance with a tall container that fits into a motorized base. The motor rotates a set of sharp blades that blend, chop, purée and liquefy foods. See Chapter 8, "A Kid's-Eye View of Appliances," to learn more about blenders.

boil   To heat liquids to the point at which bubbles begin to break the surface. This boiling point is 212 degrees F (Fahrenheit) at sea level. This also refers to cooking food in a liquid that is boiling. If a recipe calls for a *full rolling boil*, it means that stirring will not stop the bubbling. To bring a liquid to a rapid boil, turn the heat on high. To reduce the boil to a simmer, turn down the heat.

braise   To cook food gently in a covered pan with a small amount of liquid. Braised foods sometimes are first seared—cooked quickly with hot fat at high heat.

broil   To cook food by direct heat under a gas or electric broiler in an oven or above a heat source on a barbecue grill. You also can broil in a portable toaster oven with the proper setting.

brown   To make a food brown on all sides by cooking it, usually on top of a stove, in a small amount of fat. Browning gives food a rich flavor and an appetizing golden color, and it helps seal in natural juices.

chop   To use a sharp knife to cut food into small pieces. Food that is very finely chopped is called *minced* food.

coat   To cover a utensil or food with an outer coating, such as butter, oil, flour, or crumbs.

colander   A utensil used to separate and drain the liquid from foods, such as pasta and vegetables. Colanders are usually made of plastic or metal. They are shaped like a bowl and punched throughout with holes.

combine   To mix together two or more ingredients in order to distribute them evenly.

core   To cut out the stem, seeds, and middle of vegetables or fruits, such as apples. To core, you can use a sharp knife, an apple corer, or a melon baller.

cream   To mix foods with an electric mixer or spoon until they are combined into a soft and smooth mixture. This usually involves fat, such as butter, and sugar.

cube   To use a sharp knife to cut food into square chunks (cubes) of roughly the same size, usually about ½ inch.

dice   To use a sharp knife to chop food into small pieces, usually ⅛ to ½ inch in size. Diced food is smaller than cubed food.

disher   A hand-held utensil with a small round scoop at the end that is used to scoop and serve foods. Dishers are also used to shape foods, like the chocolate truffles in Chapter 30, "Holiday Happenings."

dissolve   To stir a dry ingredient, such as gelatin or yeast, into a liquid ingredient until the dry ingredient fills with liquid and loses its shape.

dough   A mixture of liquid, flour, and other ingredients, often including a leavening agent such as yeast, baking soda, or baking powder. Dough is stiff and, unlike batter, cannot be poured, but is pliable enough to be kneaded or worked with your hands.

drain   To separate a liquid, such as water, from a solid, such as rice or pasta. One method of draining is to pour everything into a colander or a strainer and let the liquid run out of the bottom.

drizzle   To slowly pour a small amount of a liquid, such as oil or vinegar, in a thin but steady stream on top of food.

dutch oven   A large pot with two side handles and a tight-fitting lid, used to make soups and stews. Dutch ovens are usually made of cast iron.

egg separator   A small tool used to separate egg whites and egg yolks. The egg is cracked and the contents are emptied into the separator, which enables the white to seep out, leaving behind the yolk.

egg slicer   A utensil with an egg-shaped hollow bottom and a hinged top made of fine steel wires. A hard-cooked egg is placed in the hollow and the top is brought down over the egg to cut it into thin slices. This tool can also be used for cutting soft foods, such as slices of bananas.

egg wash   A beaten egg, or the white or yolk only, that is brushed on top of baked goods. The wash sometimes is mixed with milk or water, and it gives a sheen to the surface of the pastry or dough when baked. The recipe for Wecke Bread (the yeast bread in Chapter 29, "The Baker's Rack") calls for an egg wash.

electric mixer   This appliance is used to whip, mix, or beat foods, such as batters, cream, egg whites, or cookie dough. There are two types: stationary (standing) or portable (held by hand). Both have beaters that fit into holes in the top of the mixer. Stationary mixers have more powerful motors and can handle heavier batters and bigger jobs. These standing mixers also have other attachments, such as whisks, hooks, and paddle-type beaters.

fold   To mix one ingredient with another by slowly and gently lifting and turning one over the other, usually with a rubber spatula. You usually fold the lighter or more fragile ingredient, such as beaten egg whites, into the heavier ingredient, such as batter, so as not to deflate the lighter ingredient. Place the lighter ingredient on top and use the rubber spatula to cut down the middle of the bowl and then bring up some of the heavier ingredient to cover the lighter ingredient. Turn the bowl slightly with your free hand and repeat this method until the ingredients are combined. Folding also is used to combine berries, nuts, or other ingredients, such as chocolate chips, into batter for cakes or muffins.

food processor   An electric appliance that performs many kitchen tasks quickly. The processor can chop, dice, shred, slice, grind, and purée most foods in seconds. Large machines can also knead dough. These machines come in several sizes, including a miniprocessor for small, everyday jobs. A food processor has a motorized base, a plastic work bowl that fits into the base, and a cover. A steel blade or dough blade fits atop the drive shaft in the center of the bowl. Ingredients are added to the bowl through a feed tube in the cover. Most processors come with discs for slicing and shredding, an S-shaped blade, and a dough blade.

fry   To cook in hot fat in an open skillet or pot. Pan-frying requires a shallow pan and a small amount of fat. Deep-frying foods, such as onion rings and french fries, requires a large amount of fat in a deep pan.

garlic press   A hand-held metal or plastic tool that reduces a whole bulb of garlic to shreds. The bulb is dropped into a small container with holes and then pressed with an attached piece of metal or plastic that fits into the container. The garlic pulp and juice come out the other end.

garnish   To decorate a finished dish by adding artistically placed and colorful food. Typical garnishes include sprigs of parsley, citrus slices, or carved fruits and vegetables as discussed in Chapter 17, "Playing with Your Food." A garnish also refers to the food used as the decoration.

grate   To rub a large piece of food against the metal blade of a food processor or a hand-held grater to reduce the food to small particles. Food can also be grated in a blender or a minichopper.

grater   A flat, multisided or hand-cranked metal tool used to reduce hard foods to thin shreds or tiny particles. The surface of the grater is perforated with sharp-edged small and medium-size holes and slits.

grease   To rub the surface of a bowl, pan, cookie sheet, or cooking utensil with butter, shortening, or margarine, or spray with nonstick cooking spray. This prevents foods prepared with the utensil from sticking to the surfaces.

griddle   A flat pan typically without sides and intended to cook foods with only a minimum of oil or fat. Griddles are used for pancakes, for example.

grind   To use a food processor, blender, food grinder, or mortar and pestle to turn food into fine, tiny particles. Cookie and cake recipes often call for ground nuts.

instant-read thermometer   A small food thermometer with a stem for use outside of the oven. When the stem is plunged into food, the internal temperature is recorded in seconds. The stem can also be placed into liquids. This handy tool takes the guesswork out of baking bread (the internal temperature should register 190 degrees F when finished) and determining if food is cooked sufficiently to ensure food safety. See Chapter 10, "What You Need To Know About Food Safety," for recommended temperatures of foods.

jelly-roll pan   A rectangular baking pan with sides about 1-inch high. While the pans were designed to make sheet cakes or sponge cakes, they are useful for other types of baking, such as making granola. The high sides prevent foods from spilling out of the pan when stirred.

julienne   To cut food, such as fruits and vegetables, with a sharp knife into small, match stick–like pieces.

kitchen scissors or **shears**   Scissors that are used to cut various foods, such as dough, herbs, dried fruit, sun-dried tomatoes, and scallions.

knead   This is the hand motion used to mix and work dough until it is smooth for breads and pizza. Some kitchen appliances, such as food processors or stand mixers, also can be used to knead. For more details about kneading techniques, see Chapter 13, "Let's Take a Cooking Lesson."

ladle   A long-handled utensil used to scoop and pour foods, such as soups, chili, and hot drinks. The ladle has a bowl at the end that is dipped into the food to collect it.

leaven   To add a leavening agent, such as yeast, baking soda, or baking powder, to a dough or batter to make it rise. These agents are intended to increase the volume and lighten the texture of baked goods.

level ingredients   To pass a straight edge, such as the straight side on a table knife blade or pastry spatula, across the top of the mounded ingredient in a measuring cup or spoon so that the ingredient is even with the top of the measuring spoon or cup.

marinate   To allow food to soak in a liquid mixture to give it flavor or make it tender.

mash   To crush or smash food (such as cooked potatoes) to form a soft, smooth, and evenly textured mass. A potato or bean masher is a good utensil for mashing food.

measuring cups   Utensils used to measure liquid and dry ingredients. Liquid cups are made of glass or plastic and have a handle and spout. Lines on the side of the cup show standard and metric measurements of 1 or more cups and part of a cup. Dry cups are made of metal or plastic, come in nested sets, and are used to measure dry ingredients, such as flour and sugar. The average set includes ¼, ⅓, ½, and 1 cup measures. Refer to Chapter 12, "Kitchen Math and Measuring," to learn more about these utensils.

measuring spoons   Spoon-shaped utensils used to measure liquid and dry ingredients. These utensils come in sets and are made of metal or plastic. Sets are nested and generally include 1 tablespoon and ¼, ½, and 1 teaspoon measures. Some sets also include smaller and larger spoons.

melon baller   A small hand-held tool with bowl-shaped forms at either end. The form is pushed into a melon and cuts it into either oval or round shapes. This tool can also be used to core apples and pears.

melt   To turn a solid substance, such as butter or margarine, into a liquid by heating it. You can melt foods in a pan on the stove, in the oven, or in a microwave oven.

mince   To cut or chop food into very tiny pieces, usually with a sharp knife, a food processor, or an electric blender. Recipes often call for minced onions, garlic, or herbs, such as parsley or basil.

mortar and pestle   A mortar and pestle are used together to grind herbs, spices, and other foods. The mortar is a bowl-shaped container and the pestle is a rounded utensil with a shape similar to the rounded end of a baseball bat. Ingredients are put into the mortar; the pestle is then pressed into the mortar and rotated to grind the ingredients.

parchment paper   A grease-, heat-, and moisture-resistant paper that is used to line cookie sheets and baking pans, to make disposable pastry bags, and to wrap foods to be baked. Lining cookie sheets and baking pans with parchment paper prevents food from sticking and thus eliminates the need to grease the pans. The paper is available in supermarkets and kitchenware stores.

peel   (verb) To use a sharp knife or a peeler to cut the skin off of a fruit or vegetable. (noun) The outermost layer or skin of a fruit or vegetable. When referring to citrus fruits, the word is often used interchangeably with zest.

pizza wheel   A hand-held tool with a handle and round metal wheel at the end. The wheel can cut pizza, tortillas, dough, and other breads.

poach   To gently cook food in barely boiling water or another liquid so that the food keeps its shape. Chicken breasts, fish, and eggs are commonly poached.

preheat   To heat the oven or grill to a certain temperature before you start cooking. By the time you're ready to cook, the proper temperature has been reached.

proof   A test to determine whether yeast is still alive. Proofing is done before making yeast breads to make sure the yeast will cause the bread to rise. Dissolve the yeast in warm water (105 to 115 degrees F) with 1 teaspoon of sugar and set it aside for 5 to 10 minutes. The mixture will become bubbly and foamy if the yeast is alive.

purée   To mash or grind food until it is a smooth, thick mixture. Foods can be puréed in several ways, including using an electric blender or food processor and pressing the food through a sieve. Food that is mashed into a smooth, thick mixture is also called a purée.

quick bread   A bread that does not require any rising time or kneading and, as a result, is quick to make. Many fruit breads, such as apple or banana bread, are quick breads.

reamer   A hand-held tool with a handle and a ridged and tear-dropped point that is designed to extract the juice from citrus fruits. The point is pressed into the halved fruit and turned while the free hand squeezes the fruit.

roast   To cook poultry, meat, or vegetables uncovered using dry heat in an oven.

roll out   To flatten and spread dough with a rolling pin until it becomes thin and even in thickness.

rounded   To fill a measuring spoon or cup until the ingredient is in a small mound slightly higher than the rim.

sauce pan   A round pot with a long handle on one side and, typically, a tight-fitting lid. These come in various sizes and are usually deep but can be as shallow as 3 inches.

sauté   To cook quickly in a small amount of fat on top of the stove in an open skillet, sauté pan, or fry pan. The food is turned or stirred often.

scoop   To cut food into round or oval pieces, often using a tool called a melon baller.

scramble   This term usually refers to a way to cook eggs. Using a fork or a spoon, stir and mix the eggs in the pan, scraping the bottom. Push the cooked eggs to the side, let the liquid cover the bottom of the hot pan, and cook until it becomes solid.

Again, push the cooked eggs to the side, let the liquid cover the bottom of the hot pan, and cook until solid. Continue this method until all of the egg is solid.

sear   To brown the surface of meat or fish quickly in order to seal in the juices. The food is exposed to very high heat in the oven or skillet or under the broiler.

shred   To reduce a large piece of food into small, thin strips either by cutting it with a knife or rubbing it against the metal blade of a food processor or hand-held grater.

sift   To pass flour or other dry ingredients, such as sugar through a sieve, strainer, or sifter to give them a fine texture or to remove any lumps. Some dry ingredients are sifted together to mix them well.

sifter   A utensil with a mesh bottom used to sift ingredients. They are usually made of heavyweight plastic or stainless steel.

simmer   To cook food in liquids just below the boiling point. Tiny bubbles will form around the edges of the pan and will slowly rise to the surface in the center.

skillet   A pan with a long handle and low sloping sides that prevent steam from collecting in the pan. Skillets come in various sizes and are also called frying pans.

slice   To use a sharp knife or a food processor to cut food into even pieces.

soften   To leave an ingredient, such as butter, at room temperature until it is soft enough to spread or to blend easily.

spatula   A kitchen utensil which comes in a variety of shapes and sizes and can be used for various kitchen tasks, including lifting, turning, flattening, spreading, and mixing foods. Metal and plastic spatulas have a long handle attached to a wide flat piece. This end piece is used to get underneath foods, such as pancakes, and turn or flip the food. These spatulas are also referred to as turners. Metal spatulas with flexible, long narrow blades are used for frosting cakes, leveling ingredients, and loosening ingredients and foods from surfaces. Rubber spatulas have a wooden or plastic handle attached to either a flat or curved blade. They are used to scrape out ingredients from bowls, cans, or appliances, such as the blender or food processor. Curved spatulas can be used to mix, scoop up, and transfer foods and fold in ingredients.

spoon   To use a spoon to pick up food or ingredients and transfer them.

steam   To cook food in a covered basket or pot by the heat of moist steam. Typically, food is placed in a steamer basket or rack and then is placed over simmering or boiling water in a covered pan. This method helps foods retain the vitamins, minerals, flavor, taste, and texture that are often lost in boiling.

steep   To soak dry ingredients, such as herbs or tea, in liquids. This softens the ingredients and allows the flavor of the dry ingredients to seep into the liquids.

stew   A method of cooking that makes tough pieces of meat tender and that increases the flavor of the food being cooked. The food usually is cut into small pieces, is covered with liquid, and is left to slowly simmer for a long period of time. The pot often is tightly covered.

361

stir   To use a whisk or a spoon in a circular motion to combine ingredients or to prevent them from sticking.

stir-fry   To quickly fry small pieces of food in a little fat over very high heat while briskly and constantly turning and stirring the food. Stir-frying usually is associated with Asian cooking and usually is done in a wok, although any large pan can be used.

strainer   A utensil with a bottom that is perforated or made of mesh and through which liquids or semiliquids are strained. These come in various sizes and shapes.

tongs   A metal or wooden utensil that has long arms and is used to grip and turn food. Metal tongs with a spring grip are particularly easy to use, especially for children.

toss   Tossing is a method used to mix a salad with a dressing or to mix pasta and other ingredients with a sauce. Quickly and lightly lift the ingredients from one section of the bowl or pot with two forks or spoons. Drop the food back into the bowl and then repeat with food in different parts of the bowl until all the ingredients are well-mixed.

whip   To mix rapidly with a whisk or an electric beater at high speed to add air to make a mixture light and fluffy and to increase its volume.

whisk   A metal utensil used to blend or beat ingredients (such as egg whites and cream) to incorporate air and increase volume. Whisks (sometimes called whips) come in many sizes and are usually made of stainless or tinned steel. A whisk has a handle that holds several metal wires that are looped and extend out in a teardrop shape. To whisk also means to use a whisk.

wok   A large metal round-bottom pan with high sloping sides used for stir-frying. This utensil is most often associated with Asian cooking. Woks are also used for steaming, stewing, braising, and deep frying. Electric woks and flat-bottomed woks for electric stovetops are also available.

yeast   A single-celled, microscopic organism that converts its food into carbon dioxide and alcohol through a process called *fermentation*. Baker's yeast is used as a leavener, or to lighten breads and enable the dough to rise.

yeast breads   Breads that use yeast and generally require time to rise before baking.

zest   The colored portion or outer layer of the peel of a citrus fruit. To zest also means to remove the colored outer layer of the peel of a citrus fruit such as lemon, lime, or grapefruit. The aromatic oils in the peel add flavor to baked goods and dishes. Zest can be obtained by rubbing the citrus fruit against the smallest holes of a grater, by using a zester, or by using a sharp knife to peel the fruit and then mince the peel.

zester   A small tool with a series of small, sharp holes which remove the peel from zitrus fruits. Press the zester firmly against the fruit and then slide it along the side of the fruit. Do not remove the white pith of the fruit as you zest.

The Resource Guide

When you page through this guide, you'll be amazed at how much information is out there for the asking. These pages are designed to enhance the material you'll find in this book and to expand your culinary world. Pick up the phone and call one of the toll-free numbers to participate in some of the many free offers or to get advice from food professionals and companies.

You'll find listings for free information, from getting food tips from a nutritionist to asking for help with food-safety and cooking questions.

Search the Web for food finds and get your kids to plug in to the many educational and interactive food games on kids' pages. The Web sites listed here point the way.

Want to know more about cooking and find more recipes? You'll get plenty of ideas and information from the cookbooks and magazines listed here. And the mail-order guide will provide you with helpful sources of products and information for projects in this book.

Companies and Organizations

These companies and organizations offer free information, recipes, and advice.

You'll also find brochures, newsletters, and cookbooks available free or for a nominal fee. Most phone listings are toll free.

American Cancer Society
1-800-227-2345
7 days a week, 24 hours a day
www.cancer.org

Cancer information specialists offer free information about cancer, and the American Cancer Society guidelines for nutrition, cancer prevention, and food choices.

American Dietetic Association
1-800-366-1655
Monday through Friday, 8 A.M.–8 P.M. Central Time
www.eatright.org

Hear timely recorded messages from registered dietitians about nutrition and food on this nutrition hot line. You'll find occasional offers of free information and brochures along with referrals to dietitians in your area.

American Egg Board
www.aeb.org

This Web site provides free brochure offers, recipes, and extensive information on eggs, including the *Eggcyclopedia*. Kids will enjoy activities and information in the kids' section.

For a free recipe brochure on kids' cooking, send SASE to:

The Incredible Edible Egg
#28 PO Box 733
Park Ridge, IL 60068-0733

American Heart Association
1-800-AHA-USA1
Monday through Saturday, 5 A.M.–11 P.M. Pacific Time
www.amhrt.org

The AHA provides information about diets in relation to heart disease, strokes, and cholesterol.

American Institute for Cancer Research
1-800-843-8114
Monday through Friday, 9 A.M.–5 P.M. Eastern Standard Time

This nonprofit organization focuses exclusively on the link between diet and cancer and publishes the *good-news-letter* (bimonthly) for kids ages 7 to 10. (The first year's subscription is free with a nominal renewal fee thereafter.) It also publishes a free quarterly newsletter with recipes, health tips, and recent research updates. Requests for publications are taken at the preceding toll-free number.

Dole

1-800-232-8888
Monday through Friday, 8 A.M.–3 P.M. Pacific Time
www.dole.com

You can receive a free *Fun with Fruits and Vegetables Kids' Cookbook* along with nutrition and product information upon request.

www.dole5aday.com

Log on to this excellent kids' Web site for games and activities with over 70 fruit and vegetable characters that teach about food and nutrition. Kids can e-mail the characters and get responses back. To order the *Dole 5-a-Day Adventures* CD-ROM, send a check for $14.95 payable to Dole Food Company to:

Dole Nutrition Program
155 Bovet, Suite 476
San Mateo, CA 94402

Fleischmann's Yeast
1-800-777-4959
7 days a week, 8 A.M.–5:30 P.M. Central Time
www.breadworld.com

The hot line offers answers to questions about yeast products, coupons, free recipes, and advice. If you want to know about yeast and learn how to knead and make bread, check out the Web site. You'll find easy step-by-step instructions with accompanying photos.

Food And Drug Administration Food Hot Line
1-800-332-4010
24-hour recorded messages
www.fda.gov
Consumer affairs specialists are available Monday through Friday, noon–4 P.M. Eastern Standard Time.

Log on to the FDA's extensive Web site where you'll find a kids' page and interactive games.

General Mills
Toll-free numbers for recipes:
1-888-ASK-BETTY
1-800-336-9331 (Bisquick)
1-800-328-6787(prerecorded recipes)
877-RECIPES (24-hour, prerecorded message)

To receive the *Alpha Bakery Book* (a baking book for kids), send a check or money order for $2 payable to General Mills to:

Gold Medal Alpha-Bakery Cookbook
PO Box 5119
Minneapolis, MN 55460-5119 (offer expires 12/31/2001)

To receive *The Rainbow Bakery* (kids' cookbook and activity book), send a check or money order for $2.50 payable to General Mills to:

Gold Medal Rainbow Bakery
PO Box 2052
Milaca, MN 56353-2052 (offer expires 12/31/2002)

The Kellogg Company
1-800-962-1413
Monday through Friday, 7 A.M.–7 P.M. Central Time
www.kelloggs.com

You'll find information about Kellogg's products along with recipes through the hotline and the Web site. The internet also features offers for free product samples.

McCormick/Schilling Company
1-800-632-5847
Monday through Friday, 9:30 A.M.–5 P.M. Eastern Time
www.McCormick.com

You can get answers to spice and cooking questions and monthly featured meal ideas with recipes, coupons, and free samples. The Web site offers spice information, cooking tips, and recipes.

National Honey Board
www.honey.com

The kids' section on the Web site includes recipes and facts about honey. For a free kids' honey recipe leaflet, send a legal-size SASE to:

National Honey Board
Department CK #229
390 Lashley Street
Longmont, CO 80501-6045

For a 96-page, spiral-bound cookbook including low-fat recipes using honey, send a check or money order for $2.95 to:

National Honey Board
Dept. CAD
PO Box 125
Wisconsin Rapids, WI 54495

National Pasta Association
2101 Wilson Boulevard, Suite 920
Arlington, VA 22201
703-841-0818
www.ilovepasta.org

The Web site offers extensive information about pasta along with a variety of recipes, cooking tips, and descriptions and uses of different kinds of pasta. Look for offers for cookbooks and free brochures.

Nestlé
1-800-851-0512
Monday through Friday, 8 A.M.–8 P.M. Eastern Standard Time
www.tollhouse.com

Nestlé offers nutritional information and answers to product questions plus free recipes through the hotline and the Web site. Inquire on the hotline about information and hotlines for other Nestlé products, such as Libby's pumpkin and Carnation Evaporated Milk. Check out the Web site for classic baking recipes, and the "valupage," with weekly specials on products and grocery coupons online.

Pillsbury
www.pillsbury.com

If you've got baking questions, log on to this Web site where you can e-mail questions and get responses to solve problems or find out general baking information.

Quaker Oats
1-800-367-6287
Monday through Friday, 8:30 A.M.–7 P.M. Eastern Standard Time
www.quakeroats.com
www.quakeroatmeal.com

Quaker provides answers to questions about nutrition and health-related issues, products, and free recipes through the hot line and on the internet. Check out the kids' corner and meal suggestions at these fun Web sites.

Red Star Yeast
1-800-445-4746

Monday through Friday, 7 A.M.–7 P.M. Central Time
1-800-368-4483 (bread machine hot line)
Monday through Friday, 8 a.m.–5 p.m. Central Time
www.redstaryeast.com

Call the hot line to get recipes and answers to your questions about baking, baking problems, and using yeast. The bread machine line focuses on use of that appliance.

The Web site offers some 30 recipes, including gluten-free recipes, and a kids' site with recipes geared toward the young baker. E-mail yeast baking questions to carol.stevens@ufoods.com.

For a copy of *The Kneaded Loaf: A Guide to Contemporary Breadmaking* (104-page cookbook with 60 recipes and 8 pages of photos), send a check or money order for $8 to:

Red Star Yeast and Products
433 East Michigan St.
Milwaukee, WI 53202

Tone Brothers, Inc.
1-800-247-5251
Monday through Friday, 9 A.M.–4 P.M. Central Time
www.spiceadvice.com

The hotline provides answers to questions about spice use and cooking with spices. Check out the Web site for recipes and an online spice encyclopedia. The Sugar and Spice Kid's Corner offers information about spices, their uses, and recipes geared toward kids.

USA Rice Federation
PO Box 740123
Houston, TX 77274
713-270-6699
www.usarice.com

Send a SASE for free brochures and recipes using rice. The Web site offers recipes and nutrition information. Learn about different types of rice and how and where it is produced. Seasonal specials are featured monthly. Look for the kids' crafts and activities on the Web site.

USDA Meat & Poultry Hot Line
1-800-535-4555
www.usda.gov

Consumer affairs specialists are available to answer questions Monday through Friday, noon–4 P.M. Eastern Standard Time. The Web site has an extensive kids section with information about Team Nutrition, food safety, agriculture, and many other interesting topics.

Vegetarian Resource Group
PO Box 1463
Baltimore, MD 21203
410-366-VEGE
www.vrg.org
e-mail: vrg@vrg.org

This nonprofit organization educates the public about vegetarianism. Free reprints of the Family Matters series discussing vegetarian families (and other brochures) are available upon request.

Kids' Cooking Classes, Programs, Activities, and Culinary Organizations

American Culinary Federation (ACF)
1-800-624-9458
www.acfchefs.org
e-mail: acf@aug.com

Chef members teach a 10-week, after-school kids' cooking program called That's Fresh Cooking Team.

American Institute of Wine and Food (AIWF)
1-800-274-2493 or 415-255-3000
e-mail: aiwfmember@aol.com
(no Web site)

Days of Taste, a nationwide program taught in schools and at community groups, is sponsored by the AIWF's 31 chapters every fall. The program includes taste and nutrition classes, visits to farmers' markets and restaurants, and cooking classes.

Chefs Collaborative 2000
282 Moody St. Suite 207
Waltham, MA 02453
781-736-0635
fax 781-642-0307
www.chefnet.com/cc2000
e-mail:CC2000@chefnet.com

The Adopt-A-School program brings the organization's chef members and non-members into classrooms for eight one-hour classes for 8- to 12-year-old students. Kids sample regional dishes and learn about healthful eating, history, geography, culture, and the environment.

If you are interested in teaching this program in your area, contact Sara Baer-Sinnott at Oldways Preservation & Exchange Trust for information. (See listing below.)

Culinary Institute of America (CIA)
433 Albany Post Road
Hyde Park, NY 12538
1-800-888-7850

This premiere culinary institute offers kids the opportunity to take classes on campus as part of the continuing education program in the spring and fall. Kids learn basic cooking and baking skills. Class age groups are divided into 8 to 11 year olds and 12 to 15 year olds. Information about course dates and fees is available at the continuing education number listed above.

International Association of Culinary Professionals (IACP)
1-800-928-IACP or 502-581-9786
www.iacp.com
e-mail: iacp@hqtrs.com

Apple Pie for Kids workshops are held in schools and community centers around the country. IACP's Kids in the Kitchen Committee provides a network for kids' cooking professionals and teachers. IACP can provide information about member cooking professionals and teachers throughout the country.

IACP is a professional society that represents virtually every profession in the culinary industry. Information on membership and upcoming events is available on the Web site or through the headquarters.

Oldways Preservation & Exchange Trust
25 First St.
Cambridge, MA 02141
617-621-3000
www.oldwayspt.org
e-mail: oldways@tiac.org

This nonprofit organization offers information and education about traditional culture-based diets through conferences, publications, and its Web site.

Oregon Dairy Council
www.oregondairycouncil.org

You can order the Cooking with Kids program for schools through the council's Web site. The program packet includes 20 simple recipes with grocery and equipment lists, 15 quick food and mealtime activities, a teacher guide, and 25 mealtime guides.

Team Nutrition
www.usda.gov/fcs/team.html

Launched by the USDA, this partnership between public and private organizations sponsors nutrition activities on many levels. The Web site offers an overview of the program and its participants, resources for teaching children about nutrition education, a student page with activities, links to agencies and organizations dedicated to healthy school meals, and much more.

Cooking School Guides

These guides are available in bookstores and by mail order:

Peterson's Culinary Schools
Peterson's Summer Opportunities for Kids & Teenagers
www.petersons.com

This summer opportunities guide lists cooking programs at summer camps.

Shaw Guides to Cooking Schools
www.shawguides.com

More Web Sites

Kids can learn about food and healthy eating on many Web sites. These are just a few fun sites. Be sure to check out the related links when you visit these sites to get even more information.

www.cspnet.org/kids/index/html

The Center for Science in the Public Interest site has lots of activities and healthy recipes for kids as well as other nutrition information and offers.

www.familyfun.com

This Disney Web site is filled with information for the whole family and includes recipes and mealtime ideas.

www.kidsfood.org/

Join in the Kids' Food Cyber Club fun at this site with interactive nutrition quizzes, food-related activities, and fun and games focused on the Food Guide Pyramid. Be sure to check out the extensive links at this site.

www.exhibits.pacsci.org/nutrition/

Step into this Nutrition Cafe for fun and games centered around what you eat every day.

www.foodsafety.gov

This site offers kids' activities to help them learn about food safety.

nppc.org/foodfun.html

This National Pork Producers Council site is specially designed for kids with lots of fun activities, recipes, and games.

www.fsis.usda.gov

This Food Safety Information Service Web site makes learning about food safety fun for kids. Check out the links to various sites relating to kids, families, and nutrition.

Selected Web and Mail-Order Resources

This is your guide to sources for baking, cheesemaking, and gardening products and information. Reading these catalogs is guaranteed to pique your interest and educate you about these different areas.

Baking and Grains

Bob's Red Mill
5209 SE International Way
Milwaukie, OR 97222
1-800-553-2258
www.bobsredmill.com

This catalog carries every grain grown in North America either whole, stone ground, or blended into mixes. Bob's also sells baking supplies, equipment, and books.

The Home Baking Association
10841 S. Parker, Suite 105
Parker, CO 80134
303-840-8787
303-840-6877 (fax)
www.homebaking.org

This association publishes an invaluable baking resource guide with recipes, tips, and baking information for $1 and a baking video and curriculum for $15 plus $5 postage. To receive information or copies, contact the HBA at the preceding address and phone numbers.

King Arthur Flour
The Baker's Catalogue
PO Box 876
Norwich, VT 05055-0876
1-800-827-6836
www.kingarthurflour.com

Whether you're an experienced baker or a novice, you'll find this color catalog filled with excellent information about baking. The color photographs accompany the commentary and descriptions of fine tools, equipment, ingredients, and books for the home baker. Recipes are featured throughout. Be sure to check out the information in the catalog and on the Web site about free baking classes held in various parts of the country.

CheeseMaking

New England Cheesemaking Supply Co.
PO Box 85
Ashfield, MA 01330
413-628-3808
fax 413-628-4061
e-mail: info@cheesemaking.com
www.cheesemaking.com

This company offers cheesemaking supplies, books, equipment, starters, and kits. The free paper catalog is available upon request. Kits include a 20-minute mozzarella and ricotta kit for about $20. The Web site offers the novice an introduction to home cheesemaking.

Children's Gardening

Gardens for Growing People
PO Box 630
Point Reyes, CA 94956-0630
415-663-9433 (phone and fax)
www.svn.net/growpepl

This company is focused exclusively on children's gardening and education through the garden. A free catalog offers information about seeds, books, equipment, music, garden games, and arts and crafts.

Seeds of Change
PO Box 15700
Santa Fe, NM 87506-5700
1-888-762-7333
www.seedsofchange.com

A free extensive catalog with color photos offers the company's organic seeds, gardening supplies, and some food products along with books for new and experienced gardeners and kids.

Shepherd's Garden Seeds
30 Irene Street
Torrington, CT 06790-6658
860-482-3638
www.shepherdseeds.com

This company's illustrated catalog for $1 will make you want to run right out and start a garden. Look for kids gardening seed packets, ornamental sunflowers, and a garden for children. The company carries seeds for flowers and vegetables, garden tools, and supplies.

Cookbooks on the Internet

Amazon.com
www.amazon.com
1-800-201-7575 (customer service only)

This Web leader provides a substantial cooking, food, and wine section and offers discounts on books. Catalog information and ordering is online only.

Jessica's Biscuit
www.jessicas.com
1-800-878-4264

You can order 24 hours a day, and the company offers frequent super sales and bonus bargains.

Ethnic Ingredients and Spices

Catalogs from these companies offer the reader an excellent introduction to ethnic ingredients and the use of spices.

Adriana's Caravan
409 Vanderbilt Street
Brooklyn, NY 11218
1-800-316-0820
www.adrianascaravan.com

Adriana's specializes in ethnic and exotic ingredients and condiments. The catalog features over 400 spices, 100 chilies, and 100 mushrooms.

373

Penzeys Spices
PO Box 933
Muskego, WI 53150
1-800-741-7787
www.penzeys.com

You'll get an education about spices when you read this attractive color catalog. The catalog offers a full range of spices and spice blends and explanations about their use along with gift box items. Recipes throughout the catalog often are aimed at things kids can eat or make and include photographs of the dish and, in some cases, techniques used to prepare the dish.

Spice Merchant
PO Box 524
Jackson Hole, WY 83001
1-800-551-5999
www.email.com/spice

Spice Merchant specializes in Asian condiments, spices, noodles, and cookware. You'll find a variety of woks and Japanese utensils used for making sushi, including a bamboo sushi mat, sushi rice molds, and a home sushi making kit.

Kitchen Supplies

This list includes sources for dishers (the scoops used for making holiday chocolate truffles in the Chapter 30, "Holiday Happenings") and various types of kitchen thermometers.

A Cook's Wares
1-800-915-9788
www.cookswares.com

This catalog features cooking supplies and cookware at discounted prices.

Boxer-Northwest Co.
Wholesale Food Service Supply and Equipment
438 NW Broadway
Portland, OR 97209
1-800-547-5700
www.boxernw.com

The catalog features a full range of kitchen equipment and is available at the Web site. The company offers discounts for purchases made on the Web. This company is the source for the disher or small hand-held scoop used to the Chocolate Truffle recipes in Chapter 30.

Chef's Catalog
PO Box 620048
Dallas, TX 75262
1-800-338-3232
www.chefscatalog.com

This catalog of fine-quality cookware and utensils offers frequent specials and sales.

Professional Cutlery Direct
1-800-859-6994
www.cutlery.com

This catalog features discounts of 25 to 50 percent off retail prices for cutlery and kitchen equipment.

Sur La Table
1-800-243-0852
fax 206-682-1026
www.surlatable.com

This gourmet kitchenware retailer's catalog features cooking tools and kitchen and tableware designed specifically for kids. Check out the kid's cooking tools sets, including the bake set, pastry making kit, and junior cooking set.

The attractive color catalog is filled with kitchen finds from the latest equipment and tabletop fashions to imported kitchen tools from around the world. Phone or fax orders 24 hours, 7 days a week, or shop online at the company's Web site.

Williams-Sonoma
1-800-541-2233
fax 702-363-2541
www.williams-sonoma.com

Keep up with the latest in kitchenware with this sleek color catalog, sprinkled with favorite recipes. Phone or fax orders 24 hours, 7 days a week or shop online at the company's Web site.

Cookbooks

Whether you're looking to start your cookbook collection or expand an existing one, the books listed below are tried and true favorites. The basic cookbooks will help you get around the kitchen and expand your culinary talents. Your kids will be happy with any one of the kids' cookbooks. The books on food science and garnishing will provide hours of kitchen fun.

General Reference Cookbooks and Reference Books

The American Dietetic Association's Complete Food & Nutrition Guide, by Roberta Larson Duyff. Minneapolis, MN: Chronimed Publishing, 1998.

Better Homes And Gardens New Baking Book, edited by Jennifer Dorland Darling and Lisa Holderness. Des Moines, IA: Meredith Corporation, 1998.

Better Homes And Gardens New Cook Book, 11th edition, edited by Jennifer Dorland Darling. Des Moines, IA: Meredith Corporation, 1996.

The Fannie Farmer Cookbook, by Marion Cunningham. New York: Alfred A. Knopf, 1997.

Joy Of Cooking, by Irma S. Rombauer, Marion Rombauer Becker, and Ethan Becker. New York: Scribners, 1997.

The New Basics Cookbook, by Julee Rosso and Sheila Lukins. New York: Workman Publishing, 1989.

The New Food Lover's Companion, 2nd edition, by Sharon Tyler Herbst. New York: Barron's Educational Series, 1995.

The New York Times Cookbook, by Craig Claiborne. New York: Harper-Collins, 1990.

Vegetarian Cooking For Everyone, by Deborah Madison. New York: Broadway Books, 1997.

The Way To Cook, by Julia Child. New York: Alfred A. Knopf, 1989.

Selected Kids' Cookbooks

American Heart Association Kids' Cookbook, edited by Mary Winston. New York: Times Books, 1993.

Better Homes and Gardens New Junior Cookbook, edited by Jennifer Dorland Darling. Des Moines, IA: Meredith Corporation, 1997.

Better Homes and Gardens Silly Snacks, edited by Jennifer Dorland Darling. Des Moines, IA: Meredith Books, 1998.

Betty Crocker's Baking with Kids. New York: Macmillan, 1995.

Betty Crocker's Boys and Girls Microwave Cookbook. New York: Prentice Hall, 1992.

Betty Crocker's Cooking with Kids. New York: Macmillan, 1995.

The Children's Step by Step Cookbook: Photographic Cooking Lessons for Young Chefs, by Angela Wilkes. New York: Dorling Kindersley, 1994.

Cooking with Children: 15 Lessons For Children, Age 7 And Up, Who Really Want To Learn To Cook, by Marion Cunningham. New York: Alfred A. Knopf, 1995.

FamilyFun's Cookbook: Irresistible Recipes For You and Your Kids, by Deanna F. Cook and the experts at *FamilyFun* magazine. New York: Hyperion, 1996.

Fanny at Chez Panisse, by Alice Waters with Bob Carrau and Patricia Curtan. New York: HarperCollins, 1992.

The Good Housekeeping Illustrated Children's Cookbook, by Marianne Zanzarella. New York: William Morrow, 1997.

A Good Soup Attracts Chairs: A First African Cookbook for American Kids, by Fran Osseo-Asare. Gretna, LA: Pelican Publishing Co., 1993.

The Kids' Multicultural Cookbook: Food & Fun Around The World, by Deanna F. Cook. Charlotte, Vermont: Williamson Publishing, 1995.

Kitchen Science

Cooking Wizardry for Kids: Learn About Food While Making Tasty Things to Eat!, by Margaret Kenda and Phyllis S. Williams. New York: Barron's, 1990.

Simple Kitchen Experiments: Learning Science With Everyday Foods, by Muriel Mandell. New York: Sterling Publishing Co., 1993.

Playing with Food and Garnishing

The Book of Garnishes, by June Budgen. Los Angeles: HP Books, 1986.

First Food Made Fun: Delicious and Healthy Fun Food for Babies and Toddlers, by Miriam Stoppard. New York: Dorling Kindersley, 1993.

Fun Foods: Clever Ideas For Garnishing And Decorating, by Wim Kros. New York: Sterling Publishing Co., 1990.

(This book is out of print but I found it in the library. If you can get a used copy, grab it. It's dated but is one of the most interesting and detailed books about garnishing I've seen.)

Play with Your Food, by Joost Elffers. New York: Stewart, Tabori & Chang, 1997.

Magazines with Regular Food Features for Kids and Families

Child

Crayola Kids

FamilyFun

FamilyLife

Healthy Kids

Parenting

Parents

Sesame Street Parents

The Food Guide Pyramids

Use these Food Guide Pyramids for easy reference when planning your daily meals and diet.

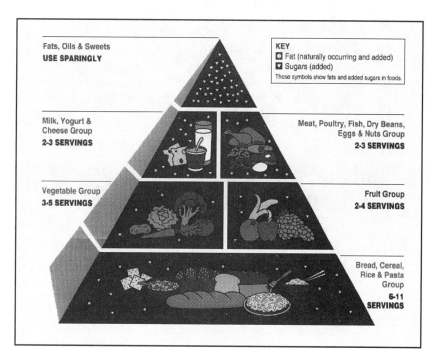

The food guide pyramid. Source: United States Department of Agriculture.

Food guide for young children (ages 2–6). Source: United States Department of Agriculture.

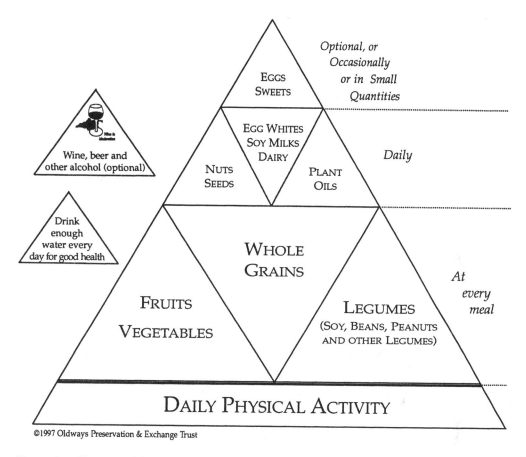

Vegetarian diet pyramid. Source: Oldways Preservation & Exchange Trust.

The Nutrition Facts Label

This sample nutrition facts label will help you understand what's in the food you buy. Read the accompanying chart to learn what the listings on the label mean.

Nutrition Facts

Serving Size 1 cup (228g)
Servings Per Container 2

Amount Per Serving

Calories 90   Calories from Fat 30

                                                    % Daily Value*

Total Fat 3g	**5%**
Saturated Fat 0g	**0%**
Cholesterol 0mg	**0%**
Sodium 300mg	**13%**
Total Carbohydrate 13g	**4%**
Dietary Fiber 3g	**12%**
Sugars 3g	
Protein 3g	

Vitamin A 80%	•	Vitamin C 60%	
Calcium 4%	•	Iron 4%	

* Percent Daily Values are based on a 2,000 calorie diet. Your daily values may be higher or lower depending on your calorie needs:

		Calories:	2,000	2,500
Total Fat	Less than		65g	80g
Sat Fat	Less than		20g	25g
Cholesterol	Less than		300mg	300mg
Sodium	Less than		2,400mg	2,400mg
Total Carbohydrate			300g	375g
Dietary Fiber			25g	30g

Calories per gram:
Fat 9   •   Carbohydrate 4   •   Protein 4

NATIONAL FOOD PROCESSORS ASSOCIATION
in cooperation with FDA and FSIS

Read the nutrition facts label; you may be pleasantly—or unpleasantly—surprised.

Behind the Fine Print

The nutrition facts label describes the amount of calories, fat, cholesterol, sodium, carbohydrate, fiber, sugars, and protein in the product. It also gives information about vitamins and minerals. The following information and guidelines are based on a 2,000-calorie-a-day diet.

Serving Size

Many people make the mistake of miscalculating nutrition information because they misinterpret the serving size on the label. Be aware that the information on the label describes only one serving. The label tells you the size of a serving and then the number of servings in the package. You'll have to ask yourself if what you're eating is the same amount contained in one serving. If you're eating more or less than a serving, you'll have to multiply or divide the facts on the label. So, if the package contains two servings and you plan to eat all of it, double the information about nutrients and caloric values.

Calories

This describes the number of calories in one serving size and how many of these come from fat.

Percent of Daily Value

You'll see this listed on the right side of the label. The information is based on a 2,000-calorie diet and tells you what percent the serving represents of the total amount you should have each day.

Your daily value goal for carbohydrate, dietary fiber, vitamins, and minerals is 100 percent. In contrast, when it comes to fat, saturated fat, cholesterol, and sodium, you should choose food with a low percent daily value because you should be eating less.

Daily Value Footnote

Some labels have a footnote that lists some daily values for a 2,000- and 2,500-calorie diet with maximum amounts for fat and saturated fat, cholesterol, sodium, carbohydrate, and fiber. At the bottom of the chart, you may see information about how many calories there are in a gram of fat (9 calories), carbohydrate (4 calories), and protein (4 calories). Notice that fat supplies more than twice the calories per gram of either carbohydrate or protein.

The following daily values are based on a 2,000-calorie diet.

Total Fat

This describes how many grams of fat are in a product and includes all types of fat, including saturated, polyunsaturated, and monounsaturated fat. A breakdown of the saturated fat is listed below the total fat because this kind of fat is key in raising blood cholesterol. High cholesterol can lead to heart disease. The recommended guideline for overall fat consumption is no more than 30 percent of your calories each day, or less than 65 grams.

Cholesterol

This shows how many milligrams are contained in the product. The recommended guideline is to eat less than 300 milligrams a day.

Sodium

This refers to the amount of salt in the product. Start zeroing in on salt content and you'll be amazed at how high it is for many canned and prepackaged goods. That's because manufacturers use salt as a preservative as well as for flavor. But too much of it can lead to high blood pressure. Follow the guidelines and limit your salt intake to 2,400 milligrams a day.

Carbohydrates

Carbohydrates are in foods like bread, potatoes, rice, pasta, cereals, corn, apples, jam, and candy bars. There are two types: simple and complex. The complex carbohydrates are the starches in grains and beans. The simple ones include refined sugars and natural sugars in fruit and vegetables.

Carbohydrates supply energy, help your body use fat, and allow protein to be used to build and repair your body.

The recommended guideline is that 55 to 60 percent of calories consumed per day should come from carbohydrates, or 300 grams.

Dietary Fiber

Carbohydrate-rich foods supply dietary fiber, which helps digestion and can offer protection from certain diseases. Fiber sources include fruits, vegetables, and dry beans. It's important to have a diet rich in fiber, with a target of 25 grams per day.

Sugars

The major problem that results from eating sugar is tooth decay. (Studies do not support the theory that too much sugar revs kids up.) Sugars are high in calories but low in nutrients. Eat them in moderation.

Protein

Protein supplies energy, maintains and builds body tissues, and helps your body fight infection. Protein comes from animal and vegetable sources. Keep in mind that animal sources will also contain fat and cholesterol. Most Americans eat much more protein than they need each day. Recommendations range from 24 grams a day for 4- to 6-year-olds to 63 grams for men 25 years of age and older.

Index

395

397